KINGDOM AND CHURCH

Dedicated to
ERNST WOLF and OTTO WEBER
of the University of Göttingen
in appreciation of their work for
a closer understanding between
the Lutheran and Reformed
Churches.

KINGDOM AND CHURCH

*A Study in the Theology
of the Reformation*

by
T. F. TORRANCE

Professor of Christian Dogmatics
University of Edinburgh

PUBLISHERS
Eugene, Oregon

Wipf and Stock Publishers
199 W 8th Ave, Suite 3
Eugene, OR 97401

Kingdom and Church
A Study in the Theology of the Reformation
By Torrance, Thomas F.
Copyright©1996 by Torrance, Thomas F.
ISBN: 1-57910-012-0
Publication date 12/2/1996
Previously published by Oliver and Boyd, 1996

FOREWORD

THE present work has been built up on the basis of a short essay contributed to *Eschatology*, Occasional Paper No. 2, of the *Scottish Journal of Theology*. The request to publish the essay in German (*Evangelische Theologie*, July 1954) and in French (*Les Réformateurs et la fin des temps*, 1955) has encouraged me to offer in this enlarged form a discussion of the relation of eschatology to the life of the Church as found in the works of Luther, Butzer and Calvin. In distinguishing their thought in terms of 'The Eschatology of Faith', 'The Eschatology of Love' and 'The Eschatology of Hope', I have followed what seems to me to be an important emphasis in each, although all three of them were united in thinking of the Kingdom of Christ in terms of faith, hope and love. The study of the theology of Butzer (reprinted from the *Journal of Ecclesiastical History*, with the kind permission of Professor Dugmore) is rather out of proportion to the others, but it is offered only as an introduction to his thought and as an indication that in his writings, particularly his Biblical expositions, the link may be found which, along with modern Biblical theology, may well serve to bring into closer understanding the Lutheran and Reformed Churches. It is to be hoped that the new and complete edition of Butzer's works now being published may help to bring about the answer to his prayer for the unity of the Churches of the Reformation.

I should like to acknowledge my indebtedness to Principal P. S. Watson for making a complete edition of Luther's *Commentary on Galatians* available in English, and to the recent work of Dr Gordon Rupp on the theology of Luther, *The Righteousness of God*, from which I have borrowed several citations. My warm thanks are also due to Mr Walter W. Beyerlin who has given me generous help with the proofs. The Publishers, Oliver and Boyd of Edinburgh, and the Printers, Robert Cunningham and Sons Ltd of Alva, have shown to me great kindness and patience for which I am deeply grateful.

T. F. TORRANCE

May 1955

CONTENTS

		PAGE
	Foreword	v
I	The Eschatology of the Reformation	1
II	The Eschatology of Faith: Martin Luther	7
	Justus et Peccator	10
	The Two Kingdoms	16
	The Kingdom of God	22
	The Kingdom of Christ	25
	The Eschatological Perspective	29
	Christian Order?	32
	The Orders of Creation	34
	The Christian Persona	37
	Verbum Dei	40
	The Kingdom of Faith	45
	The New Man	48
	The Church	52
	Form and Order	57
	The Sacramental Analogy	60
	The Church under the Cross	64
III	The Eschatology of Love: Martin Butzer	73
	Regnum Christi	75
	The Kingdom and the Church	79
	The Eternal Kingdom	83
	The Christian Community	87

	CONTENTS	
IV	THE ESCHATOLOGY OF HOPE: JOHN CALVIN	90
	Early Views	90
	The Word and the Spirit	97
	Union with Christ	100
	Election	104
	The Ascension of Christ	108
	Between the Advents	113
	The Two Conditions of the Kingdom	122
	The Ministry	125
	Order in the Kingdom	134
	The Difference between Calvin and Luther	139

ABBREVIATIONS

W.A. *Weimarer Ausgabe* of Luther's Works, Wein ar, 1883-.
W.M.L. *Works of Martin Luther*, Philadelphia, 1943.
Op. Lat. *Martini Buceri Opera Latina*, Paris, 1955.
O.R. *Corpus Reformatorum, Opera Calvini*, Brunswick and Berlin, 1863-1900.
O.S. *Calvini Opera Selecta*, München, 1926-1952.

I

THE ESCHATOLOGY OF THE REFORMATION

IN a recent work Jacob Taubes discusses the transition in eschatological thought from the mediaeval to the modern world in terms of the Copernican revolution.[1] In the mediaeval cosmology the Ptolemaic world-view was dominant. The Ptolemaic earth had a heaven overarching it as the ultimate reality which the earth in its transitory existence was designed to reflect. Everything that happened on earth corresponded in some way to an eternal pattern in the heavens, so that the whole purpose of life could be described in terms of *imitatio* or conformity to the heavenly reality. The publication in 1543 of the main work of Copernicus marked the climax of a transitional period characterised by the discovery that the earth is engaged in the planetary revolutions of the heavens. That meant in effect that the secret of the heavens had been discovered, for the heavenly bodies which had so long cast their spell upon men were disclosed to be only other 'earths'. Thus in the Copernican cosmology there is earth with no heaven overarching it; there is no imaging by earth of heavenly realities. The purpose of life is not the imitation of a fixed pattern in a heavenly world but the fulfilment of some future ideal. Heaven above loses its supernatural character and humanity begins to concentrate on an earthly and historical end.

That revolution in science, however, was made possible, as Professor John Baillie has pointed out in his address to the British Association,[2] by a profounder change in theology, a revolution in the doctrine of God and His relation to the world. In the old Greek notion of God, which was deeply embedded in the theology of the mediaeval world, God was regarded as impassable and changeless. Accordingly, nature also was held to be changeless and even eternal, and because men thought of it as impregnated

[1] *Abendländische Eschatologie*, pp. 87f.
[2] *Natural Science and the Spiritual Life*, pp. 18f.

with final causes, they imagined that the eternal pattern could be read off the book of nature, thus in effect substituting nature for God. With such a doctrine of God and nature behind it, medieval thought was essentially deductive and left no room for the element of contingency in nature, to the recognition of which modern empirical science owes its very existence. This science had to wait until the period of the Reformation, when men learned from the Biblical revelation and more particularly from the Christian doctrine of creation that the world is contingent upon the divine will, and that the pattern of nature, while intelligible to us in principle, is essentially hidden and cannot be known in advance but only from the other end, through empirical observation. Thus the great difference between the more or less static science of the ancient and medieval world and the great movement of modern science rests upon a difference in the doctrine of God.

It is with the same profound revolution in the doctrine of God and His relation to nature and history that we are concerned in the transition from mediaeval thought to the eschatology of movement that characterised the Reformation. In the mediaeval Roman Church the Greek view of God and nature was carried over into the relation of heaven and earth, the Kingdom of God and the Church. Nature was regarded as impregnated with final causes, so that the eternal pattern embedded in nature could be read off by natural theology or deductive science. Likewise the Church was regarded as impregnated with the Kingdom of God, so that the pattern of the Kingdom embedded in the earthly structure of the Church could be read off the historical consciousness of the Church by the teaching office. Here the *Eschaton* is so domesticated and housed within the Church that, far from standing under final judgment, the Church dispenses it by her binding and loosing, far from being repentant and reformable, the Church can only develop according to her own immanent norms which correspond to the fixed pattern of the Kingdom. To this theology the idea that eschatology is concerned with history is almost 'totally alien'.[1] That is nowhere more apparent than in the decided reaction of the Roman Church against the great attempt of Joachim of Fiore and his followers to revive 'the historical perspective' and to reimpose 'the temporal

---

[1] E. L. Tuveson, *Millennium and Utopia*, p. 19.

relevance of the last things'.¹ By stressing the heavenly character of the ultimate consummation, by returning to a more Hellenic notion of heaven and earth, which were regarded rather like parallel lines that only appear to meet when produced to infinity, so postponing indefinitely the occurrence of the last things, the Church stressed the permanence of her institutions and the unchangeableness of her state. When St Thomas, for example, considered the questions raised by Joachim, he removed the eschatological end to a realm beyond history, and concluded that the Church, which has the pattern of that end embedded within it, is as static as history.

In contrast, the Reformation stands for the rediscovery of the living God of the Bible, who actively intervenes in the affairs of men, the Lord and the Judge of history, and with that comes a powerful realisation of the historical relevance of eschatology. The Reformation thinks of the ends of the world as having already overtaken humanity, so that even now the Church on earth lives in the last times and even now the last things are being wrought out in history.² Here we have a return to the realist, historical perspective of Biblical eschatology which envisages both a new heaven and a new earth, an ultimate end in which the fulness of the creation is maintained unimpaired in union with a heavenly consummation.

In mediaeval theology, nature, which was never regarded as existing in tension with supernature from which it fell, was to be redeemed not by recreation but by transfiguration, through a state of *gratia* into a state of *gloria*, as the doctrine of transubstantiation in the Mass makes so clear, but in this transfiguration nature was to lose much of its original character. Thus in the *Supplement* to the *Summa Theologica* of St Thomas we are told that in the final consummation the movement of the heavenly bodies will cease, the transfigured earth will bear little resemblance to the original creation, for dumb animals and plants, being incapable of renewal, will no longer exist, while even the resurrected bodies of the blessed will cease to have many of their most human characteristics. In

---

[1] Karl Löwith, *Meaning in History*, pp. 154f, where we are given a 'most illuminating interpretation of Joachim of Fiore. I am much indebted to this work.
[2] Cf. Calvin, *Comm. on Hebrews*, 1.1, C.R. 83, p. 10; on Heb. 2.5f, C.R. 83, p. 23; on Heb. 9.26, C.R. 83, p. 119.

the last resort nature is transmuted into supernature, the earthly into a heavenly reality.[1]

Against such a docetic interpretation of redemption and eschatology the Reformers were in full revolt. By their return to the historical perspective of the Bible, by their emphasis upon the humanity of Christ and upon the Church as His Body in history, they brought back the original expectations of the Apostles and the early Fathers for a new age in which an earthly future figures as prominently as a heavenly.[2] Moreover that new age was linked once again with the mission of the Church on earth, so that in their proclamation of the Gospel, in their service of the Word made flesh, they believed the new age was already at work in their midst, and that all history was moving under the impact of God's Word towards its goal in Jesus Christ. The new creation was already present within history, and if its presence meant tumult and commotion throughout the world and the Church, that was to be interpreted as the travail of its full appearing. In this way the movement of the Reformation was itself given eschatological interpretation, as an imperfect anticipation of the final movement through which the perfect age was soon to dawn upon the world.

There can be no doubt that this eschatology played a significant part in the development of the new movement in science, particularly towards the end of the sixteenth century in France and England, but even before 1543 Lutherans like Osiander gave considerable help to Copernicus in working out his revolutionary conceptions. At the same time the eschatology of the Reformation stands in marked contrast to the Copernican world-view with its expectation only of an earthly future. By their continued belief in a heavenly reality overarching the earth and its history, and by their doctrine of the temporal relevance of the heavenly realm, they taught that the earthly future is divinely governed through the mission of the Church. By that they do not mean that the Church on earth is impregnated with the patterns of the heavenly Kingdom, nor do they return to a doctrine of predestination as *pars providentiae*, as taught by St Thomas,[3] but nevertheless it is by thinking election and eschatology into each other that the Re-

---
[1] *Summ. Theol. Supplementum*, p. 91., art. 4 and 5; *Scriptum s. Sent.* IV, dist. 48, q. 11., art. 1 et seq.; cf. E. L. Tuveson, *Millennium and Utopia*, pp. 18f.
[2] See Luther's *Preface to the Prophet Ezekiel*, 1545, and *Tischreden* (F.B.) 4.51.
[3] *Summa Theol.*, I, q. 22 and 23.

formers found their answer to Romanism on the one hand and to Copernicanism on the other. Predestination does not mean that there is a predetermined pattern which can be read off the structure of the Church on earth, but that the whole of the history of the Church like nature is contingent on the will of God, and that while the pattern is discernible in principle, as it were, in Christ, in the Word of the Gospel, it remains essentially a *mysterium* and cannot be known in advance, but only from the final end, by apocalyptic manifestation at the advent of Christ. Until then the history of the Church is essentially ambiguous, for the perfect face of the new creation, while partially disclosed in the Church, does not yet fully appear. That election always wears a double aspect in history is the answer of the Reformation to the Copernican striving after only an earthly end. There is an earthly future and an earthly consummation, but because the heavenly end in election has moved into time and travels through time, the meaning of history is fulfilled against itself, against its secular interpretation, and even, it may be, against its ecclesiastical trends. It is only by faith that we may discern the signs of the times, the faith which has discerned the perfect pattern of the Kingdom in Jesus Christ, 'the mirror of election', as Calvin called Him, and may therefore penetrate behind the outward façade of history to discern the face of the new creation that is about to be revealed.

This gives us a general picture of the eschatology of the Reformation, but within that unity there were highly significant differences, particularly between Luther and Calvin. Broadly speaking, their divergence may be characterised by saying that while Lutheran eschatology was mainly an eschatology of judgment, going back to early Latin Fathers like Cyprian with their emphasis on the decay and collapse of the world,[1] Reformed eschatology was mainly an eschatology of the resurrection, going back to the early Greek Fathers with their emphasis upon the renewal of the world through the Incarnation of Christ. That line cannot be drawn very sharply, for Luther had much to say of the resurrection of the Church, though he rarely speaks about the renewal of the world. When a baby's head is born, says Luther, the worst is over. Because Christ the Head is already risen, we must think of the

[1] Cf. Cyprian's *De Immortalitate* and his *Epistle to Demetrianus*, and see W.A. 34/2, p. 475; W.A. 29, p. 617ff; *Augsburg Conf.*, XXIII; *Apology*, XXIII.

resurrection of the Church which is His Body as more than half accomplished.[1] Typical of his thought, however, is the *Tessaradecas Consolatoria*, in which he describes the blessing above in terms of Christ risen from the dead who is our righteousness, and the future blessing in terms of death as release from this wretched world, a joyful negative, but no attempt is made to think the two blessings into each other. Calvin, on the other hand, constantly speaks of the resurrection as the chief article of our faith, and even when he speaks of justification the emphasis is laid on our participation in the new humanity in Christ. And yet the eschatology of the new man in a new world meant for Luther[2] that Christian theology, like the parables of Jesus recorded in the Gospels, must make use of new language and new thought-forms with which to express the new and wonderful reality disclosed in the resurrection—'*ein seltsame sprache und newe Grammatica*', he called it. '*Denn er wil, weil wir sollen newe menschen sein, das wir auch ander und new gedanken, verstand und sinne haben und kein ding ansehen nach der vernunfft, wie es fur der welt stehet, sondern wie es fur seinen augen ist, und uns richten nach dem zukünfftigen, unsichtbaren newen wesen, des wir zu hoffen haben und nach diesem leiden und elenden wesen folgen sol.*'[3] It is eschatology that accounts for the incredible boldness of Luther's language, but it is also eschatology that keeps Calvin within the sober limits of the revealed Word of God in the Holy Scripture.

---

[1] W.A. 36, pp. 547f and also pp. 162f.
[2] W.A. 40/1, p. 46.   [3] W.A. 34/2, p. 480f.

II

THE ESCHATOLOGY OF FAITH: MARTIN LUTHER

IN turning from the literature of medieval theology to the works of Martin Luther one is arrested immediately by an expression such as '*Regnum fidei*', and the contrast it presents to the whole of mediaeval thought. For almost a millennium the eschatology of the Scriptures and the Early Fathers had been adapted to the prevailing cosmology. The language of primitive cosmology had certainly been used in the Scriptures in the communication of the eschatological message of the Bible, but not in such a way that eschatology was redacted to a particular cosmology or determined in its main features by it, for the very nature of Biblical eschatology made that impossible. But in the mediaeval world it was quite a different story; eschatology was almost wholly determined by a pre-Copernican geography of heaven and hell, with its dominating conception of purgatory. The whole of that way of looking at things was torpedoed by Luther's doctrine of the *Regnum fidei*, and Purgatory was regarded as '*ein lauter Teufelsgespenst*', for the perverse eschatology it enshrined turned the Mass into sheer *Abgötterei*.[1]

Typical of this position was Luther's interpretation of the parable of Dives and Lazarus.[2] 'Abraham's bosom' was not to be understood in any corporal sense, but solely in terms of the Word of God, and as nothing else than God's Word in Gen. 22.18, in which Christ was promised to Abraham: 'Through thy seed shall all the nations of the earth be blessed.' All the fathers who believed this Word of God were blessed, that is, were redeemed from sin and death and hell. They belonged therefore to 'Abraham's bosom', and having died in faith they remain there until the day

[1] W.A. 30/2, pp. 367ff; 34/1, pp. 536f.
[2] W.A. 10/3, pp. 191ff. At this period (1522), however, Luther had a milder view of Purgatory than that which he adopted after 1530. See W.A. 7, pp. 149, 453.

of judgment. Similarly, when we die, we must die believing in the Word of Christ: 'He who believes in me shall never die' (John 11.26), for then we are embraced in the 'bosom of Christ' and are kept in Him until the day of judgment. That is the same Word of God that was spoken to Abraham, so that the *sinus Abrahae* is fulfilled in the *sinus Christi*.[1] On the other hand, 'just as Abraham's bosom is God's Word, within which believers through faith rest and sleep, and are kept until the last day, so hell must be understood on its part as where God's Word is not, where the unbelieving through unbelief are expelled until the last day. That can be nothing else than an empty, unbelieving, sinful, evil conscience'.[2] By that Luther means, as he goes on to explain in the same sermon, that when a man dies his conscience is opened up so that even in his unbelief he sees 'Abraham's bosom' and those in it, that is, the Word of God, in which he ought to have believed and has not and from which he suffers the greatest pain and anguish without any help or comfort. That does not mean that Luther simply interprets hell in subjective terms, but that he refuses to understand it in the terms which 'carnal reason' had so long supplied.

The difficult thing to grasp in Luther's thought here is that he should think of the 'bosom of Abraham' or the 'bosom of Christ' in terms of the generations of history of those who have believed the Word of God, and in terms of the ultimate refuge of the believing beyond history—and yet it is just this very fact that injects into Luther's theology the utmost eschatological concentration and urgency. In answer to the question whether Dives continued daily to suffer such torments, Luther declared that here we have to put out of our minds all notions of time, for in that world '*nicht Zeit noch Stund sind, sondern alles ein ewiger Augenblick*'.[3] In another sermon on the same passage preached during the following year, 1523, Luther speaks of the fact that *coram Deo* a thousand years are not even a day, so that when a man rises from the dead Adam and the fathers will rise with him just as if they had been living but half an hour before. '*Dort is kein Zeit . . . Es ist vor Gott alles auf einmal geschehen. Est ist nicht weder vor noch hinter, jene werden*

---

[1] See also the *Exposition of Genesis* 22.18, W.A. 43, pp. 245ff; Gen. 25, W.A. 43, pp. 351ff; and W.A. 42, pp. 67f.
[2] W.A. 13, p. 192.
[3] W.A. 10/3, p. 192.

THE ESCHATOLOGY OF FAITH: MARTIN LUTHER

nit eh kommen an den jüngsten Tag denn wir.'[1] The impact of that eternal moment (in which all action is concentrated) upon the life of the believer in time gives it intense eschatological potency, for it is life in the 'hour' when the mighty last things knock at the door. That is what Luther characteristically called the *Stündlein*.[2] Nowhere is the eschatological perspective which this brings better expressed than in his Commentary on Peter and Jude.[3] 'There are two ways of viewing things—one for God, the other for the world. So also this present life and that to come are twofold. This life cannot be that, since none can reach that but by death—that is by ceasing from this life. This life is just to eat, drink, sleep, endure, bring up children, etc., in which all moves on successively, hours, day, year, one after another: if you wish now to apprehend that life, you must banish out of your mind the course of this present life; you must not think that you can so apprehend it, where it will all be one day, one hour one moment. Since then in God's sight there is no reckoning of time, a thousand years must be before Him, as it were, a day. Therefore the first man, Adam, is just as near to him as he who shall be the last born before the last day. For God sees not time lengthwise but obliquely, just as when you look at right-angles to a long tree which lies before you, you can fix in your view both place and parts at once—a thing you cannot do if you only look at it lengthwise. We can, by our reason, look at time only according to its duration; we must begin to count from Adam, one year after another, even to the last day. But before God it is all in one heap; what is long with us is short with

---

[1] W.A. 12, p. 596. Cf. W.A. 36, p. 349: '*Asbald die Augen zugehen, wirst du auferweckt werden. Tausend Jahre werden sein, gleich als wenn du ein halbes Stündlein geschlaffen hättest. Gleich wie wir, wenn wir nachts den Stundenschlag nicht hören, nicht wissen, wie lange Zeit wir geschlaffen haben, also noch viel mehr im Tode sind tausend Jahre hinweg. Ehe sich einer umsiehet, ist er ein schöner Engel.*'

[2] W.A. 33, pp. 404f, W.A. 36, pp. 687f, etc. Compare the beginning and end of the long *Exposition of Genesis* throughout which he expounded again and again the *Regnum fidei* and the *Ecclesia* in terms of *sinus Abrahae, sinus Christi*. At the beginning: '*Dominus noster Ihesus Christus perficiat opus suum quod incepit in nobis, et acceleret diem illum redemptionis nostrae, quem (Dei gratia) levatis capitibus petimus, suspiramus et expectamus.... Veni Domine Ihesu. Et qui te amat, dicat: Veni Domine Ihesu, Amen*' (W.A. 42, p. 2). And at the end: '*Das ist nu der liebe (liber?) Genesis. Unser Herr Gott geb, das andere nach mir besser machen. Ich kann nit mehr, ich bin schwach, orate Deum pro me, das er mir ein gutes, seliges stündlin verleihe*' (W.A. 44, p. 825). Those are the eschatological brackets within which all Luther's life, work and thought are to be understood.

[3] But cf. also the sustained exposition of Titus 2 (W.A. 34/2, pp. 108ff).

Him—and again, here there is neither measure nor number.'¹

To refer back again to the exposition of the parable of Dives and Lazarus, the ultimate division which the *Stündlein* reveals between the 'bosom of Abraham' and 'hell', so sharp that an impassable gulf is seen to exist between them, is read back into our life before the day of judgment, so that Lazarus and Dives represent the Kingdom of faith with its poor despised Church on the one hand, and the kingdom of this world with its external wealth and splendour on the other. It was in those terms that he expounded the Book of Genesis, his longest and most sustained exposition, for throughout it the whole of history, life and theology is interpreted in the light of ultimate judgments and distinctions. That, then, is the idea that dominates Luther's thought and makes it eschatological through and through—the dialectic between heaven and earth, grace and nature, gospel and law, the true Church and the false.

Justus et Peccator

All this, however, is also rooted in Luther's own spiritual pilgrimage, which made him react against a superficial conjunction of heaven and earth and against the easy relation of grace and nature² or the easy transfiguration of nature which he found in mediaeval theology, both in its Dominican and in its Nominalist form. His Augustinian training, his searching experience in the monastery, and his lectures on Scripture all combined to convince him that grace and nature as we know it in this world today are in the sharpest tension, a tension which goes down into the depths of man's being³—so he interpreted Romans 7⁴ and Galatians 5⁵.

---

¹ W.A. 14, pp. 7of. Judging by this, Luther's own calculations in the *Supputatio annorum mundi* (*vide infra*) were exercises of the reason, not of faith!

² Cf. the last four *Theses* of 1517. 'Away, then, with those prophets who say to Christ's people, "Peace, peace", where there is no peace. Hail, hail to all those prophets who say to Christ's people, "The Cross, the Cross", where there is no cross. Christians should be exhorted to be zealous to follow Christ, their Head, through penalties, deaths, and hells; and let them thus be more confident of entering heaven through many tribulations rather than through a false assurance of peace' (W.A. 1, p. 38). See also the Sermon on *Ablass und Gnade*, W.A. 1, pp. 239ff; and the Sermon *de Poenitentia*, W.A. 1, pp. 317ff.

³ This becomes increasingly clear in the early series of lectures on the Bible, Psalms (1513-14; W.A. 3 and 4, and 9, pp. 116f), Romans (1515-16; W.A. 56 and 57), Galatians (1516-17; W.A. 2, pp. 436ff), Hebrews (1517-18; W.A. 57), and Psalms (1519f; W.A. 5). For the importance of his own experience in this connexion see especially W.A. 1, pp. 525, 558; 19, pp. 210, 226; 54, 179ff. The tension Luther interpreted wholly in terms of the death and resurrection o

THE ESCHATOLOGY OF FAITH: MARTIN LUTHER 11

Furthermore, Luther's conflict with a Papacy hostile to the proclamation of the Biblical Gospel of grace shocked him into the conviction that the same tension ran clean through the official Church from top to bottom.[1] The inner conflict of his soul had a counterpart within the Church on earth.[2]

Luther's own inner conflict found its answer in the doctrine of justification by faith through which the believer, though *semper peccator*, knew himself in Christ to be *semper justus*.[3] The outstanding characteristic of this teaching is that justification was understood as the eschatological act of pure grace which anticipated Christ's ultimate vindication of the sinner at the final judgment. And so with reference to the words from John's First Epistle, 'If our hearts condemn us God is greater than our hearts', Luther wrote: 'Greater, infinitely greater, is the counsel for the defence than the counsel for the prosecution. God is the Defender, the heart is the accuser. What, is that the proportion? Thus, thus, even thus, it is. "Who shall lay anything to the charge of God's elect? Nobody. Why? It is Jesus Christ (who is very God) who died, nay, rather, who is risen again. If God be for us, then, who can be against us?"'[4] No wonder Luther came to long for the day of judgment as *'lieben jüngsten Tag'*.[5]

As early as his lectures on Romans Luther had come to use the terms *'reputatio'* and *'imputatio'* to describe that act of pure grace.[6] 'The saints are inwardly always sinners and thus outwardly they are always justified. The hypocrites inwardly are always just, and thus outwardly they are always sinners. By inwardly, I mean, as

---

Christ, His descent into Hell and His ascent into Heaven. '*Sic Deus dum vivificat facit illud occidendo: dum justificat, facit illud reos faciendo; dum in coelum vehit, facit id ad infernum ducendo*' (W.A. 18, p. 633). That was against Erasmus in the *De Servo Arbitrio*, but earlier he had written: '*vivendo, immo moriendo et damnando fit theologus, non intelligendo, legendo aut speculando*' (W.A. 5, p. 163).
[4] W.A. 56, pp. 334f; W.A. 8, pp. 99f.   [5] W.A. 40/2, pp. 1ff.

---

[1] W.A. 6, pp. 322-329. See also the letter to Spalatin about his horrified conviction that the Pope is Antichrist (W.A., *Briefe*, II, p. 48).
[2] W.A. 8, p. 106. Cf. the *Sermons on the Law and Gospel* (W.A. 36, pp. 8ff, 25ff).
[3] W.A. 56, p. 442. Cf. also pp. 252, 287, 298, etc., and W.A. 54, pp. 179ff. For a more mature exposition see *Comm. on Gal.* 3.6, W.A. 40/1, pp. 362ff.
[4] W.A. 56, p. 204.
[5] WA. 34/2, p. 465: '*Wenn der Tag nicht ein mal kommen solt, so wolt ich eben so mehr nie geboren sein.*' Cf. W.A. 8, p. 719; W.A. 10/1, p. 142.
[6] See the valuable discussion by Dr Gordon Rupp, *The Righteousness of God*, pp. 158ff.

we are in ourselves, in our own eyes, in our own estimation. But outwardly what we are in God's sight, in His *reputation*. Therefore we are outwardly just when we are just, not of ourselves or of our own works, but only by the reputation of God.'[1] 'Since therefore the saints always have their sin in view and implore righteousness from God according to His mercy, by this fact they are always *reckoned* just by God on account of this confession of sin. For they really are sinners, but they are just by the merciful *reputation* of God. Ignorantly they are just, they know themselves as unjust: sinners indeed they are none the less just in hope.'[2] 'For righteousness and unrighteousness are taken in Scripture very differently from the way in which the philosophers and lawyers interpret them. For they assert it to be a quality of the soul, but in the Scriptures righteousness consists rather in the *imputation* of God than the essence of the thing itself. He is a possessor of righteousness, not only who has a certain quality, nay rather, he is altogether a sinner and unjust, but whom God on account of the confession of his unrighteousness and his imploring mercifully *reputes* the righteousness of God and wills to regard as just in His presence. Thus we are all born and die in iniquity, i.e. in unrighteousness. We are just by the sole *reputation* of the merciful God by faith.'[3]

It was in the great *Commentary on Galatians* that that teaching was fully developed and the eschatological character of *imputation* was powerfully brought out. In the *Lectures on Romans* Luther had been concerned to emphasise the fact that justification is on the ground of Christ's substitutionary and atoning exchange, thus involving the believer in objective righteousness, the righteousness of God, so that it is God's righteousness which is the real heart and substance of man's righteousness, but in the *Commentary on Galatians* Luther is also concerned to emphasise the fact that we can only understand justification in terms of a duality which reaches out to the advent of Christ, when our perfect righteousness in Christ will be revealed. 'Christian righteousness consists in two things, faith in the heart and God's imputation.'[4] Faith is a

---

[1] W.A. 56, p. 268.
[2] W.A. 56, p. 269. See the whole section on Rom. 4.7, and also pp. 20, 30, 42, etc.
[3] W.A. 56, p. 287; cf. W.A. 8, p. 92.
[4] Cf W.A. 40/1, p. 367: 'Christian righteousness consists in these two things: faith which gives glory to God, and in God's imputation. For faith is weak, and

formal righteousness (*formalis iustitia*), and yet this righteousness is not enough, for after faith, there still remain remnants of sin in our flesh. This sacrifice of faith began in Abraham (Rom. 4.20-22), but at the last it was finished in his death. Wherefore the other part of righteousness must be added also, *to finish the same in us*, that is to say, God's imputation. We have received the first fruits of the Spirit, but not yet the tenths.... We conclude, therefore, that righteousness indeed begins through faith, and by the same we have the first fruits of the Spirit; but because faith is weak, it is not made perfect without God's imputation. Wherefore faith begins righteousness, but imputation makes it perfect unto the day of Christ.'[1] Or again: 'Hereby we may see how faith justifies without works, and yet how imputation of righteousness is also necessary. Sins do remain in us, which God utterly hates. Therefore it is necessary that we should have imputation of righteousness which we obtain through Christ, and for Christ's sake, who is given unto us and received of us by faith. In the meanwhile as long as we live here, we are carried and nourished in the bosom of the mercy and longsuffering of God until the body of sin is abolished and we are raised up as new creatures in that great day. Then there shall be new heavens and a new earth in which righteousness shall dwell.'[2]

Here it is clear that *imputation* is essentially an eschatological concept. Certainly it indicated that justification is forensic in the sense that it is grounded on the judgment of Christ on the Cross, for He the Just dies for the unjust that we may be made the righteousness of God in Him, but it also indicated that what happened in the judgment and death of Christ for us is yet to be fully disclosed at the advent of Christ. *Imputatio* is the concept which holds together those two moments, the forensic and the

---

God's imputation must be joined with it. Thus a Christian man is both righteous and a sinner, holy and profane, an enemy of God and yet a child of God.' Luther goes on to point out that such contraries are not acceptable to the philosopher or the natural reason or the wisdom of the flesh. 'Here we see that every Christian is a high priest: for first he offers up and slays his own reason —the wisdom of the flesh; then he gives glory to God, that He is righteous, true, patient, pitiful, and merciful. And this is the daily sacrifice of the New Testament which must be offered evening and morning. The evening sacrifice is to slay reason, the morning sacrifice is to glorify God. This is therefore a strange and wonderful definition of righteousness that it is the imputation of God.'

[1] W.A. 40/1, p. 364. '*Fides ergo incipit, reputatio perficit usque ad illum diem.*'
[2] W.A. 40/1, p. 372; W.A. 8, pp. 77, 88f, 96f, 104f.

eschatological, in one.¹ That the believer is imputed righteous means that he possesses a righteousness which is *real (justus)*, though not yet fully *realised (justificandus)*,² as real as Christ who dwells in his heart by faith, but who as yet is discerned only by faith and not by sight.³ *Imputatio* describes the *hic et tunc* of our salvation in Christ,⁴ and tells us not to judge our actual righteousness by the appearance of the flesh, for it is concealed under hope until Christ comes. 'We through the Spirit wait for the hope of righteousness by faith' (Gal. 5.5). Every word here is pithy and full of power. . . . Hope after the manner of the Scriptures is taken two ways: namely, for the thing that is hoped for, and for the affection of him that hopes. For the thing that is hoped for, it is taken in the first chapter to the Colossians: 'For the hope that is laid up for you in heaven' (v. 5), that is, the thing we hope for. For the affection of him who hopes it is taken in the eighth chapter of Romans (v. 24): 'For we are saved by hope.' So also in this place hope may be taken in two ways: first, 'we wait in Spirit, through faith, for the hope of righteousness', that is, the righteousness hoped for, which shall be revealed when the Lord will; the second, we wait in Spirit by faith for righteousness, with hope and desire. That is to say, we are righteous, although our righteousness is not yet revealed, but hangs yet in hope. For so long as we live here,

---

¹ Therefore the counterpart to the duality of imputation is the duality involved in repentance, which Luther thinks of as a 'medium between unrighteousness and righteousness'. 'Thus he is in sin as a *terminus a quo* and in righteousness as a *terminus ad quem*. If we are always repenting, we are always sinners, and yet at the same time we are just and justified, *partim* sinners, *partim* just, i.e. nothing save penitents' (W.A. 56, p. 442). Cited from Gordon Rupp, *The Righteousness of God*, p. 180.

² W.A. 4, p. 364: '*Semper peccamus, semper immundi sumus. Et quia spiritus et caro unus homo est, sine dubio culpa hominis est, quod caro tam mala est et male agit. Quare . . . semper sumus in motu, semper iustificandi, qui justi sumus. Nam hinc venit, ut omnis iustitia pro presenti instanti sit peccatum ad eam, que in sequenti addenda est. Quia vere dicit b. Bernardus: "Ubi incipis nolle fieri melior, desinis esse bonus. Quia non est status in via dei: ipsa mora peccatum est." Quare qui in presenti instanti se iustum confidit et stat, iam iustitiam perdidit, sicut in motu similiter patet: terminus, qui in isto instanti est ad quem ipse in sequenti instanti est terminus a quo. Terminus autem a quo est peccatum, a quo semper eundum est. Et terminus ad quem est iustitia, quo eundum est.*'

³ W.A. 40/I, pp. 229, 280ff; p. 545.

⁴ Cf. W.A. 40/I, p. 377f. 'We look for Christ to come again in glory to judge both the quick and the dead, whom we believe to have come already for our salvation. At this day also Christ is present to some, to others He is to come. To all believers He is present; to the unbelievers He is not yet come, nor does He profit them at all, but if they hear the Gospel and believe that He is present to them, He justifies and saves them

THE ESCHATOLOGY OF FAITH: MARTIN LUTHER

sin remains in our flesh; and there is also a law in our flesh, and members rebelling against the law of our mind, and leading us captives unto the service of sin (Rom. 7.23). Now, when these affections of the flesh rage and reign, and we on the other side wrestle against them, then there is room for hope. Indeed, we have begun to be justified through faith, whereby we have also received the first-fruits of the Spirit, and the mortification of the flesh is also begun in us, but we are not perfectly righteous. It remains, then, that we be perfectly conformed, and this is what we hope for, so our righteousness is not yet in actual possession but lies under hope (*nondum est in re, sed adhuc in spe*).[1] Or, as Luther puts it a little later in the same *Commentary*: 'We possess Christ by faith and in the midst of our afflictions through hope we wait for that righteousness which we possess already by faith.'[2]

That is the relation between *having* and *not-having* which lies at the heart of Luther's eschatology.[3] It is thus neither a realised eschatology, for the *having* here and now is offset by a *not-having*, nor is it a futurist eschatology, for the *not-having* is a *not-yet-having* which is offset by a present *having*. It is the eschatological dialectic of *justus et peccator*.[4]

It is with the same doctrine that Luther faced the conflict with the official Church. At first he believed that the hostility of the Papacy to his doctrine of grace must be due to a misunderstanding, that it was only temporary, and that he would be vindicated in his difference at a General Council of the Church, because the Church itself was sound. But then when he saw that the tension between grace and nature ran right through the fabric of the institutional Church, he knew that the only General Council which would vindicate him would be the final judgment of Christ at His advent.[5] As he recovered from his shock of horror at the conflict of the Church with the Church, Luther could only interpret the conflict

---

[1] W.A. 40/2, p. 23f; W.A. 34/2, p. 118.   [2] W.A. 40/2, p. 30.
[3] W.A. 38, p. 567. '*Talis est natura regni Dei, ut alius videatur possidere et non possidet. Alius possidet et tamen non videtur possidere.*' Cf. also W.A. 34/2, pp. 110f.
[4] Cf. W.A. 40/2, p. 27. 'Faith is the *dialectic* which conceives the idea of whatsoever is to be believed. Hope is the *rhetoric* which amplifies, urges, persuades, and exhorts to constancy, to the end that faith should not fail in the time of temptation but should keep hold of the Word and firmly cleave to it.'
[5] Cf. W. A., *Tischreden*, Vol. 1, § 491; *Von den Konziliis und Kirchen*, W.A. 50, pp. 509-653; and *An die Herren deutschen Ordens*, W.A. 12, pp. 232-244; W.A. 42, pp. 276f.

as an adumbration of the final judgment when the children of light would be divided from the children of darkness.[1] To Luther the Reformation was a divine act[2] which startled him into the realisation that he was living in the last times, so close to the impending judgment that already he could see the Church of Jesus Christ being unmasked of its anti-Christian secularisation. 'If the Last Day were not so close at hand it would be small wonder if heaven and earth were to fall at such blasphemy. The fact that God can tolerate such things as this is a sign that the Great Day is not far off. And yet they laugh at that, unmindful that they have made God out to be blind, crazy, mad, and foolish, and they think that their doings are wise and manly. I, too, would be as carefree as they are, if I regarded only their raging; but the wrath of God, which is shown upon them, terrifies me sorely, and it is high time that we all wept and prayed earnestly, as Christ did over Jerusalem, when he bade the women weep not for Him, but for themselves and their children. For they do not believe that the time of their visitation is near, and they will not believe it, even though they see it, hear it, smell it, taste it, touch it, and feel it.'[3]

The Two Kingdoms

The characteristic way in which Luther stated his whole position was his doctrine of the two kingdoms, the *'geistliches Regiment'* and the *'weltliches Regiment'*.[4] That was his way of expressing the Biblical doctrine of the two ages, the αἰὼν οὗτος and the αἰὼν μέλλων. The Christian who is *simul justus et peccator* lives, as Luther puts it, in two kingdoms, two ages, or 'two worlds, the one heavenly, the other earthly'.[5] But there are differences between Luther's

---

[1] *Tischreden*, IV, 51.13.
[2] 'God alone is in this business. We are carried away by Him. We are led rather than lead.' W.A., *Briefe*, II, p. 39; p. 41; cf. W.A. 2, p. 399.
[3] *Von den Konziliis und Kirchen*, W.A. 50, pp. 509ff. Cf. *An den christlichen Adel deutscher Nation*, W.A. 6, p. 411. And also *Colloquia*: 'It is my firm belief that the angels are getting ready, putting on their armour and girding their swords about them, for the last day is already breaking, and the angels are preparing for the battle.' Cited from H. T. Kerr, *Compend of Luther's Theology*, p. 244.
[4] See Gustaf Törnvall, *Geistliches und weltliches Regiment bei Luther* (Münich, 1947), and Edmund Schlink, *Theologie der lutherischen Bekenntnisschriften* (Münich, 1947), pp. 306ff.
[5] *Comm. on Gal. Introd. Argument*, W.A. 40/1, p. 46. Of special importance for Luther were the New Testament passages, John 18.36, W.A. 6, p. 293; and Luke 17.20f, W.A. 6, p. 293. See also W.A. 7, pp. 683f.

understanding of the two ages or worlds and that of the primitive Church. The New Testament writers and the early Fathers thought of the two aeons in terms of a *Heilsgeschichte*, in terms of a divine action within, as well as transcending, the course of history. In that historical perspective the age of the Kingdom of God is partially telescoped into this present age, so that there is an area in which they overlap each other. The Church on earth has her existence in that overlap of the two ages, living at once in the time of this present age and in the time of the Kingdom of God.

In contrast to that historical perspective, Luther's doctrine of the two ages or regiments is primarily dialectical.[1] The historical element, however, is by no means wanting in Luther's thought. It is apparent, for example, in the temporal order in which he expounded the relation of Law and Gospel, although these two times, of Law and Gospel, are also thought of as persisting side by side in the present, cleaving the Christian himself in two, as it were. 'A Christian is divided into two times. In that he is flesh, he is under the law; in that he is spirit, he is under grace. But these days must be shortened, or else no flesh should be saved. The time of the law is not perpetual, but has an end, which is Jesus Christ. But the time of grace is eternal.'[2] The same historical perspective is to be found in Luther's notion of the *novum regnum* which Christ came to set up in distinction to the old kingdom[3] which has persisted ever since God said to Adam: 'Be fruitful, and multiply, and replenish the earth and subdue it and have dominion over the fish of the sea, and over the fowls of the air and over every living thing that moves upon the earth' (Gen. 1.28). That 'old kingdom' founded in Adam concerns our temporal life and relates to *die weltliche Oberkeit*. But afterwards God has established another *Regiment* which is *zweierley*. On the one hand, it is the regiment of the law which was founded through Moses to reveal

---

[1] 'The conception of the Church as a *civitas Dei* on earth Luther called '*ein grawsamer yrthum*' (W.A. 6, pp. 293f).
[2] *Comm. on Gal.* 3.23, W.A. 40/1, p. 525. Cf. p. 522: 'Therefore we must join two things together which are most contrary, to fear and to fly from the wrath of God, and again to trust in His mercy and goodness. The one is hell, the other heaven, and yet they must be nearly joined together in the heart.'
[3] W.A. 34/2, p. 504. '*Christus venit auffzurichten novum regnum, nicht auffzuheben das alte, auch nichts genomen, sed gegeben, was gebuhrt. Ipse utitur mundo, sed non regit, nimpt ein bissen brods, sed non docet.*'

sin but it has little to do with grace. On the other hand, however, there is '*alterum regnum, das resurrectio Domini hat gestifftet, wil ein new Reich, wesen einsetzen*'. This is the Kingdom of Christ, who is enthroned as King to have dominion over life and death and to reign over sin and death, which we have inherited from Adam, but in distinction to the temporal nature of the old kingdom this is the '*regnum coelorum, non terrestre*'.[1] It is the '*regnum remissionis peccatorum*' through which heaven is opened and hell is closed.[2]

Luther has another way of speaking of the historical perspective of the two kingdoms, the *duplex ecclesia* which dates from the beginning of history[3]. We shall examine that later, but here it must be noted that the *geistliches Regiment* as even *novum regnum* is not thought of in positive relation to the temporal kingdom of this world but is sharply distinguished from it like the *sinus Abrahae*. That kingdom has no need of the Gospel,[4] no need of the Word of God, for it has its own *ratio*.[5] And yet there is no doubt that Luther does think of this temporal kingdom as taking on through sin the form of the law[6] upon which, therefore, the *geistliches Regiment* supervenes as a *novum regnum* in a mighty operation of the Word of God. The *novum regnum* is involved in history, therefore, so that Luther sometimes interpreted it in terms of the prophecies of Ezekiel and Daniel,[7] but his attempt to relate eschatology to the actual course of history was strangely confused. Nowhere is that more apparent than in his second preface to the book of Revelation written in 1545, in which he sought to give it a detailed historical interpretation.[8] The fact is that on the one hand Luther was powerfully influenced by the popular apocalyptic literature in which the later Middle Ages abounded, literature from Wyclifite England, from Taborite Bohemia, and above all from

---

[1] Cf. W.A. 41, p. 483. '*Et quod hoc factum ideo, ut ostenderet suum regnum non debere esse mundanum, potens, dives in terris. Sed omnia da hin gerichtet, quod aliud regnum, quod nach der weltlichen ehr . . . prius dedit mundanum regnum Adae.*'
[2] W.A. 49, pp. 137-139.   [3] W.A. 43, p. 3.   [4] W.A. 41, p. 483.
[5] '*Deus dedit rationem, ut regamus corporales res, educare liberos, administrare domos etc. ad hoc non opus scriptura, hoc donum Deus proiecit inter omnes gentes. Non opus ergo, ut demittat verbum de celo*' (W.A. 16, p. 353).
[6] W.A. 36, p. 358; 20, p. 530.
[7] See the Prefaces, W.M.L., VI, pp. 412-423. Cf. the work of Melanchthon, *In Danielem Prophetam Commentarius* (1543), C.R. 13.
[8] Op. cit., pp. 479-488. In the 1522 Preface Luther had written: 'My spirit cannot fit itself into this book.'

THE ESCHATOLOGY OF FAITH: MARTIN LUTHER 19

the many successors of Joachim of Fiore and the Fraticelli,[1] and yet, on the other hand, his training in scholastic philosophy and theology had so indoctrinated him with a conception of eternity as '*totum simul, alles auf einmal*',[2] or 'all in one heap', as he put it in the Commentary on Peter and Jude,[3] that he found it extremely difficult to think of duration or time in the Kingdom of God, and had to think in terms of mathematical points and lines.[4] Consequently, apocalyptic for Luther pointed not so much to the engagement of the Kingdom of God with history, as to its abrupt termination, '*consummans et abbrevians*' (Rom. 9.28), for the nearer the day of judgment comes the fewer will be the faithful, as in the days of Noah.[5] That is to say, Luther's was an apocalyptic view in the Donatist or sectarian rather than in the Biblical sense, for to him 'the whole world is evil and among thousands there is scarcely one true Christian'.[6] As early as 1530 Luther was so convinced that the end was about to break in with catastrophic swiftness that he resolved to publish his translation of the book of Daniel right away in order that it might do its work before the mighty and terrible day of the Lord, so full of fear for the godless, and so full of consolation for the believing.[7] 'Therefore we commend all earnest Christians to read the book of Daniel, to whom it will be a consolation and a great profit in these wretched last times: but to the godless he is of no profit, as he himself says, in the end, "The godless remain godless and do not heed" (Dan. 12.10).... As Christ in Luke 21 encouraged His own with terrible news, and says, "When ye shall see all these things, then look up

[1] This is apparent also in the commentary of Francis Lambert published in 1528, *Exegeseos in sanctam divi Ioannis Apocalypsin*, which appears to have influenced Luther's second preface of 1545; and in the work of Andreas Osiander, *Coniectura de ultimis temporibus ac de fine mundi* (1544), which was undertaken at the request of Melanchthon.
[2] W.A. 12, p. 596.   [3] W.A. 12, pp. 70f.
[4] See W.A. 40/2, p. 526; W.A. 39/2, p. 299; W.A. 40/3, p. 572.
[5] '*Quid futurum putamus ante diem extremum, siquidem nunc revelato Euangelio tanta contemptorum est copia, ut verendum sit, ne brevi praevaleant et repleant Mundum erroribus et Verbum omnino extinguitur?*' (W.A. 42, p. 246; cf. p. 279).
[6] On Secular Authority—To what extent it should be obeyed, IV, W.A. 11, pp. 229ff.
[7] Cf. 'These and similar thoughts caused us to publish this Prophet Daniel before the others, which have to be published still, that he may see the light of day before the elements shall melt, and he may do his work and console the distressed Christians for whose sake he was written and spared to these last days' (*Luthers Schriften*, Walch edition, 6, p. 893). Cf. the letter to Hausmann of 25th February 1530: '*Nos iam Danielem formamus edendum pro solatio istius ultimi temporis*' (W.A., *Briefe*, V, p. 242).

and lift up your heads, for your redemption is near" (21.28), so here too we see that Daniel always ends all his visions and dreams, however terrible, with joy; namely, with Christ's Kingdom and Advent, and it is on account of this Advent, as the most important and final thing in them, that these visions and dreams were given, interpreted and written.'[1]

Throughout the year 1530 Luther was working and writing in *'Johannine haste' (in festinantia Ioniana)*.[2] He was afraid that the advent would take place before he had finished translating the Scriptures. 'The world runs and hastens so diligently to its end that it often occurs to me forcibly that the last day will break before we can completely turn the Holy Scriptures into German.[3] For it is certain from the Holy Scriptures that we have no more temporal things to expect. All is done and fulfilled: the Roman Empire is at an end; the Turk has reached his highest point; the pomp of Papacy is falling away and the world is cracking on all sides almost as if it would break and fall apart entirely. It is true that this same Roman Empire now under our Emperor Charles is coming up a bit and is becoming mightier than it has been for a long time, but I think that that shows it is the last phase, and that before God it is just as when a light or wisp of straw is burnt up and about to go out, then it gives forth a flame as if it was going to burn brightly and even at the same moment goes out: even so Christendom now does with the light of the Gospel. Moreover all prophets in and out of the Bible write that after this time, namely, after the present year of 1530, things will go well again. That which they so rightly point to and prophesy will be, I hope, the last day, which will free us from all evil and help us to everlasting joy. So I reckon this epoch of the Gospel light as none other than the time in which God shortens and restrains tribulation by means of the Gospel, as Christ says in Matthew 24: "If the Lord shortened not these days, no man would be saved." For if

---

[1] *Preface to Daniel*, Erlangen edition, 41, pp. 321f.
[2] Letter to Melanchthon, of 2nd June 1530, W.A., *Briefe*, V, p. 346.
[3] Luther declares he did not want to 'force others to believe as I do; neither will I permit anyone to deny me the right to believe that the last day is near at hand. These words and signs of Christ (Luke 21.25-36) compel me to believe that such is the case' (cited from H. T. Kerr, *Compend of Luther's Theology*, p. 246). But surely this was to judge according to the carnal reason, the very thing Luther condemned so often! Three years later, in 1533, Luther had to deal severely with Michel Stifel for calculating that the world would end at 8 a.m. on 19th October 1533! (*Tischreden*, IV, 51.2.)

the world had to stand longer as it has hitherto stood, the whole world would become Mohammedan or sceptical, and no Christian would be left, as Christ says (Luke 18.8): "When the Son of Man comes, shall He find faith on the earth?" And, in fact, there was no more right understanding nor doctrine in the Christian faith present, but mere error, darkness and superstition with the innumerable multitude.'[1]

That fervid eschatological expectation kept up its force until Luther's death, but it became more and more calculating. In 1541 he published a book called *Supputatio annorum mundi*, which he reissued in an enlarged edition in 1545.[2] In it he calculated in old Patristic style, finding that the year A.D. 1540 corresponded to the year 5500 after creation. There were still five hundred years to go before the eternal Sabbath, but the Lord had promised to shorten the time for the sake of His elect, and as the Lord Himself did not stay the full three days and nights in the grave, the day of the Church's resurrection would be hurried on. There might be no more than a hundred years to go![3] It was during the Easter season that Pharaoh was overthrown in the Red Sea and Israel was redeemed out of Egypt. It was during the same season that the world was created, and that Christ rose again from the dead. Perhaps it will be at Easter too, thought Luther, that the Last Day will arrive, when God's gracious *imputation* will be fulfilled crowned with glory.[4]

There can be no doubt that Luther's realistic eschatology revived a Biblical emphasis which he preached with great power and comfort to the flock of Christ hungering for the righteousness of the Kingdom of Heaven. There were also these other aspects of his eschatology which were rather unfortunate and came to have too great an influence, particularly in England, but after all they are but a minor aspect of his theology. More important than any correlation between prophecies and contemporary events was his apocalyptic cast of thought which allowed him to see movement and divine intervention in history, for the Word of God preached throws the world into tumult. 'The world and its god cannot and

---

[1] Erlangen edition, 41, pp. 321f.   [2] W.A. 53, pp. 1ff.
[3] See also *Tischreden* (F.B.), IV, 49f and 51.4, 8: '*Diese jtzige Zeit, wenn man sie hält gegen die vorigen, vergangenen Zeit, so ist sie kaum einer Hand breit, oder wie ein ubrig Aepfelchen, das an einen Baume ein wenig hanget*' (ibid., IV, 51.3).
[4] *Tischreden* (F.B.), IV, 51.9.

will not bear the Word of God: and the true God cannot and will not keep silence. While, therefore, these two gods are at war with each other, what else can there be in the world but tumult? Therefore to wish to silence these tumults is nothing else than to wish to hinder the Word of God, and to take it out of the way. For the Word of God, wherever it comes, comes to change and renew the world.'[1] And that is the *'Verbum Dei* by which we receive testimony of future and invisible things'.[2] Indeed, it is just because the Word of God is the sceptre of His Kingdom that by bringing the future things into the present it creates *commotiones*.[3] *'Verbum non est opus nostrum, sed est regnum Dei efficax et potens in cordibus nostris.*[4] *Regnum habet fundamentum, columnam in verbo Dei.'*[5] That, however, is the very fact that determines the dialectical character of eschatology for Luther. 'Here thou hearest that His Kingdom is on earth, and that it is not visible but is in Word.'[6] Just because the Word of God is His sovereign and mighty action, His Kingdom operates wherever the Word is heard —that is the '*Regnum fidei*',[7] as he is so fond of calling it. But, as a *hearing Kingdom*, it is not a *seeing Kingdom*.[8]

The Kingdom of God

At this very point, however, Luther sometimes speaks of *'duplicia regimina dei*".[9] One is the *Regnum dei invisibile*, the invisible Kingdom of the invisible God. Because it concerns the hidden will and council of God it is utterly incomprehensible to us, for His eternal decisions and judgments are far beyond our knowledge and he who would pry into that Kingdom will only 'break his neck'.[10] The other Kingdom is the Kingdom of the Incarnate

---

[1] *De Servo Arbitrio*, 19. W.A. 18, p. 626: '*Sermo enim Dei venit mutaturus orbem, quoties venit.*' Cf. the letter to Spalatin, February 1520: '*Obsecro te, si de Evangelio recte sentis, noli putare, rem eius posse sine tumultu, scandalo, seditione agi. Tu ex gladio non facies plumam, nec ex bello pacem: verbum Dei gladius est, bellum est, ruina est, scandalum est, perditio est, venenum est, et (ut Amos ait) sicut ursus in via et leaena in silva*' (W.A., *Briefe*, II, pp. 43f).
[2] W.A. 3, p. 386.   [3] W.A. 28, p. 314.   [4] W.A. 39/1, p. 332.
[5] W.A. 40/2, p. 196; cf. W.A. 30/2, pp. 539 and 554; 27, p. 417.
[6] *Sermon on John* 1.5f, W.A. 15, p. 542.
[7] See for example, W.A. 40/1, p. 427; W.A. 36, pp. 568f. '*Er redet von dem Reich Christi jtst auff erden, welches ist ein Reich des glaubens, darin er regiret durch das Wort, nicht inn sichtlichem, offentlichen Wesen, sondern ist gleich, wie man die Sonne sihet durch eine Wolcken, da sihet man wohl das liecht, aber die Sonne selbst sihet man nicht.*'   [8] W.A. 51, p. 11.
[9] W.A. 45, p. 280; cf. 28, p. 281.   [10] W.A. 45, pp. 252, 282, 290.

THE ESCHATOLOGY OF FAITH: MARTIN LUTHER   23

Son, 'the visible God', '*Gottes Regiment auff Erden, das sichtbar Regiment Gottes, welches uns Christen angehet und heisset das Reich Christi*'. This is the revealed Kingdom in which Christ as King and Lord rules through the Word of the Gospel, through the Spirit and the Sacraments; it is the Kingdom of the Incarnation and the mighty deeds of Christ for our salvation.[1] Jesus Christ is God, Creator and Lord over all, and He participates in God's invisible Kingdom as well as rules over the visible Kingdom of God on earth. *Secundum Deitatem* Christ rules in the invisible Kingdom along with the Father, for He is equal to the Father, but *secundum humanitatem* He reigns in the *Kirche* and *Christenheit* on earth, although He is also Head of the whole worldly regiment on earth because of His Deity.[2] In so far as Christ's Kingdom is involved '*in den heimlichen, verborgenen Rath und in das unsichtbar, unbegreiflich und unerforschlich Regiment Gottes*,' it is beyond us, but what concerns us is the visible Kingdom of God on earth, where we have to do with the Humanity of Christ.[3] That is the Kingdom which is the object of our faith and which therefore Luther calls '*Regnum fidei*'. This is the revealed Kingdom visible to faith, but in contrast to the worldly regiment it is invisible because it is not discerned through our senses or by our natural reason. The visible Kingdom on earth is invisible because it concerns hearing rather than seeing, faith rather than works, Gospel rather than Law. That takes us back in our discussion to Luther's primary emphasis upon the eschatological tension between *believing* and *seeing*, between *having* and *not-having*, which assumes its large and masterful aspect in the dialectical relation between the two Kingdoms, *geistliches Regiment und weltliches Regiment*.[4]

Luther employs a wealth of expression to distinguish the two kingdoms, such as '*regimen spirituale/regimen corporale*',[5] '*regnum gratiae/regnum rationis*',[6] '*regnum fidei/regnum operum*',[7] '*regnum Christi/regnum Caesaris*',[8] '*regnum aeternum/regnum seculare*',[9] '*Reich des Glaubens/Reich der Tat*',[10] '*Hörreich/Sehreich*',[11] '*regnum*

[1] W.A. 45, pp. 280ff.   [2] W.A. 45, pp. 291f.   [3] Cf. W.A. 42, p. 625.
[4] See, for examples, W.A. 19, p. 629; 30/2, p. 554; 32, p. 159; 49, p. 30; 50, p. 652.
[5] W.A. 45, p. 253; 40/1, p. 293; 51, pp. 21, 239; 11, p. 262; 27, p. 417.
[6] W.A. 40/2, p. 292; W.A. 40/1, p. 292; 45, p. 252.   [7] W.A. 40/1, p. 427.
[8] W.A. 28, p. 311; 32, p. 183; 45, p. 252; 34/1, p. 178.
[9] W.A. 28, p. 281; W.A. 16, p. 254; 34/1, p. 178; 40/1, p. 395; 45, p. 252.
[10] W.A. 51, p. 11; 36, p. 385.   [11] W.A. 51, p. 11; 20/2, pp. 394f.

coelorum/regnum mundanum',[1] '*regnum dei/regnum humanum*',[2] etc. It is clear that Luther does not think of these two regiments as two magnitudes excluding each other or competing with each other for rule, but as two overlapping aspects of the one *Regnum Dei invisibile*.[3] The Kingdom of God in the supreme sense, '*das hoch Regnum der Göttlichen Majestet*',[4] assumes a dual aspect within this world, and each aspect is unthinkable without, and inseparable from, the other.[5] 'There are two kinds of regiment in the world (*zweyerley regiment auff der wellt*), as there are also two kinds of people (*wie auch zweyerley leut sind*), the believing and the unbelieving. Christians yield themselves to the control of God's Word; they have no need of civil government for their own sake. But the unchristian portion require another government, even the civil sword, since they will not be controlled by the Word of God. Yet if all were Christians and followed the Gospel, there would be no more necessity or use for the civil sword and the exercising of authority; for if there were no evil doers there certainly would be no punishment. But since it is not to be expected that all of us should be righteous, Christ has ordained magistracy for the wicked, that they may rule as they must be ruled. But the righteous He keeps for Himself, and rules them by His Word.'[6]

Both these Kingdoms are involved in our relation to God the Creator and Redeemer. In the spiritual realm the relation to God is direct, in the secular realm it is indirect, but even the *regnum seculare* or '*weltliches Regiment* is spoken of as *Gottes Reich*, for God wills it to remain and wishes us to be obedient within it. It is the Kingdom of God's left hand', says Luther, 'where God rules through father, mother, Kaiser, king, judge, and even hangman, but His proper Kingdom, the Kingdom of His right hand, is where God rules Himself, where He is immediately present and His Gospel is preached'.[7] 'As Christians we must not place the

---

[1] W.A. 49, pp. 30, 40, 227.   [2] W.A. 40, pp. 293f.
[3] W.A. 45, pp. 280, 292.   [4] W.A. 45, p. 252.
[5] When Luther thought of the relation between the Kingdom of God and the concrete life of this world he thought of the Kingdom as assuming *three* visible forms or regiments, which he called '*ecclesia*', '*politia*', and '*oeconomia*', the latter being the *Hausregiment*, but because this belonged essentially to the worldly kingdom as distinct from the spiritual kingdom, it was not regarded as a third in the wider dialectic. See W.A. 47, p. 853.
[6] W.A. 45, p. 252.
[7] *Sermon for the third of Advent*, on Matt. 11.2-10, *Predigten*, edition by Kreutzer, p. 26f. Cf. W.A. 36, p. 385; 20, p. 530; and 52, p. 26.

Datum of our life here on earth, but know that He will come from heaven, and so we are to be ready to expect His coming every hour. Therefore we are only half and with the left hand, within the life of this world, for with their right hand and their whole heart they live in expectation of the hour of His Coming.'[1] When, therefore, Luther speaks of one Kingdom as 'spiritual' in contrast to the other, which is 'corporal', it does not mean that one has to do with pure spirit and has nothing to do with our physical life on earth. 'Spiritual' distinguishes this Kingdom of Christ or of faith in two main respects: (*a*) It is spiritual in that its *end* is different, for its end reaches beyond the earthly life as we know it into a new existence beyond death and sin and all corruption. The spiritual Kingdom is thus essentially an eschatological expression for the fact that in God's redeeming purpose this present evil world is to be renewed through the Spirit—it is with that *causa finalis* that the spiritual Kingdom is supremely concerned.[2] In contrast the worldly or secular kingdom is concerned with earthly matters only and with earthly peace. (*b*) It is spiritual in that a different means is employed for its operation in the world: the Word and Spirit of God or the sword of the Spirit, as against the sword of steel which is employed by the *Obrigkeit*.[3] This division is also an essentially eschatological expression, for it means that in His mercy God wills that His power shall operate through preaching of the Gospel, and that the Omnipotent Judgment of God is suspended until the Last Day.[4]

The Kingdom of Christ

To these two differences in end and method between the *geistliches Regiment* and the *weltliches Regiment* there correspond two other distinctions which Luther constantly makes: (*a*) The spiritual Kingdom is distinguished as the *new Kingdom*, as we have already seen. That is well expressed in the Preface to the Book of

---

[1] *Sermon for the second Sunday of Advent*, W.A. 36, p. 379; W.A. 34/2, p. 111; W.A. 33, p. 681.
[2] '*Christi regnum ist geordnet, hat, finalis causa, endlich darum eingesetzt ut homines nati in peccatis et morte, ut illis geholffen, ut a peccato et morte ad vitam et iustitiam . . .*' (W.A. 45, p. 252).
[3] W.A. 27, p. 417: '*Sepe audistis, quod praedicemus spirituale et corporale regimina. Spirituale per verbum, seculare per gladium regit.*'
[4] W.A. 34/2, pp. 128f. See also W.A. 51, p. 261; W.A., *Briefe*, V, p. 413; W.A. 10/1, p. 142.

Ezekiel. 'The old, worldly, temporal regiment remains in all the world, and does not at all prevent the establishment of the new, spiritual, everlasting rule and Kingdom of Christ under it and within it, though this Kingdom has its own peculiar nature. Especially is this the case where there are righteous kings and princes, who tolerate this new, everlasting Kingdom of Christ under their old government, or accept it themselves, promote it, and desire, as Christians, to be in it. Otherwise the greater part of the kings, princes and lords hate the new covenant and kingdom of Christ as poisonously and bitterly as the Jews at Jerusalem, and persecute it and would wipe it out, and like the Jews, they go to destruction because of it. That is what happened to Rome, and will happen to others also, for it is promised that Christ's new Kingdom shall be an everlasting Kingdom, and the old Kingdom must perish in the end. It is well to remember, too, that since God Himself calls this Kingdom a new Kingdom, it must be a far more glorious Kingdom than the old Kingdom was or is, and that it was God's will to make it a far better Kingdom than the old one; and even though it had no other glory, this alone would be enough to make it glorious beyond measure—that it is to be an everlasting Kingdom that will not come to an end like the human kingdom.'[1]

(b) This very Kingdom of Christ, however, just because it has moved into history, and operates under and in this old world reaching out in its *causa finalis* beyond, must itself be considered as two-fold. '*Regnum Christi est duplex*. On the one hand, it is the Kingdom which Christ has from eternity with the Father and the Holy Spirit which He will never lay down. On the other hand, it is the Kingdom which He now has, which is the Kingdom of remitting sins and governing His Church. This Kingdom Christ will lay down at the Last Judgment, for no more will there be sin or death or any calamity or misery.'[2] Another way Luther had of speaking of that was to distinguish between the *Regnum gratiae* (or *Regnum fidei*) and the *Regnum gloriae*. 'The *Regnum gratiae* is the *Regnum fidei* in which Christ reigns as Man, set over all things by God the Father. The *Regnum gloriae* is the Kingdom in which God Himself through Himself (*Deus ipse per se*) will reign no longer through humanity in faith. *Non quod aliud et alius sit Regnum, sed aliter et aliter. Nunc in fide et aenigmate per humani-*

[1] W.M.L. 6, pp. 417f.   [2] W.A. 39/2, p. 281, on 1 Cor. 15.24.

tatem Christi, tunc in specie et revelatione divinae naturae.'[1] This was a theme on which Luther was fond of preaching in connexion with 1 Cor. 15.24. Thus in 1532 he declared: 'All Scripture shows that this worldly life will cease, the nasty devil with his regiment, and all worldly regiment and all spiritual *Aemter*, for that life is ordered very differently from this. "He will hand over the Kingdom to God the Father" refers then to the Kingdom of faith. Christ now rules through the Word, in faith. Christ and God are already reigning, for there is only one Kingdom of Christ and God. The difference is this, that now it is a Kingdom that is made secret and invisible (*heimlich und nicht sichtbar*), hidden, covered, veiled and grasped in faith and Word. That is how Christ rules now.'[2] Luther goes on to say that because the Kingdom now operates in this way through the Word, 'we see nothing but the Gospel, the Sacrament, Baptism, and that we ought to honour our parents',[3] but when we see God in His majesty without Word and Faith, that will mean that 'the eternal Kingdom of Light will bring the Kingdom of faith to an end. *Das Weltreich will er zerstören, und das Reich Christi wird aufhören.*'[4] In the following year Luther preached again from the same text. 1 Cor. 15.24 'speaks of the Kingdom of Christ now upon earth which is a Kingdom of Faith, wherein He rules through the Word, not in a visible, public character (*Wesen*), but like the Sun which we see through a cloud, for then we see the light but the sun itself we do not see. But when the cloud is removed we see both light and sun together, *in einerlei Wesen*. And so Jesus Christ now rules along with the Father, and there is *einerlei Reich*. The only difference is that it is now dark and hidden, or veiled and covered, grasped in Faith and in the Word so that we do not see any more of it than Baptism and the Sacrament, or hear any more than the external Word: *das ist alle seine Kraft und Macht, dadurch er regieret und Alles ausrichtet . . . bis so lange das Stündlein kommt*, when Christ will make an end and openly manifest Himself in His Majesty and Power. . . . Then it will be called the Kingdom of God.'[5]

Sometimes it looks as if Luther held that with the coming of

---
[1] *Comm. on Gal.* 1.3, 15. Jena edition, 4, p. 394f. Cf. W.A. 40/1, pp. 72f, 139; W.A. 14, p. 28.
[2] W.A. 36, pp. 568f.   [3] Ibid.   [4] Ibid.
[5] Cited from Baier, *Compendium*, IIIa, p. 130f; W.A. 34/2, pp. 128f.

that absolute Kingdom of God the *regnum corporale* will be completely set aside for some empyrean heaven, but that is not the case. In the sermon just cited, for example, he explains the words 'and then God will be all in all' to mean that each one will then himself have in God everything he now has, for when God manifests Himself, '*werden wir alle genug haben an Seele und Leib, und nicht mehr so mancherlei bedürfen, wie wir jetzt auf Erden müssen haben*'.[1] Both the Kingdom of Christ which is described as 'spiritual' and the Kingdom of God in glory have to do with the *whole man, body and soul*,[2] and indeed with the whole of creation.[3] Like the other Reformers Luther held that the whole of nature would be re-created in the Kingdom of God, but so long as this fallen world remains in its present state, the one invisible Kingdom of God at work in it *necessarily* wears a dual aspect in which the direct action of God's grace appears under the contrary aspect of sight and might. If we live in sin and the midst of death and hell, then it is into sin and death and hell that the Word made flesh has come, made like us in our condition that we through grace may be made like Him in glory. That is the *wonderful exchange* that lies at the heart of Luther's theology, the *theologia crucis*.[4]

The Kingdom of grace means that God's Kingdom has penetrated into the midst of our life and taken on the aspect of our life, so that its very hiddenness in the darkness of our sin is the token of its real presence and activity on earth. 'If we follow the judgment of reason, God sets forth absurd and impossible things, when He sets before us the articles of the Christian faith. Indeed it seems to reason an absurd and foolish thing that in the Lord's Supper is offered to us the Body and Blood of Christ, that Baptism

---

[1] Cf. also W.A. 36, pp. 661f.
[2] Cf. the Sermon in the previous year on 1 Cor. 15.44f (W.A. 36, pp. 666f): '*Du wirst nicht allein an der Seelen getauft und gepredigt und durch Euangelion gesegnet, sondern am Leibe. Es wird dir Christi Leib und Blut am Altare nicht allein in die Seele gegeben, sondern in den Leib. Er soll nicht dahinten bleiben. Und soll werden ein geistlicher Leib gleichwie Christi Leib am Tage der Auferstehung.*' See also the Sermon on 1 Cor. 15.20-22, 1532 (W.A. 36, pp. 547f and W.A. 49, pp. 395f).
[3] W.A. 34/2, pp. 126f. Cf. *Tischreden* (F.B.), IV, 49, 51. '*Im künftigen Leben, will ich sagen, da werden Kirchen, Weinbeer, Vögel, Bäume, usw, so solls bald da stehen*' (IV, 51.10). '*Wenn wir nur Gottes Gnade haben, so lachen uns alle Creaturen Gottes an!*' (IV, 49.5).
[4] W.A. 40/1, p. 442; cf. *amabilis permutatio*. W.A. 38, p. 527; and see W.A. 5, pp. 598-673, the *Exposition of Psalm 22*; *Disputatio Heidelbergae habita*, 1518 (W.A. 1, pp. 361f): '*In Christo crucifixo est vera theologia et cognitio Dei.*'

is the laver of the new birth,[1] and of the renewing of the Holy Spirit, that the dead shall rise at the Last Day, that Christ the Son of God was conceived and carried in the womb of the Virgin Mary, that He was born, that He suffered the most reproachful death of the Cross, that He was raised up again, that He now sits at the right hand of the Father, and that He has power both in heaven and in earth. For this cause Paul calls the Gospel of Christ crucified the word of the Cross and the foolishness of preaching which to the Jews was offensive, and to the Gentiles foolish doctrine. Wherefore when God speaks reason judges His Word to be heresy and the word of the devil, for it seems unto it absurd and foolish.'[2] That is the way in which Luther understands the *Regnum fidei*, understands Christ as the object of faith. 'Christ is the object of faith, nay, He is not the object of faith but, as it were, in the faith itself Christ is present (*imo non objectum, sed, ut ita dicam, in ipsa fide Christus adest*). Faith therefore is a certain obscure knowledge or rather darkness which sees nothing, and yet Christ apprehended by faith sits in this darkness: as God in Sinai and in the Temple sits in the midst of darkness (Exod. 19.9; 20.21; 1 Kings 8.10, 12).'[3] '*Ut ergo fidei locus sit, opus est, ut omnia quae creduntur abscondantur. Non autem remotius abscondantur, quam sub contrario objectu, sensu, experientia.*'[4] 'For our good is hidden, and that so deeply that it is hidden under its contrary. Thus our life is hidden under death, our joy under our hatred, glory under our shame, salvation under perdition, the Kingdom under exile, heaven under hell, wisdom under foolishness, righteousness under sin, strength under infirmity.'[5]

The Eschatological Perspective

Since this is so, that the Kingdom of Christ has come to us in the midst of our wretchedness and sin and weakness, then the very measure of its hiddenness is the measure of its penetration and actual presence. But that makes it imperative that we learn how

---

[1] Throughout the sermon on Titus 2 Luther emphasises the fact that through Baptism Christians are 'inserted into the Kingdom of God', where the new and eternal life is not to be understood according to the judgment of reason (W.A. 34/2, pp. 108ff, 118ff).
[2] W.A. 40/1, p. 361. 'Faith said, I believe O God when Thou speakest. And what does God say? Impossible things, lies, foolish, weak, absurd, abominable, heretical, and devilish things, if ye believe reason' (ibid.). Cf. also W.A. 31/1, p. 249.   [3] W.A. 40/1, p. 227.
[4] W.A. 18, p. 633.   [5] W.A. 56, p. 392. Cf. also pp. 377f.

to distinguish between the Kingdom of Christ and the aspect which it wears in our corporal and earthly existence, for unless we distinguish them, we lose the Kingdom of Grace by losing its identity in our sin and shame under law and the worldly kingdom. 'In this life God does not deal with us face to face, but veiled and shadowed from us. That is, as Paul said in another place: "We see Him now through a glass darkly" (1 Cor. 13.12). Therefore we cannot be without veils in this present life. But here wisdom is required which can distinguish the veil from God himself, and that is the wisdom the world does not have.'[1] Though the creation which has been deformed and demonised by sin comes under judgment, it belongs nonetheless to God's Kingdom, and there are not two Kingdoms of God but one. The fact, however, that God has reserved to the last day the renewal of all creation and 'has reserved the displaying of His greatness and majesty, His glory and His effulgence', so that we have but a 'narrow view' of Him,[2] means that we have to exercise faith within that action of divine *reserve*. We must not therefore confound the two realms which God deliberately keeps apart in His eschatological purpose. To confuse the two kingdoms, to join together in the present hearing and seeing, heaven and earth, word and power, *religio* and *politia*, *fides* and *mores*, *gratia* and *opera*, *iustitia Christiana* and *iustitia civilis*, etc., is to usurp the Kingdom of God or to force God's hand—and that is the very mark of Antichrist.[3] '*Das ist invadere regnum et majestatem Dei*.'[4] The two realms or kingdoms may be confounded either by the subordination of the spiritual kingdom to the worldly kingdom as among the Turks, or by the subordination of the worldly kingdom to the spiritual, as in the Papacy, but whether the movement comes from the one side or the other it is really the same act of the devil, for what he seeks to do in each instance is to gain the mastery by anticipating the final judgment and usurping the prerogative of God. Precisely the same attempt to force the Kingdom of God Luther saw in the *Schwärmer*. 'There are two kingdoms, one the Kingdom of God,

---

[1] W.A. 40/1, p. 173: '*Iam adhuc agimus cum Deo velato, in hac enim vita non possumus cum Deo agere facie ad faciem. Universa autem creatura est facies et larva Dei. Sed hic requiritur sapientia quae discernat Deum a larva. Hanc sapientiam mundus non habet, ideo non potest discernere Deum a larva.*'
[2] Cited from H. T. Kerr, *Compend of Luther's Theology*, pp. 247f (Lenker edition of Luther's works, vol. VII, p. 36). See also W.A. 43, p. 393.
[3] W.A. 40/1, pp. 51, 175-178.   [4] W.A. 40/1, p. 106. Cf. 49, p. 30.

the other the kingdom of the world. I have written this so often that I am surprised that there is anyone who does not know it or note it. . . . God's Kingdom is a kingdom of grace and mercy, not of wrath and punishment. In it there is only forgiveness, consideration for one another, love, service, doing of good, peace, joy, etc. But the kingdom of the world is a kingdom of wrath and severity. In it there is only punishment, repression, judgment and condemnation, for the suppressing of the wicked and the protection of the good. For this reason it has the sword, and a prince or lord is called in Scripture God's wrath, or God's rod (Isa. 14). . . . Now he who would confuse the two kingdoms—as our false fanatics would do—would put wrath into God's Kingdom and mercy into the devil's kingdom; and that is the same as putting the devil in heaven and God in hell.'[1]

On the other hand, it is the part of faith to maintain the eschatological perspective by distinguishing sharply between the two kingdoms, the *Reich der Gnade* and the *Reich der Tat*, the Kingdom of God and the kingdom of this world. In this way the Church of Christ waits in faith for God's final action and does not attempt to usurp His power by execution or to force His hand by a preliminary decision.[2] To distinguish the two kingdoms is an act of humility before the impending judgment, and that carries with it the recognition that the final judgment sets limits and boundaries to our obedience in time in respect both of the Church and of the State, the representatives of the two kingdoms on earth. Neither the Church nor the State can assume absolute power. Both are under the judgment, both will pass away in their present forms, and that final judgment relativises and restricts the authority of each.[3] Rebellion against that limitation is apparent in the welding of spiritual and worldly authority into one, the *potestas tyrannica* which Luther discerned in the action of the Papacy on the one hand and the action of the *Schwärmer* on the other.[4]

[1] W.A. 18, p. 389. [2] Cf. W.A. 10/3, pp. 14f; and W.A. 38, p. 144.
[3] W.A. 36, pp. 568ff. Cf. W.A. 43, pp. 393, 425f; 19, pp. 652f; 2, pp. 27.
[4] W.A. 51, p. 239. 'Denn der leidige teuffel hoeret auch nicht auff diese zwey Reich inn einander zu kochen und zu brewen. Die weltlichen herrn wollen ins teufels namen imer Christum leren und meistern, wie er seine kirche und geistlich Regiment sol fueren. So wollen die falschen Pfaffen und Rottengeister nicht inn Gottes namen imer leren und meistern, wie man solle das weltliche Regiment ordenen, Und ist also der Teuffel zu beiden seiten fast seer unmuessig und hat viel zu tun. Gott wolt im weren, Amen, so wirs werd sind.' Cf. W.A. 15, p. 220; 18, pp. 168f; 6, p. 430; 11, p. 271. W.A., *Tischreden*, 4635 and 6234.

At the same time, this does not mean that the two realms are to be separated from each other, for the visible and outward realm is also under Christ and belongs to the Kingdom of God, and therefore must listen to the Word of God's Kingdom as proclaimed in the Gospel.[1] But just because Christ's Kingdom is inward (*internum Regnum*[2]) and spiritual it has no right to rule over the corporal realm or to exercise authority over it as though it were itself an external kingdom.[3] That would be to act against its own essential law and to confound the kingdoms again.[4] Though distinct the two realms are involved in each other and must not be separated; they are differentiated and yet unified under the overarching *Regnum Dei*.[5]

Christian Order?

That brings us to ask an important question, and for Luther's eschatology it is perhaps the most significant. Apart from the ultimate unity between the two kingdoms which will be revealed only in the advent of Christ in glory and power and the over-all rule of the Word of God, is there no positive connexion between the two kingdoms in history, no *tertium comparationis* which faith at least may discern here and now in this world?[6] In answer to that question we may turn to Luther's conception of *Christenheit* which stretches over the whole mass of the people in the world who are baptised and are Christian in name.[7] This does not mean that

---

[1] W.A. 40, p. 8. Cf. W.A. 5, p. 217: '*Alle hönige und fürsten, wenn sie der natur und höchsten Weisheit folgen, müssen Gottes feinde werden und sein Wort verfolgen*'; and W.A. 30/1, pp. 189ff.   [2] W.A. 17/1, pp. 193f.

[3] Cf. W.A. 8, p. 539f, where Luther makes it clear that the 'law' of the *Regnum Christi* is spiritual: '*das lebendige gesetz Christi, welchs ist der geyst gotts, der nicht gegeben wirt, denn durch das wort des Euangelii.*' Cf. W.A. 11, p. 235: 'He is a King over Christians and rules by His Spirit alone, without law.'

[4] W.A. 6, pp. 293ff; W.A. 2, p. 73.

[5] Cf. W.A. 6, p. 297: '*nit das wir sie voneinander scheydenn wollen.*' The spiritual and corporal realms are to be understood on the analogy of spirit and body in the whole man (p. 295f). See also W.A. 12, pp. 275f, 331. Cf. W.A. 11, p. 255: '*Also gehets denn beydes Seyn miteinander, das du zu gleich Gottis reich und der wellt reych genug thuest, eusserlich und innerlich, zu gleich unrecht und Ubel leydest und doch ubel und unrecht straffest, zu gleich dem Übel nicht widderstehist und doch widderstehist. Denn mit dem eynen sihestu auff dich und auff das deyne, mit dem ander auf den Nehisten und auff das seyne.*'

[6] For a *tertium comparationis* in the future compare W.A. 51, p. 261: '*Aber unsers Herr Gotts rat ist der beste, das er gedenckt himel und erden jm einen hauffen zu stossen und eine andere newe welt machen, denn diese welt taug nicht, der buben ist zu viel und der fromen zu wenig drinnen.*'

[7] W.A. 11, p. 251.

Luther held that there could be any Christian regiment in or over the world or over any country.[1] So that even with *Christenheit* Luther has to draw a distinction between the true believers and those who are nominally Christian,[2] and the true *Christenheit* which is free of all external things,[3] and nominal believers who must come under the external jurisdiction of the sword.[4] Far from providing any real *tertium comparationis*, the notion of *Christenheit* tends to move in the direction of an *ecclesiola*, that is, of an inner community of believers within the larger mass which Luther always thought of as unchristian.[5] The notion of *Christenheit* does carry with it, however, the idea that the Kingdom of God is actually present within this world, within history, as well as future. '*Idem Christi regnum hic et in futuro: hic per fidem incoatum, in futuro consummandum per gloriam.*'[6]

To answer the question as to a *tertium comparationis* we have to inquire whether the *geistliches Regiment* ever assumes order and concrete form within the world of here and now. It is not often that Luther uses the term '*ordo*'.[7] No doubt the two regiments do acquire some kind of *ordo* in history, and so far as they do, that is in the nature of the case only observable empirically, but an empirical *ordo* cannot be the object of faith, cannot in the nature of the case belong to the *Regnum fidei*, so that such *ordo* as is acquired in history comes under the judgment of the last day. The real nature of the two regiments, however, Luther preferred to understand in terms of a divine *ordinatio*,[8] that is, in terms of the Word of God,[9] the Word which created heaven and earth, the Word which has broken into our estranged world in Jesus Christ and clothed itself once and for all with His humanity. While therefore Luther makes a sharp distinction between the two regiments, he thinks of the mighty, active, living divine-human Word as operating behind both and it is through that Word that God's

---

[1] W. A. 11, p. 251.   [2] W.A. 10/3, p. 49; W.A. 11, p. 271.
[3] W.A. 12, pp. 275f, 331; cf. also p. 50.
[4] W.A. 27, p. 417. And see W.A. 11, pp. 53, 251.
[5] See especially W.A. 12, p. 485.
[6] Letter to Spalatin, de Wette edition, *Briefe*, II, p. 492.
[7] Cf. Luther's part in the *Promotionsdisputation* of Johannes Macchabäus Scotus, W.A. 39/2, pp. 52, 175, 181. In the Exposition of Genesis Luther speaks frequently of the *tres ordines vitae huius, oeconomia, politia et ecclesia*—see Chs. 19, 21, 43, W.A. 43 and 44.
[8] See the *Disputatio anno 1539 habita*, W.A. 39/2, pp. 52ff.
[9] '*Ubi verbum Dei est ordinatio Dei*' (W.A. 31/2, p. 614).

will is performed. It is the Word of God which is the third dimension between heaven and earth, between spiritual regiment and earthly regiment, and it is through that Word of God that the heavenly realm is made relevant to the earthly, and the last things are made relevant to the present, and the present things of the earth are taken in control and ordered in accordance with God's final purpose for the renewal of heaven and earth.

The Orders of Creation

To see how Luther works out that idea we must examine his difficult doctrine of the '*larva dei*', a term which he apparently took over from mediaeval theology.[1] '*Larva*' means at once a mask or a veil and a ghostly presence. In the world which God has created all creatures and all ordinances are designed to be veils or masks of God's presence,[2] but in this life or in this world that mask or veil can never be removed so that we may see God face to face.[3] The Creator is concealed behind the creature as his *larva* or his *persona*.[4] '*Universa creatura eius larva.*'[5] But this world is estranged from God and the powers of evil have entered to extend their kingdom in it, so that while the whole realm of creation (*universa creatura* or *tota creatura*)[6] is to be regarded as *larva*, and to be nothing in itself but only what it is with respect to the Word of God,[7] yet it may be turned into its opposite by corruption and may even be spoken of as devilish. In this way Luther can speak of *weltliches Regiment* and even of the Law as devilish.[8] As a matter of fact sin has entered creation and therefore all the *larvae* are involved in this demonic perversion and cannot be used directly without correction and judgment, i.e. without the

[1] Cf. Calvin, *Instit.* 4.17.13, and his reference to Peter Lombard in this connection. In his early days Luther lectured on the *Sentences* of Peter Lombard, the notes of which are still extant (W.A. 9, pp. 1-94).

[2] W.A. 40/1, p. 463: '*Omnes ordinationes creatae sunt larvae dei.*' Because theology has to use creaturely words and concepts, Luther adds: '... *larvae, allegoriae, quibus rethorice pingit suam theologiam.*'

[3] '*Nuda facie non possumus agere cum Deo*' (W.A. 40/1, p. 174). '*Iam adhuc agimus cum Deo velato, in hac enim vita non possumus cum Deo agere facie ad faciem*' (ibid.).

[4] W.A. 40, pp. 175f. Luther recalls that both *larva* and *persona* were used of the painted mask of the actor on the Roman stage.

[5] Op. cit., p. 174.

[6] Loc. cit., p. 173. The first edition of this passage (*Comm. on Gal.* 2.6) had *universa*, the final edition, *tota*.

[7] W.A., p. 376: '*Omnes creaturae coram Deo nihil erga Verbum.*'

[8] W.A. 40/1, pp. 553f.

realisation that at the final judgment as they are now, perverted and twisted masks, they will be done away with. Meanwhile, however, the *larva dei* veils the presence of God, not just because it is creaturely but because it is impregnated with evil. Estrangement and perversion therefore turn the *larva dei* into a ghostly presence,[1] so that now *larva* becomes, so to speak, a haunted mask, and it is only an angry God who can be known behind it and only God's strange work which can be encountered through it apart from the Gospel.[2]

This concept Luther also applies to official persons ('for *persona* is properly speaking only "face" or "countenance" or "*larva*", and is that quality or quantity by which a man may be considered from without'),[3] offices and authorities, capacities and institutions, for God uses them as His 'instruments' of action and communication—though there is a difference here between the way He uses them in religion and in the worldly realm.[4] 'So the prince, the magistrate, the teacher, the schoolmaster, the scholar, the father, the mother, the children, the master, the servant, the maid, are *personae*, *larvae* which *religiose* God will have us to acknowledge, love, reverence as His creatures.[5] We must have them in this life, but He does not wish divinity to be ascribed to them.' We must not so reverence them that we forget Him. In order that we may not magnify the *personae*, or put any trust in them, God leaves in them offences and sins, yes, great foul sins, to teach us what a difference there is between the *persona* and God Himself.[6] Everything depends then on the way these *larvae* and *personae* are used. '*Personae, larvae debent esse, Deus dedit eas, sed non debeo*

---

[1] We have to remember that in Latin literature *larvae* was used to describe the *noxiae infernorum umbrae* and the *daemones aerii*. See Stephanus, *Thesaurus Linguae Latinae*, and Dufresne et du Cange, *Glossarium* in *art. cit.* Cf. the incredible statements of Luther in W.A. 31/1, p. 249, and 40/1, p. 361; 40/2, p. 53.

[2] Cf. W.A. 40/1, pp. 500f; pp. 553f; 1, pp. 105f; pp. 112ff etc.

[3] W.A. 57, 67.

[4] '*In religione loquimur aliter de rebus quam in politia in qua vult honorari istas personas ut suas larvas et instrumenta per quae excercet et regit mundum*' (W.A. 40/1, p. 176).

[5] Although they have to be used *religiose*, these distinctions do not obtain in the Kingdom of God, for *before God* all are equal. Therefore we are not baptised into these distinctions (W.A. 34/2, pp. 116f).

[6] 'When it is a question of religion, conscience, the fear of God, faith, and the service of God, we must put no fear in these outward *personae*, we must put no trust in them, look for no comfort from them, or hope for deliverance by them, either corporally or spiritually' (loc. cit., p. 175).

accipere, respicere. Es ligt in usu rerum.'[1] It belongs therefore to theology to draw the proper distinction between the *larva* or *persona* as a God-given *creatura*, and then to pass behind it to God Himself. Thus when we hear the word in St Paul we adore it as Christ Himself speaking; it is not that we adore St Paul. But this is only possible through the Spirit. It does not belong to political man, naturally grounded. 'Only a spiritual person distinguishes acutely the appearance from the Word, the divine *larva* from God Himself and God's work. Hence our science, to distinguish divinity from *larva*. *Hoc non facit mundus.*'[2] This is of prime significance for the whole realm of the Church and the two kingdoms on earth, for it means that we must not be 'respecters of persons' —that is, must not render to the *persona* an importance in himself which he does not have but exercises only as a servant of God, to whom it is his duty to point.[3] That is particularly the case in religion and with respect to the Word of God. 'But out of religion, and in matters of *politia*, we must have regard to the *persona*: for otherwise there will necessarily be confusion and an end of all respect and order. In this world God will have order, a reverence and a difference of *personae*. For else the child, the scholar, the servant, the subject would say: I am a Christian as well as my father, my schoolmaster, my master, my prince. Why then should I reverence him? Before God, then, there is no respect of persons, neither Greek nor Jew, but all are one in Christ—although not so before the world.'[4]

Luther attacks both the Papacy and the *Schwärmer* on the ground that they fail to make the proper theological distinction between the *larva* or *persona* and *divinitas*. 'Scripture is full of examples to warn us not to put our trust in the person and not to think that when we have the person we have all things, as it is in the Papacy where they judge all things according to the outward

---

[1] W.A. 40/1, p. 174. Cf. p. 176: '*Deus dedit omnes creaturis usum, utilitatem, sed non in cultum et religionem. Sicut utor pane, vino, veste, sic fruor omnibus creaturis dei, sed non debeo ea timere, confidere, in eiis gloriari.*' See especially Luther's letter to Amsdorf, de Wette edition, V, p. 431.

[2] W.A. 40/1, p. 173. Cf. the 1535 edition, p. 174: '*Universa creatura est facies et larva Dei. Sed hic requiritur sapientia quae discernat Deum a larva. Hanc sapientiam mundus non habet, ideo non potest discernere Deum a larva.*'

[3] '*Larva est nec res seria.... Sed nosti, quod Deus has personas seu larvas nihil curat, ut quae non sint regnum Dei, ita ut Paulus audeat etiam Apostolatum appellare larvam Gal. II: Deus personam non respicit*' (De Wette, *Luthers Briefe*, V, p. 431).   [4] W.A. 40/3, p. 177.

larva, and therefore the whole Papacy is nothing else but a mere respecting of persons. God has given us His creatures for our use and to do us service, and not as idols that we should do service to them. Let us then use bread, wine, apparel, possessions, gold, silver, and all other creatures. But let us not trust or glory in them; for we must trust and glory in God alone. He only is to be loved. He only is to be feared and honoured.'[1] 'We could be content to suffer the dominion of the Pope, but because he abuses the same so tyrannously against us, and would compel us to deny and blaspheme God, acknowledging the Pope only as our lord and master, clogging our consciences and spoiling us of fear and trust which we should have in God, therefore we are compelled by the commandment of God to resist the Pope: for it is written: "We must rather obey God than men" (Acts 5.29). Therefore without offence of conscience, which is our singular comfort, we contemn the authority of the Pope. Müntzer and other mad heads desired the destruction of the Pope, but they sought to accomplish this with arms, not with the Word; and so they withstood him for the sake of his person, and not for God's sake. We for our part would gladly show favour to Behemoth and his scales, with all the persons and dignities which they have, if they would but leave us Christ. But because we cannot obtain this of them, we contemn their persons and say boldly with Paul: "God respects no man's person." '[2]

The Christian Persona

These passages, mostly from the great *Commentary on Galatians*, show us how extremely important this idea was for Luther, for it is nothing else than the fundamental distinction between the two kingdoms and indicates clearly why that distinction is to be made. But Luther was not content to leave the distinction in this dialectical contrariety, and it is at this point that we see how deep is the significance of the conception of *larva vel persona*. And here once again he has in mind the significance both of *larva* and of *persona* on the stage, where an actor assumes a rôle and a public face which he does not have privately, so that he can be spoken of as having '*two persons*'.[3] That is particularly true of the Christian

---

[1] W.A. 40/1, p. 175.   [2] W.A. 40/1, p. 177.
[3] W.A. 32, p. 390: '*die zwo personen odder zweyerley ampt auff einen menschen geraten und zugleich ein Christ und ein Furst....*'

who has become a new man in Christ. Thus, for example, he is at once a member of the *geistliches Regiment* and yet also participates in the *weltliches Regiment*.¹ In the *geistliches Regiment* he may also be a preacher²; and even as an individual Christian is 'a person for himself who believes for himself and for no one else',³ and yet we must speak of him 'not as one Christian but *in relatione* as bound in this life to another person'.⁴ The fundamental distinction here is between the person which a man is *coram Deo* and the person he necessarily is *coram mundo*, for he lives in the world and uses the Kaiser's world and goods as well as any heathen.⁵

The supremely important fact here, however, is Christological, for the Eternal Son of God, the second Person of the Trinity, came down and wore our humanity and suffered under Pontius Pilate. He did that 'not for His own *Person* but for our person'.⁶ 'Thus making a happy exchange with us, He took upon Him our sinful *person*, and gave unto us His innocent and victorious *person*, with which we are now clothed and are freed from the curse of the law. For Christ was willingly made a curse for us, saying: As touching my own *person* both as human and divine (*pro mea persona humanitatis et divinitatis*) I am blessed and need nothing. But I will humble myself (*exinanibo*) and put upon me your *larva*,⁷ that is to say, your human nature, and I will walk in it among you, and will suffer death and deliver you from death. Thus when bearing the sin of the whole world in our *larva* He was taken, suffered, was crucified and put to death, and became a curse for us. But because He was a divine Person and eternal, it was impossible that death should hold Him. Wherefore He rose again the third day from death, and now lives for evermore. And there is neither sin nor death in Him any more (*nec amplius invenitur peccatum, mors et larva nostra*) but mere righteousness, life and everlasting blessedness.'⁸ Through faith, that is, reason enlightened by faith (*ratione illuminata fide*), we lay hold of this victory of Christ and enjoy it.⁹ 'If you believe sin and death to be abolished they are

---

¹ W.A. 32, p. 473. ² W.A. 32, p. 475.
³ W.A. 19, p. 648. ⁴ W.A. 32, pp. 390, 475f.
⁵ Cf. W.A. 32, pp. 391, 440; 34/1, p. 122, etc. ⁶ W.A. 40/1, pp. 442f.
⁷ Luther uses *larva* to indicate that he is using the term *person* not univocally of Christ's *eternal Person* and *our person*. ⁸ W.A. 40/1, p. 443.
⁹ At this point Luther presupposes the idea that faith contains at its heart union with Christ, fully expounded earlier in this Commentary on Gal. See, for example, on 2.16, W.A. 40/1, p. 228: 'Christian faith is not an idle quality

THE ESCHATOLOGY OF FAITH: MARTIN LUTHER   39

abolished. For Christ has overcome and taken away these in Himself, and will have us to believe that as in His own person there is now no *larva peccatoris, nullum vestigium mortis*, so there is none with us since He has accomplished and performed all things for us.... Therefore the victory of Christ is most certain, and there is no defect in the thing but in our incredulity: for to reason it is a hard matter to believe these inestimable good things.'[1] 'If we look upon our own person or the person of our brother, we see that it is not holy, but Christ has sanctified and cleansed His Church.'[2] 'If therefore in the matter of justification you separate the Person of Christ from your person, then you are in the law, you remain in it, and live in it yourself and not in Christ, and so you are condemned by the law and are dead before God.'[3] 'By faith, however, you are so entirely and closely joined to Christ that He and you are made, as it were, one person.'[4] 'By the inseparable union and conjunction Christ and I are made as it were one body in Spirit.'[5]

The Christian then is two persons because of union with Christ. 'He uses the world and all creatures so that outwardly there is no difference between him and the infidel. "In outward appearance they are like", as Paul says also of Christ: "In outward appearance he was found as a man" (Phil. 2.7). Yet, notwithstanding there is a great difference.'[6] In so far as the Christian is one person with Christ he is hid with Christ in God and his union with Christ is '*in medio tenebrarum*',[7] but in so far as he still lives *in mundo* he presents to the eyes of the world a person that is to all appearances sinful. But faith discerns that that person is *larva*, and behind it faith discerns the new man in Christ. At the very heart of this teaching is the fact that the eternal Son or Word of God was found

---

or empty husk in the heart, but a firm consent whereby Christ is apprehended: so that Christ is the object of faith or rather, He is not the object, but as it were *in faith itself Christ is present.*' See especially the discussion of Gal. 2.20 of the *unio hominis cum Christo*, W.A. 40/1, pp. 280-290.

[1] W.A. 40/1, p. 443.   [2] W.A. 40/1, p. 444.   [3] W.A. 40/1, p. 284.
[4] Ibid., p. 285.   [5] Ibid., p. 283.   [6] W.A. 40/1, p. 288.
[7] W.A. 40/1, p. 229. Cf. *Luthers Vorlesung ueber den Hebräerbrief*, 1515/16, edition by E. Hirsch and H. Rückert, p. 235: In a comment to Psalm 30, '*Abscondes eos in abscondito faciei tuae*', Luther says: '*Hoc incipit quidem in hac vita, sed perficietur in futura. Magna itaque res esse Christianum et vitam suam habere absconditam non in loco aliquo ut eremitae nec in corde suo quod est profundissimum sed in ipso invisibili deo, scilicet inter res mundi vivere et pasci eo quod nusquam apparet nisi modico verbi indicio soloque auditu, ut Christus Matth. 4 dicit:* "*Non in solo pane vivit homo sed in omni verbo*", etc.'

as a man wearing our *persona* and *larva* in order that we might be translated into the Kingdom of Christ. It is an operation of the *Verbum Dei*.[1]

Verbum Dei

Fundamentally the Word of God is Christ Himself,[2] but Christ's Word, Christ Himself, comes to us through the Holy Scriptures as the Word of God. Here our human words are used as *instrumenta* or *larvae* by means of which the mighty living Word of God communicates Himself to us and acts upon us.[3] In the passages from the *Commentary on Galatians* cited above we say that Luther regarded the Apostles, Paul for example, as *larva* or *persona* through which *Christus loquens* comes to us speaking through the mouth of the Apostle.[4] A proper theology distinguishes between the person of the Apostle and Christ Himself. So in the Scriptures the *Verbum Dei* comes to us using creatures as His *larvae*, but here we must think of *larva* in a different sense from the general sense in which all creation is *larva* haunted by the presence of a strange God, or in which we have to deal very indirectly with a distant God. 'God is indeed to be left to remain in His own nature and majesty, for in this respect we have nothing to do with Him, nor does He wish us to have, in this respect, anything to do with Him: but we have to do with Him as far as He is clothed in and delivered to us by His Word, for in that He presents Himself to us.'[5] Here the *larva* is filled with the gracious presence of God, and so Luther speaks of it as *iucunda larva* through which God reveals Himself directly. That is His 'proper Kingdom where He rules Himself, where He is Himself, for there the Gospel is preached to the poor.'[6] And yet, because this Word is none other than Christ Himself who was crucified and resurrected for us, this

---

[1] Luther even speaks of faith as imparting *divinitas* to us, '*non in substantia dei sed in nobis*' (W.A. 40/1, p. 360).
[2] Cf. *Luthers Vorlesung über den Römerbrief*, II, p. 65: '*Deus nos facit, quale est verbum suum, hoc est justum, verum, sapiens, etc. Et ita nos in verbum suum, non autem verbum suum in nos mutat. Facit autem tales tunc, quando nos verbum suum tale credimus esse scilicet justum, verum. Tunc enim iam similis forma est in verbo et in credente, id est veritas et justitia.*' Cf. also p. 160.
[3] W.A. 42, p. 8; 10/1, p. 158, etc.
[4] Luther speaks of the *outward word* in distinction but not in separation from the *inward Word* which is in Christ (W.A. 40/1, pp. 141, 571).
[5] *De Servo Arbitrio.* W.A. 18, p. 685.
[6] W.A. 52, p. 26. Cf. W.A. 40/1, pp. 500f.

THE ESCHATOLOGY OF FAITH: MARTIN LUTHER 41

is the Word which slays and makes alive, and operates law and Gospel, by crucifixion and resurrection.[1] It is through that operation of the Word that the Christian is united to Christ according to Gal. 2.20.

But that mighty Word of God, that slays and makes alive, comes not simply to the individual believer, but is injected into the whole situation, where every creature is *larva dei*, and where all the *ordinationes* are *larvae dei*.[2] When that Word comes to us in this creaturely context we can discern the presence and glory of God in nature and behind it, and so the *larvae* become not veils that conceal a terrifying ghostly presence but such veils that, while they cover the majesty of God, they serve as a means to unveil to us His will and His purpose of love in our human life. But in order to do that the Word of God must intervene as it did in Jesus Christ in mercy and judgment, in death and resurrection.[3] Under this activity of the Word Luther can speak of Preachers of the Word and Sacraments, and of the Church itself, as well as of Apostles and Holy Scriptures, as *larvae Dei*, for through their instrumentality Jesus Christ is preached and delivered over to men and His Kingdom is established.[4]

Luther was particularly concerned to apply this teaching to the whole secular life and regiment of man. He gives a sustained discussion of this in his exposition of the 82nd Psalm: 'God stands among the congregation and is judge among the gods', etc.[5] In accordance with his teaching elsewhere,[6] he speaks of 'the whole temporal estate as an ordinance of God which everyone ought to obey and honour'. Within this temporal estate the ruler is God's minister, for God as Creator, preserving His own creatures, works and ordinances, has instituted and preserved rulership. But God

---

[1] *'Mortificat et vivicat, deducit ad inferos et reducit'* (1 Sam. 2.6). These words had the profoundest impact on Luther. Cf. W.A. 56, p. 450.
[2] Cf. W.A. 40/1, p. 543: *'Unser Herr Gott habet varias ordinationes quando venit Christus....'*
[3] Therefore it still comes under a contrary aspect. Cf. W.A. 56, p. 446: *'Verbum Dei, quoties venit, venit in spetie contraria menti nostrae, que sibi vera sapere videtur; ideo verbum contrarium sibi mendacium iudicat adeo, ut Christus verbum suum appelaverit adversarium nostrum.'*
[4] W.A. 40/1, p. 173.   [5] W.A. 31/1, pp. 189-218.
[6] Cf. W.A. 6, p. 410, where he speaks of the worldly rule as part of the *Corpus Christianum*: *'Seyntemal weltlich hirschaft ist ein mitglid worden des Christlichen Corpers unnd wie wol sie ein leyplich werck hat doch geystlichs stands ist, darumb yhr werck sol frey unvorhindert gehen in alle glidmass des gantzen corpers.'*

D

Himself stands in the congregation and is the ruler of rulers and the judge of these 'gods' whom He has set over the temporal estate. That temporal estate and its whole ordinance rest ultimately upon God's creation but special communities were formed in the fallen world by a 'special Word of God'—the communities of the people of Israel. But the temporal estate is 'established anew through Christ by a special Word'. For Christ says: 'Give unto Caesar what is Caesar's' (Matt. 22.21); 'Be subject to every ordinance of man' (1 Pet. 2.13); and 'Let every man be subject to his rulers' (Rom. 13.1). Luther then reminds us that the 82nd Psalm says nothing good about the rulers or gods and their virtues. God stands in their midst and judges them. He rebukes them. It is His will that they should be subject to His Word and either listen to it or suffer all misfortune. It is enough that they have to rule over all else, but over God's Word they have no control. For God's Word appoints them and makes them gods and subjects everything to them. 'Therefore they are not to despise it, for it is their instituter and appointer; but they are to be subject to it, and allow themselves to be judged, rebuked, made, and mastered by it.' How does that take place? Through the preaching of the Gospel in the midst of the congregation, for it is there that God stands: in the midst of the congregation, and He judges through the preaching of His Word. God stands behind the congregation over against the rulers, for the congregation is His ordinance; but God stands behind the rulers over against the congregation, for they are His ordinance as well. And in the midst of both is the mighty Word of God. 'He who does not heed and keep the Word of God, sets God Himself at naught. He who would honour and have God, must have Him in and through His Word, otherwise it is impossible to get Him, have Him, or know Him.'

On the other hand, 'the Word of God hallows and makes divine everything to which it is applied. Therefore those estates that are appointed by God's Word are all holy, divine estates, even though the persons in them are not. Thus father, mother, son, daughter, master, mistress, servant, maid, preacher, pastor, etc., all these are holy and divine positions in life even though the persons in these positions may be knaves and rascals. So, because He here founds and orders the office of rulership, the rulers are called "gods" and "children of God", for the sake of the divine office and the divine Word and yet they are wicked knaves, as He here calls them.'

Because they are wicked 'God will depose them and take away their godhead so that they die and go to destruction not as "gods" or "children of God" but as men, so that both in life and death they may be like men who are without God's Word, and are lost. For God's Word makes a distinction among the children of Adam. Those who have God's Word are not merely men, but holy men, God's children, Christians, etc.; but those who are without God's Word are merely men, that is, in sin and eternally imprisoned in death, under the power of the devil and are altogether without God.... A Prince who is without God and His Word is also assuredly lost, and when he falls and passes away, he loses his godhead, that is God's appointment, and passes away as tyrants are wont to pass.'

'The Psalmist therefore prays for another government and kingdom in which things will be better, where God's name will be honoured, His Word kept, and He Himself will be served: that is the Kingdom of Christ. Therefore he says: "O God, come and be the Judge upon earth. Be Thyself King and Lord. The gods have a lost cause. For to thee belongs the kingdom among all the heathen in the whole world, as is promised in the Scriptures." This is the Kingdom of Christ: this is the true God who has come and is judging: that is to say, He is Lord in all the world, for no empire has spread so far among the heathen as has the Kingdom of Christ.... Arise O God and judge the earth.... For the righteousness of this world has an end, but the righteousness of Christ and those who are within His Kingdom abide for ever.'

Such preaching of the Word of God was certainly mighty. Whenever that Word is injected into the Church and State, the representatives of the *geistliches Regiment* and of the *weltliches Regiment*, there is inevitably tumult and upheaval, for, as we have seen, the Word challenges their disobedience to the divine *ordinatio* and calls in question their compromised and hardened institutional patterns. The Word of God does not destroy the *ordinationes* but it comes to reshape them in obedience to the Word and Will of God.[1] This is the point where we can see most clearly both the

---

[1] '*Non tollitur per Verbum Dei ulla ordinatio Dei, sed tantum praefectur Verbum*' (*Opera Omnia*, Jena edition, III, p. 545b). '*Ubi Verbum Dei est,*

greatness and the weakness of Luther. In contrast to Erasmus, who was afraid of tumult, Luther insisted that the Kingdom of God is only taken by violence and determined action, and yet when Ulrich von Hutten wanted to unsheath the sword for the sake of the Reformation, Luther wrote powerfully against it.[1] 'By the Word the world was conquered, by the Word the Church has been preserved, and by the Word also she shall be restored. Antichrist, as he began with violence, will be crushed without violence, by the Word.'[2] But if the Word inevitably creates tumult, even when it comes not to destroy the ordinances of the world but to restore them, how can you avoid violence? That was the problem which Luther never succeeded in facing properly; in the last resort he appears to have been afraid of the consequences of the mighty Word of God.

Perhaps the most significant of his smaller writings in this respect is the *Second Wittenberg Sermon*, in which he says: 'We should give free course to the Word and not add our works to it. We have the *jus verbi*, but not the *executio*. We should preach the Word, but the consequences must be left to God's own good pleasure.'[3] In the actual situation foretold by the Zwickau prophets to which this particular Word was preached Luther achieved a remarkable result, and yet the failure to go beyond the Word had a great deal to do with more extreme action by the *Schwärmer* later. What is at stake here? Luther sees quite clearly that the Word exercises in our human situation a critical, eschatological action in anticipation of the final judgment, for the final judgment of the Word of God is suspended until the last day. It is the duty of the Church therefore simply 'to let the Word work alone, without our work',[4] to work in its own time, but for Luther that actually means that before the last judgment the Word uses the *weltliches Regiment*, which is entrusted by God with the power of the sword to enact a temporary judgment, but only such a temporary judgment as to preserve the *status quo* and make room for the free course of the Word of God. In this way, as we have seen

---

ordinatio Dei et Deus vult bonam politiam.' W.A. 31/2, p. 614; cf. p. 608, 'Politia a Verbo Dei instituta et donata.'
    [1] See also the *Short Reply to Duke George*, cf. 1533, W.A. 38, pp. 141ff.
    [2] De Wette, *Luthers Briefe*, I, p. 543.
    [3] W.A. 10/3, p. 15. Cf. de Wette, op. cit., II, pp. 137f and 141ff.
    [4] W.A. 10/3, p. 15.

from Luther's *Exposition of the 82nd Psalm*, the Word addresses itself critically to all the *larvae Dei*, to every ordinance and aspect of human life in this world, calling them in question and refashioning them in accordance with their own true end and authority, and it is through them alone and their co-operation with the Word that the Word becomes action in the world. In the last resort Luther appears to resign the *executio verbi* to the secular power, for in so far as anything is *larva* it belongs to the *weltliches Regiment* and comes under its authority. And yet the difficulty Luther found here, as expressed in the *Exposition of the 82nd Psalm*, is that 'the princes and lords, who ought to be advancing God's Word, do the most to suppress, forbid and persecute it'.[1] Quite clearly Luther did not give sufficient attention to the corporeal embodiment of the Word here and now within the world, an embodiment which already spans the distinction between the two kingdoms as a *tertium datur*.

The Kingdom of Faith

Corresponding to that view of the Word is Luther's view of faith. Faith is the dimension of Christian existence over against the Word, an existence on the frontiers of the two kingdoms where the Word bears down upon this world and calls man into such obedience to it that he finds the real substance of his life in the Word, not in himself but in the Kingdom of God. 'Therefore faith in Christ is the most arduous of all things, for it is a *translatio et raptus* from all things of sense, within and without, into those things beyond sense within and without, into the invisible, the most high and incomprehensible God.'[2] The believer therefore lives and moves between two realms. He is involved by the Word in a world which is hid with Christ in God[3] and yet he is involved in this visible and tangible fallen world where God has placed and called him. The Christian, in fact, as we have seen, is divided between two times, and the two times are spoken of as the time of heaven and the time of earth, or the time of grace which is eternal and the time of the law which is not perpetual but which

---

[1] W.A. 31/1, pp. 204f.
[2] W.A. 57.3, p. 144. Cf. W.A. 5, p. 69: '*Conjungit enim fides animam cum invisibili, ineffabili, innominabili, aeterno, incogitabili verbo Dei simulque separat ab omnibus visibilibus, et haec est Crux et phase Domini.*' Cf. W.A. 40/1, p. 283.
[3] W.A. 57, pp. 144, 214; W.A. 3, p. 150.

has an end.¹ Faith is an existence therefore in which man hangs between heaven and earth, without any earthly security, but in sheer trust in God alone.² Because Christian existence is found at a point where two times meet or two worlds meet, Luther can even speak of faith as a *punctus mathematicus*,³ on the analogy, however, of the relation of God and Man in Christ.⁴ Faith is always encounter, always the tangential point where the divine bears upon the human, grace upon nature. Faith is the point where the invisible and the visible meet, where the invisible reality is given to us '*sub contrario objectu sensu, experientia*', as he says in the *De Servo Arbitrio*.⁵

There is no doubt that the tendency of Luther is to think of the encounter of faith as a timeless event within time, like the notion of continuous crisis and critical decision with which we are familiar in modern theology, but in spite of that the Christological analogy is all-important in Luther's thought. It is Christ Himself, the Word made flesh, who bears upon us and encounters us in this way, so that the 'mathematical point' is really Christ Himself, into union with whom believers enter by faith and sacramental incorporation. That does not only mean that in and through faith the Christian is formed anew in Christ and refashioned according to His image so that his true form is the form of Christ,⁶ but, as we have seen, that Christ Himself sits in faith, so that faith encompasses Christ.⁷ 'Christ is formed in us for the life of the Christian is not of himself but of Christ living in him—although that does not mean that Christ is formed in any one *personaliter*.'⁸

The Christological analogy means that faith has two aspects to it. On the one side it is union with Christ, the invisible Head of the Church, so that faith is a translation into the invisible realm of the risen and ascended Christ. But on the other hand, just as Christ was found as a man and came down to our earthly life, so

---

¹ W.A. 40/1, pp. 525f. On the other hand the timelessness of the Kingdom of God is emphasised in contrast to the temporality of this worldly kingdom (W.A. 34/2, pp. 110f).
² See especially W.A. 1, p. 199; 25, p. 238.
³ W.A. 40/1, p. 291; W.A. 40/3, p. 572.
⁴ W.A. 39/2, p. 299. He also uses the expression *linea mathematica* here.
⁵ W.A. 18, p. 633.
⁶ *Comm. on Gal.* 4.19, W.A. 40/1, pp. 648f.
⁷ W.A. 40/1, pp. 281f.
⁸ W.A. 57, p. 93. In some real sense faith is *substantia*, but not in the same way that a body is *substantia* (W.A., *Tischreden*, V, n. 5345).

faith is involved in a physical context. As there is no disembodied Word, so there is no disembodied faith. To have faith, then, means on the one side to be involved in the spiritual Kingdom of Christ which cannot be felt or grasped by the finger, any more than the forgiveness of sins can be grasped in my fingers—it has to be believed.[1] But nevertheless this takes place only in a bodily context—that is the sphere of the external Word and Sacraments. Even here it is a spiritual event, but it is not apart from seeing, hearing, speaking, grasping, eating, drinking, etc.[2]

In the *Commentary on Galatians* Luther works out this Christological analogy very fully in the relation between faith and works, in terms of a *'tertium datur'*, a *'fides operans'* which is a new *thing*, a new *doing*, unknown to the philosophers or to reason.[3] It must be understood therefore in quite a different way: on the analogy of the Incarnation of the Word.[4] Luther makes a distinction then between a *'fides abstracta vel fides absoluta'*, on the one hand, and a *'fides concreta, composita seu incarnata'*, on the other.[5] When the Scriptures speak of justification or imputation they are speaking of faith as abstract or absolute, but when they speak of rewards or works they speak of faith as composed, concrete and incarnate. In the same way the Scriptures speak of Christ. When they speak of His whole Person as God and Man they speak of Christ *compound and incarnate* (*composita et incarnata*, that is, of the divine nature united in one person to the human nature). When they speak of the two natures apart they speak *absolutely*. On this analogy then, in terms of this *new theological grammar*,[6] we must speak of faith first as naked, simple and abstract like the divinity spread throughout the humanity of Christ. Like His divinity, faith is the *'divinitas operum'*, the divinity which is diffused throughout the works, and so faith is the supreme agent (*est Fac totum, ut ita loquar*).[7] 'Faith is universally the divinity in work, person, members, as the one and only cause of justification, which nevertheless is attributed to the matter because of the form, that is to the work because of the faith.[8] Eternal and infinite power is given unto the man, Christ,

---

[1] W.A. 20/2, p. 408.   [2] W.A. 23, p. 189.   [3] W.A. 40/1, pp. 411f.
[4] That is, *secundum novam et theologicam grammaticam*, in which *substance*, *nature* become altogether new words and acquire a new signification (ibid., p. 417).
[5] W.A. 40/1, pp. 414f.
[6] Cf. W.A. 34/2, pp. 480f: *'mirabilis est Christi grammatica.'*
[7] W.A. 40/1, p. 415.
[8] This is on the analogy of the *communicatio idiomatum*, ibid., pp. 414f.

not because of His humanity, but because of His divinity. For the divinity alone created all things, without any help of His humanity; nor did the humanity conquer sin and death, but the hook under the worm, whereon the devil did fasten, conquered and devoured the devil, which sought to devour the worm. Therefore the humanity alone would have effected nothing, but the divinity, joined with the humanity because of the divinity. So here faith alone justifies and does all things: and yet notwithstanding the same is attributed to works but because of faith.'[1]

On this ground we may speak of faith in its other aspect as concrete, composed, and incarnate, as 'faith that incorporates the doing and gives it its form (*ut fides incorporet et informet "facere"*). ... First ought reason to be enlightened by faith before it works, but when a true opinion and knowledge of God is held as right reason, then the work is incarnated and incorporated into it, so that whatsoever is attributed to faith is afterwards attributed to works also, but on the ground of faith alone.'[2]

The New Man

This is a highly significant account of faith, for it shows that Christologically Luther passes beyond a merely dialectical relation and thinks of faith as involving a *new operation*; but just because it is new, it is not discerned by the natural reason, so the dialectical relation between believing and seeing remains.[3] Behind this lies also Luther's doctrine of the *new man* in Christ, that is, of regeneration, spiritual resurrection, or the new creation. In his *Third Disputation against the Antinomians* of 1538 Luther spoke of it in this way. 'In Christ who is arisen there is certainly no sin, no death, no law, to which He was subjected so long as He lived. But the very same Christ is not yet fully resurrected in His believers; rather has He only begun in them as a first-fruit, to be resurrected from the dead.'[4] 'So far as Christ is risen in us, we are without law, sin and death. But so far as He is not arisen in us,

---

[1] W.A. 40/1, p. 417.
[2] Pp. 417f: ' *Oportet enim primum rationem illustratam esse fide, antequam operetur; habita autem vera opinione et notitia Dei, tanquam recta ratione, incarnatur et incorporatur ei opus, ut quicquid fidei tribuitur, postea etiam operibus tribuatur, sed propter solam fidem.*'
[3] Cf. W.A. 3, p. 182: The Christian as a new man is '*homo spiritualis et interior coram Deo*', but as a member of this world he is '*homo peccati, homo carnalis coram mundo*'.   [4] W.A. 39/1, p. 354.

we are under law, sin and death.'¹ Those were some of the theses Luther set himself to defend and maintain, but in the discussion that followed he expanded them as follows: 'A Christian is a person who is buried with Christ in His death, he has died to sin, the law and death, and every other such tyrant. But we do not see that, for it is hidden from the world; it does not appear, does not strike us in the eye (1 Pet. 3.4 and John 3.8 are then cited). For the Christian is not in this world. He does not live, he is dead. He stands in another life, the heavenly, which is far beyond that which we have here. And yet what troubles and work and what plagues we shall have to experience before we reach there.... But the Christian lives here as there through God's imputation, righteous and holy under the wings which like a hen He spreads over us. And yet, so far as the Christian is a fighter and is engaged on military service, he is still under the law here and under sin, for he is still in this life. Daily he feels and experiences the struggle with his flesh and lives only too close to it (Rom. 7.23, 25).... A man who believes in Christ is through divine imputation righteous and holy; he already lives in heaven for he is surrounded with the heaven of mercy. But here while we are embraced in the Father's arms, clothed with the best robe, our feet stick out from below the mantle, and Satan tries to bite them if he can. Then the child whimpers and cries and feels that it still has flesh and blood, and the devil is still there.... Thus we are holy and free in the Spirit, not in the flesh.... For the feet have still to be washed, for they are unclean and so Satan bites and attacks them until they are clean. You must pull your feet under your cloak else you will have no peace.'²

Two particular points must be emphasised in this connexion:

(a) Luther distinctly thinks of the resurrection of the body as in some real sense begun in the believer. 'This is done by the Holy Spirit who sanctifies and awakens even the body to this new life, until it is completed in the life beyond.'³ It was in line with this that Luther expounded the meaning of the 'spiritual body' of the resurrection. *Spiritual* does not mean *of spirit* simply, but that the body, the same body which we have now, will be controlled

---

¹ W.A. 39/1, p. 354.   ² W.A. 39/1, pp. 519ff.
³ *On the Councils and the Church*, III, W.A. 50, p. 627; cf. W.A. 32, pp. 468f; 2, p. 728.

by the Spirit, potentiated by it and clothed with light.[1] Commenting on John 3.3: 'Except a man be born again he cannot see the Kingdom of God', and John 3.6: 'That which is born of the flesh is flesh', Luther says: 'But that flesh and blood that is baptised in Christ is no more flesh and blood (for it is born anew of the Spirit) even although it was flesh and blood. Naturally it is flesh and blood, but spiritually it is not, because through Christ it is become clean in baptism and is taken into the Kingdom of God. Therefore it cannot be called mere flesh and blood any more, externally according to the body. For properly speaking flesh and blood mean *der alte Mensch nach seiner Vernunfft*.... Because flesh and blood cannot enter into the Kingdom of God it must cease, die and pass away and rise in a new spiritual being in order to reach heaven. Therefore He warns them as Christians that they must become new men, so that on that day they may not be found as flesh and blood.'[2]

This renewal of flesh and blood, the renewal of the whole man in the unity of body and soul, has already been begun. 'Let us learn to understand and distinguish these words properly, "natural" and "spiritual" according to the Scriptures—not as though the body is to be separated from the soul, but that the body must become spirit or live spiritually, as we have already begun to do through Baptism: so that we live spiritually in the soul, while God looks upon the body and reckons it to be spiritual, although it must take its departure from this temporal life and be fully renewed and be wholly spiritual living only by and through the Spirit. Jesus Christ our Lord is the second Adam, resurrected to a spiritual life, so that He no longer suffers from bodily wants, as He did when He was on earth, but He has a proper and true body with flesh and blood, as He showed to His disciples. He it is who has in His own person established the heavenly, spiritual life in order that He might first begin it in us and complete it altogether on that day.'[3] '*Non solum habebimus in futurum sed etiam iam habemus, sed in fide.*'[4] That follows from the fact that we are joined to Christ as members of His Body, for 'the whole body hangs together'. 'Because Christ has begun our resurrection more than half has already

---

[1] See *Sermons on 1 Cor. 15* of 1532, and especially W.A. 36, pp. 661-675; and W.A. 23, p. 189.
[2] W.A. 36, p. 673.   [3] W.A. 36, pp. 665f.   [4] W.A. 38, p. 554.

THE ESCHATOLOGY OF FAITH: MARTIN LUTHER

taken place.'[1] That teaching comes out with particular force in the doctrine of Baptism.[2] The Sacrament was not to be thought of as '*momentaneum negotium*' but as '*perpetuum*', whose reality (*res*) reaches out already to the future life.[3] 'It is nothing else than the killing of the old man in us and the resurrection of the new man, both of which will continue in us all our life long. Hence a Christian life is nothing else but a daily Baptism once begun and daily continued.... Therefore everyone should regard Baptism as a garment for daily use.'[4] 'We begin then to leave behind this corporal life, so that there is already a *realis et corporalis transitus* from this world to the Father.'[5] As the outward man perishes the inward man is renewed, but the very renewal of the inward man already spells judgment to the outward man in effective anticipation of the final judgment when we shall be made over again completely.[6] 'Spiritual birth takes its rise in Baptism, proceeds and increases, but only in the last day is its significance fulfilled. Only in death are we rightly lifted out of Baptism by the angels into eternal life.'[7]

(*b*) Between Baptismal resurrection and death or the resurrection of the body at the last day Luther thinks of the Christian's life in terms of progress and advance, 'so that he can meet the coming Saviour'.[8] Here we see that for Luther faith is not simply pure encounter *vis-à-vis* the Word of God but in relation to the Incarnate Word it has permanence in time, reaching out through time towards future fulfilment in the resurrection. That dynamic view is applied to the whole Kingdom, for '*das Reich Christi stehet im Werden, nicht Geschehen*'.[9] The believer must not imagine that he is perfect, but like St Paul must forget the things that are behind and reach out towards the things that are ahead, counting not that he has apprehended. Thus '*Christianus non est in facto, sed in fieri. ... Summa, proficiendum est, non standum et secure stertendum.*

---

[1] W.A. 36, pp. 547f; also pp. 665f. '*Du wirst nicht allein an der Seele getauft, sondern am Leibe. Er soll nicht dahinten bleiben. Und soll werden ein geistlicher Leib gleichwie Christi Leib am Tage der Auferstehung* (W.A. 36, p. 666). See also W.A. 34/2, pp. 122ff; 49, pp. 395ff.
[2] W.A. 49, pp. 403f.   [3] W.A. 6, p. 534; W.A. 30/1, pp. 218f.
[4] *The Greater Catechism*, W.A. 30/1, pp. 218f.   [5] W.A. 6, p. 534.
[6] W.A. 2, pp. 724f, cf. pp. 728, 734.
[7] Ibid. Cf. W.A. 6, pp. 534f, and W.A. 2, pp. 724ff.
[8] W.A. 44, p. 776; cf. pp. 82f.
[9] Cited from *Baieri Compendium Theologiae Positivae* (edited by Walther), vol. II, p. 255.

Homo noster vetus debet de die in diem (ut Paulus) renovari' (2 Cor. 4.16).[1] Thus 'sanctification once begun daily increases, for the Holy Spirit is continually at work in us, by means of the Word of God, and daily bestowing forgiveness on us, till we reach that life where there is no more forgiveness, all persons there being pure and holy, full of piety and righteousness, delivered and free from sin, death, and all misfortune, in a new immortal and transfigured body.'[2] 'Thus we constantly grow in sanctification and ever do become more and more "a new creature" in Christ. The Word is *Crescite* (2 Pet. 3.18) and *Abundetis magis* (1 Thess. 4.1).'[3]

Both of these two points Luther regards in a corporate way, though this emphasis is not so strong. The resurrection of the new man is to be understood as part of the resurrection of the whole body already begun in Christ, in which the individual's resurrection is already implicated; and so the progress or daily renewal of the believer is thought of as operating through the sacramental ministry of the Church as the Body of Christ, which as a whole daily grows in cleansing and sanctification.[4] 'Our Lord Jesus Christ has begun the resurrection in His own Body, but that resurrection is not yet complete for we must also rise again. Just as His suffering and death are not complete, so that we follow on and suffer and die with Him as members of whom He is the Head. As St Paul says, he makes compensation in his flesh for what is yet wanting in the affliction in Christ (Col. 1.24). Similarly His resurrection is not yet complete, for we follow on and rise from the dead. He is our Head, and we are the members of His Body.'[5]

The Church

This brings us to the point where we must examine Luther's doctrine of the Church, but we may say now that Luther's doctrines of imputation, regeneration and Baptism point to the new life in Christ as an enduring new creation in and under our existence in the two kingdoms. That helps to underpin his sharp distinction between the spiritual and the corporal, between grace

---

[1] *Annotationes in aliquot capita Matthaei*, 1538 (W.A. 38, pp. 568f). Cf. also W.A. 56, p. 239.   [2] W.A. 30/1, p. 191.
[3] *On the Councils and the Churches*, W.A. 50, p. 64. Cf. W.A. 42, p. 248.
[4] See the *Exposition of Genesis* 49.11, 12, W.A. 44, pp. 774-778; W.A. 36, pp. 681ff.   [5] W.A. 49, pp. 395f.

THE ESCHATOLOGY OF FAITH: MARTIN LUTHER   53

and nature, but those distinctions are still maintained in their sharpness. That is apparent, for example, even in the doctrine of Baptism, which means mainly Baptism into the death of Christ, burial in the grave of Christ, so that the new creation remains wholly concealed until the advent of Christ.[1] There is a distinct failure at crucial points to give the doctrine of the resurrection its full significance and weight. Thus even when speaking of the resurrection, he tends to interpret it dialectically as crucifixion, as a death to death, and therefore as life. 'Against my death which binds me, I have another death, that is to say, life which quickens me in Christ: and this death looses and frees me from the bonds of my death, and with the same bonds binds my death. So death which bound me is now fast bound, which kills me is now killed itself by death—that is to say, by the very life itself.'[2] 'I live for I am quickened by His death and crucifixion through which I die: that is, forasmuch as by grace and faith I am delivered from the law, sin, and death, I now live indeed. Wherefore that crucifying and that death whereby I am crucified and dead to the law, sin and death and all evils, is to be resurrection and life. For Christ crucifies the devil, He kills death, condemns sin and binds the law and I believing this, am delivered from the law, etc. The law therefore is bound, dead, and crucified unto me, and I again am bound, dead, and crucified unto it. Wherefore by this very death and crucifixion, that is to say, by this grace or liberty, I now live.'[3] And yet on the other hand this means that so long as we are in this life waiting for the manifestation of Christ, we can never leave the death of Christ behind, even though we are risen with Him. Even though we are *justus* we are still to be considered *justificandus*, as we saw earlier. So that the very fact that Luther keeps up the dialectic of death and life to the very end is an indication of the dynamic character of Christian faith; its progress is through continuous death and resurrection.[4] In other words, the progress envisaged does not cease to be eschatological, for the progress itself comes under judgment, real though it is. It is progress toward the last day. '*Reformamini in novitate sensus vestri* (Rom. 12.2). *Hoc pro profectu dicitur. Nam loquitur iis, quia iam incoe-*

[1] See especially the *Treatise on Baptism* of 1519, W.A. 2, pp. 724-737; W.A. 36, pp. 543-554; 97f; W.A. 34/2, pp. 108-137.
[2] W.A. 40/1, p. 277.   [3] W.A. 40/1, p. 281.
[4] W.A. 42, p. 146-147: '*aliquosque procedimus.*'

perunt esse Christiani. Quorum vita non est in quiescere, sed in moveri de bono in melius velut egrotus de egritudine in sanitatem, ut et Dominus ostendit in homine semivivo in curam Samaritani suscepto. . . . Semper homo est in non esse, in fieri, in esse, semper in privatione, in potentia, in actu, semper in peccato, in justificatione, in justitia, i.e. *semper peccator, semper penitens, semper iustus.*'[1] Therefore 'progress is not by sight, but always unto clearer faith, from faith to faith, always by believing more and more so that '*qui iustus est, justificetur adhuc*' (Rev. 22.11).[2]

A better word than *progress* to express this kind of eschatological advance is another word that Luther uses, *pilgrimage*. That way of expressing it is more frequently taken by Luther towards the end of his life, for example in the exposition of Genesis, where certainly the material lends itself to this interpretation, but where too more and more he is to be found using the Epistle to the Hebrews, in which the thought of the Church as the pilgrim people of God is powerfully set forth. But here is a description from a sermon of 1531 which is very clear: '*Zu solchem ewigen Leben sind wir getaufft. Dazu hat uns Christus durch sein Tod und Blut erlöset, Und dazu haben wir das Evangelium empfangen. Als bald man ein Kind aus der Taufe hebet und im das Westerhembd anzeucht, So wirds von stund an eingeweihet zum ewigen Leben, das es hinfurt die zeit seines Lebens nur ein Pilgerim und Gast sey in dieser Welt Und sich also drein schicke, das es dis zeitlich Leben gedencke zu lassen und auff jenes unvergengliche Leben imerdar hoffe und warte.*'[3] We are not baptised for this life but are by Baptism so inserted into the Kingdom of God that we live our life in this world as those who really have a new life already in Christ, hidden from this world which can only be according to the natural *Vernunfft*, and who therefore enter upon a pilgrimage towards the manifestation or appearing of our new life in body and soul at the coming of Christ.[4] We can undertake this pilgrimage toward His glorious appearing if we die daily with Him and daily rise with Him in faith and hope, if we realise that in this world we are sown like seed into the ground that we may receive our new body and new life in the harvest of the new world.[5] Because through Baptism we are already inserted into the Kingdom of God, our life in this

[1] W.A. 56, pp. 441f.   [2] W.A. 56, p. 173.
[3] W.A. 34/2, p. 116.   [4] W.A. 34/2, pp. 117ff.   [5] W.A. 34/2, pp. 121ff.

THE ESCHATOLOGY OF FAITH: MARTIN LUTHER 55

world is such a pilgrimage that any moment of it may be the *Stündlein* when hope will yield to sight.

This is the perspective within which Luther thinks of the Church. It is essentially the Church of the baptised, but as the operative power in Baptism is the Word of God,[1] the Church as baptised is essentially correlative to that Word, and corresponds to the *Regnum fidei*, where the Word is heard and believed, and the *regnum visibile*, where through preaching and Sacraments 'the visible God', Christ the Incarnate Son, is King and Lord.[2] 'Wherever the Word of God is preached and believed, there is the Church; and where the Church is, there is the Bride of Christ.'[3]

Such a view carries with it a number of important implications:

(*a*) Because the Church is correlative to the Word of God and is 'constructed' in it,[4] the real life and essence of the Church are lodged beyond itself. '*Tota vita et substantia Ecclesiae est in verbo dei.*'[5] As such, however, grounded beyond itself in the Word, the Church is essentially an eschatological community, for 'the Word of God is that by which we receive testimony of future and invisible things.'[6] The definition of faith in the Epistle to the Hebrews: 'Faith is the substance of things hoped for, the evidence of things not seen' (Heb. 11.1), had very great influence on Luther. It is precisely because the Church is essentially *de fide* correlative to the Word as its creation,[7] that he thought of the Church as hid with Christ in God and waiting for its manifestation in the coming of Christ.[8] Until then the Church continues to exist in history as it proclaims the Word, for it lives by its proclamation. It can even be said that the Church is *praedicatio*. But this means that the Church lives through continuous dynamic movement, through the continuous creation of the Word acting from beyond the Church and impinging on it. '*Ecclesia semper nascitur et semper mutatur in successione fidelium, alia et alia est ecclesia et tamen semper eadem.*'[9] As such the Church lives wherever God dwells, and whenever

---

[1] W.A. 37, pp. 630ff. [2] W.A. 45, pp. 280f, 291f.
[3] W.A. 2, pp. 208, 239; 5, p. 547; 9, p. 505; 38, p. 352; 39, p. 176 etc.
[4] W.A. 4, p. 189. [5] W.A. 7, p. 721.
[6] W.A. 3, p. 386. This is of course prominent in the Sacrament of Baptism, where the Word assumes the form of *promise*.
[7] W.A. 42, p. 334: '*Ecclesia est filia nata ex verbo, non est mater verbi.*' Cf. W.A. 8, p. 491; 3, pp. 259, 454; 4, pp. 173, 179.
[8] W.A. 44, p. 109; 9, p. 577. [9] W.A. cf. 4, p. 169;. W.A. 5, p. 58.

through the Word the gate of heaven is opened, as Jacob found at Bethel. As such the Church is bound to no time or place and therefore to no 'carnal succession', certainly bound to no *personae*, but it is bound to the Word and the Sacraments of the Word. It is essentially the eschatological community where the Word of God sounds summoning people to a life above and beyond,[1] and where the Sacraments are the signs of the reign and activity of the invisible King.[2] '*Ut sit integra definitio Ecclesiae, quae est habitatio Dei in terra, non ut in terra maneamus: Sed ideo administrantur Sacramenta, ideo docetur verbum, ut introducamur in regnum coelorum, et per Ecclesiam ingrediamur in coelum.*'[3]

(b) The Word of God which is creative of the Church is Jesus Christ Himself, the Word that became incarnate in His historical body. Through the preaching of the Gospel that Word is now embodied in the Church, but embodied in a spiritual way—i.e. through faith—so that the Church is the *corpus vivum*.[4] This doctrine of the Church as the Body of Christ, livingly united to Him the invisible Head of the Body,[5] meant for Luther that the whole conception of the Church built up on a purely historical and physical structure is false.[6] The Church cannot exist except within the realm of physical things and events,[7] any more than it can be understood except in terms of the *regnum visibile* of the Incarnate Son and His mighty deeds of redemption, but the Church is to be understood in terms of His action through the Word upon men within this corporal realm, and therefore even this physical and visible embodiment of the Church in the world has to be understood in terms of the Spirit, i.e. *spiritually*.[8] The Church is at once a '*corpus naturale*' and a '*corpus mysticum*'.[9] At this point the Church in Luther's thought has to be thought of in

---

[1] '*Cuius vita in fide, spe et charitate, totus scil. pendens ex invisibilibus*' (*Luthers Vorlesung über den Galaterbrief*, edited by Schubert, p. 48).
[2] See especially the exposition of Gen. 28.16 and 17, W.A. 43, pp. 597, 601f, and W.A. 42, p. 424.   [3] W.A. 43, p. 601.   [4] W.A. 5, p. 289.
[5] W.A. 43, p. 582: '*Nos ergo per fidem rapimur, et efficimur una caro cum ipso, sicut inquit Christus Ioannis 17 (21). Ita in ipsum ascendimus, et rapimur per verbum et spiritum sanctum, et ipsi adhaeremus per fidem unum existentes corpus cum eo, et ipse nobiscum. Ipse caput: nos membra. Rursum ipse descendit ad nos per verbum et Sacramenta docendo et exercendo nos in sui cognitione. Prima igitur coniunctio est patris et filii in divinitate. Altera divinitatis et humanitatis in Christo, tertia Ecclesiae et Christi.*' Cf. W.A. 2, p. 239; 4, pp. 715f, 597; 12, p. 488; 26, p. 506, etc.
[6] Cf. W.A. 42, p. 424; 43, pp. 596ff, 600f.
[7] W.A. 7, p. 719.   [8] W.A. 23, p. 189.   [9] W.A. 4, p. 289.

THE ESCHATOLOGY OF FAITH: MARTIN LUTHER

terms of the *duplicia regimina*, the *Regnum invisibile* and the *regnum visibile* of Christ discussed above.[1]

(c) As a living body correlative to Christ the Church is the '*corpus fidelium*', the body of believers.[2] In other words, the Church is to be understood in terms of actual people, the people of God, rather than as a great juridical institution.[3] This emphasis upon people believing the Word and united to Christ is most characteristic of Luther and very prominent in all his sermons. 'Where God's Word is there must be the Church; so also where Baptism and the Sacrament are, there must be God's people and vice versa.'[4] 'God's Word cannot be present without God's people, and God's people cannot be without God's Word.'[5] The Church is thus essentially a communion of persons who are of one heart in Jesus Christ,[6] for 'He has set up and founded His Church not on external power and authority or on temporal things but on inner love, and humility and unity'.[7] It is a fellowship or communion of love rather than a historical structure sacramentally impregnated with grace.[8]

Form and Order

Does this community of believers have any historical form and structure essential to its nature, and therefore in some way a manifestation here and now of what it shall be in the new world?

When Luther expounded the nature and form of the Church in opposition to the worldly and temporal institution of the Papacy he tended to stress the conception of the Church as *Christenheit*, the universal communion of believers scattered throughout the world, spiritually joined to, and correlative to, the ascended and invisible Christ[9]; but when he opposed the 'spiritualising' of the Church by the *Schwärmer* who wanted to resolve away the physical or material aspect of the Church, he insisted that the Church even as *Christenheit* comes under orderly and constitutional forms of

---

[1] Cf. W.A. 6, p. 408: '*Christus hat nit zwey noch zweyerley art corper, einen weltlich den andern geistlich. Ein heubt ist und einen corper hat er.*'
[2] W.A. 4, p. 191; 11, p. 53, etc.
[3] Cf. W.A. 7, pp. 683f; 50, pp. 624f; Erlangen edition 12, p. 50.
[4] W.A. 50, p. 631.   [5] W.A. 50, p. 629.
[6] W.A. 3, p. 169.   [7] W.A. 2, p. 73.
[8] W.A. 4, pp. 607f; 2, pp. 273f, 742ff; 7, p. 69.
[9] W.A. 12, pp. 275f; 44, p. 110; Erlangen edition 12, p. 50.

human life.¹ Like the family (*oeconomia*) and like the State (*politia*), the Church (*ecclesia*) is one of the three hierarchies that make up our human life.² These are not to be regarded on the same level. Before there was any *oeconomia*, or any *politia*, says Luther, the *ecclesia* existed, and has therefore spiritual ascendancy. To that the *oeconomia* was added, so that it was the *oeconomia* that was the form which the *ecclesia* originally took in God's creation.³ But after sin entered the world *politia* (which might well be called '*regnum peccati*') was added as a 'necessary remedy for corrupt nature'.⁴ In the fallen world the Church comes to be actualised as a community of believers by submitting to these three social structures⁵—and here the *oeconomia* is of special importance as the '*seminarium non solum politiae, sed etiam Ecclesiae et regni Christi usque ad finem mundi*'.⁶ Of the three hierarchies *ecclesia*, because of its other aspect as *Regnum Christi*, retains a transcendent character. It is the '*porta coeli*',⁷ for through it we are called to another end beyond that of this world, and through it we enter into the eternal life of the Kingdom of God.⁸ Conformity with the laws and regulations of the social structures of human life does not produce the Church as *communio sanctorum*, but it does enable it under the creative impact of the Word of God to come into being, and to take part in the on-going life of the world.

This participation in the on-going life of the world Luther speaks of in terms of *Beruf* or calling, so far as the individual believer is concerned. Through Baptism every believer is a member of a community where *coram Deo* all are equal, and each has a priestly responsibility for his neighbour or brother,⁹ but in this world he has an office or a function to perform, and in it he is commanded by God to do good works. Just because he is by Baptism inserted into the Kingdom of God and given to hope for eternal life he must carry out his calling in this world in accordance

---

¹ W.A. 15, p. 220; 18, pp. 168ff.
² W.A. 47, p. 853; 42, pp. 79f, 159f, 217, 320, 414, 422, etc.
³ W.A. 42, p. 79.   ⁴ Ibid.
⁵ Cf. W.A. 30/2, p. 427. 'Take away out of the world *veram religionem, veram politiam, veram oeconomiam*, i.e. true spiritual life, true temporal government, and true conduct of the home; what is left in the world, but flesh, world and devil?' —i.e. *no church*, except what Luther calls 'the devil's *ecclesia*'.
⁶ W.A. 42, pp. 178, 179.   ⁷ W.A. 42, pp. 79f.   ⁸ W.A. 43, pp. 600f.
⁹ See, for example, W.A. 7, p. 28: '*Ubir das seyn wir priester, das ist noch vil mehr, den Kuenig sein, darumb das das priesterthum uns wirdig macht fur gott zu treten und fur andere zu bitten.*'

with the Word of God, so that his good works issue out of his faith and are well-pleasing to God.[1] If a man does not believe that he is baptised into the victory of Christ and made an heir of eternal life, then he will not be happy or peaceful in this life or in the performance of his duties; rather will he tend to be impatient, will murmur against God, and find his daily life hard and sour; but if he does believe in his Baptism, and looks forward to the new life beyond, then he will fulfil his calling happily and joyfully in the service of God's Word and will actually find his life in this world to be sweet. Thus the hope of eternal life and our daily calling in this life belong together and must not be separated. Eschatology carries with it a joyful ethic within the social structures of this world.[2]

When we come to seek the parallel to that in the life of the corporate community of the faithful, it would appear that this is to be found in *ecclesia* considered as one of the three social structures, along with *oeconomia* and *politia*, and as bound up with them. In this sense the Church does have visible structure in history, but Luther's experience with the Papacy particularly made him feel that the Church as the creature of the Word and as the community of the faithful was constantly threatened and obstructed by historical and visible structure, especially when that laid any claim to institutional independence, for that was to give the Church a *schema mundi* and to drag it down within the world that passes away, thus wrenching it from the Kingdom of God that is neither visible nor temporal.[3] What is at stake here is the self-transcendence of the Church, which knows that its true life under the impact of the Word of God is lodged beyond the external structure of history in the risen Christ Himself. Thus against the whole tendency of the Papal Church Luther insisted that room must be created within the visible and physical world for a Church whose essential nature is determined by union with Christ. It must have freedom

[1] W.A. 34/2, pp. 133ff.
[2] W.A. 34/2, p. 136: '*Ein Christ, der diese zwey stück weis* (i.e. heavenly hope and worldly calling), *hat hie ein süss Leben auff Erden und dort das ewig Leben durch Christum unsern Heyland. Ob er schon viel mühe und unlust hat in seinem Stande, So hat er doch bey seiner Mühe und Erbeit Frewde im Hertzen und ein gut Gewissen, Denn er weis, das sein werck und erbeit eitel gute werck und Gottesdienste sein. Ist er ein Knecht, so ist er frölich und guter ding, Wenn er ins Holtz feret, Auff den Acker reitet, so singet er, Ist sein Herr wünderlich, schilt in und thut im unrecht, So hat er gedult und wartet auff ein ander Leben.*'
[3] W.A. 30/1, p. 100; 34/1, p. 176.

to live within the *regnum corporale* in a way appropriate to its inherent spiritual nature, freedom to live within the historical and corporal world and yet to transcend it and to look for its true life and true form in a new world where all that is corporal would be glorified and come under the full control of the Spirit of God.

It is in this light that we are to interpret Luther's stress upon the fact that there is a *duplex communio* in the Church—'*externa et corporalis communio*' and '*interna et spiritualis communio*'[1]— which corresponds to the two regiments we have already discussed, and the two times in which the Christian lives, as '*homo carnalis et exterior*' and '*homo spiritualis et interior*'.[2] How are these two related to each other? There is no doubt that they are thought of as overlapping each other, for the spiritual is not that which is necessarily opposed to, or beyond, the corporal, but the relation of the corporal to the Spirit of God which is mediated and determined by the Word of God. '*So fort an alle· das ienige, so unser leib euserlich und leiblich thut: wenn Gotts wort dazu kompt und durch den glauben geschicht, so ists und heisst geistlich geschehen, Das nichts so leiblich, fleischlich odder eusserlich sein kan, es wird geistlich, wo es ym wort und glauben gehet, Das geistlich nicht anders ist, Denn was durch den geist und glauben ynn und durch uns geschicht, Gott gebe, das ding, da mit wir umb gehen, sey leiblich odder geistlich. Scilicet in usu non in obiecto spiritus est. Es sey sehen, hören, reden, greiffen, geberen, tragen, essen, trincken odder was es wölle.*'[3]

The Sacramental Analogy

Sometimes Luther tends to speak of this in terms of the body and soul,[4] which allowed him to draw a distinction between the corporal and the spiritual in the Church without separating them.[5] A clearer and a more frequent analogy, however, is taken from the Sacraments. According to this he thinks of the communion of saints in Christ as forming an invisible and spiritual body with an

---

[1] W.A. 1, p. 639; 3, pp. 752f; 6, p. 64, etc.   [2] W.A. 3, p. 182.
[3] W.A. 23, p. 189. Cf. W.A. 7, p. 719: '*Quamquam ecclesia in carne vivat, non secundum carnem vivit, Paulus dicit in Gal. 1 and 2 Cor. 10. Ita in loco, rebus, operibus mundi versatur, sed non secundum haec aestimatur . . . sicut enim ecclesia sine esca et potu non est in hac vita et tamen regnum dei non est esca et potus secundum Paulum, ita sine loco et corpore non est ecclesia et tamen corpus et locus non sunt ecclesia neque ad eam pertinent.*'
[4] W.A. 6, pp. 293-297. Cf. 3, pp. 103, 199; 4, p. 24.
[5] W.A. 6, pp. 296f.

external sign.¹ The internal communion is here the communion of faith, hope and love, while the Sacraments are the signs of faith, hope and love.² On this analogy, then, the Church is thought of as 'involved in external things' or 'in the flesh', on the one hand, and 'involved in spiritual things', on the other hand.³ Just because the Church is involved in the flesh it can only exist in a context where there are unjust or unbelievers⁴—which carries with it a *duplex ecclesia* in another sense, the Church of true believers and of hypocrites.⁵

The application of the sacramental analogy to the doctrine of the Church throws light upon the fundamental difficulty in Luther's thought. This helps, in part, to explain why Luther insisted so strongly that the '*Hoc est corpus meum*' involves a direct identity between the elements and the Body of Christ, for that sacramental identity nailed the two communions, the corporal and the spiritual, together—even though that identity appeared to contradict the all-important distinction between the two realms or regiments. But if Luther refused to speak of a spiritual Body and a spiritual eating of the Body in the Sacrament, how could he consistently speak here of the Church as a spiritual Body or a spiritual and inner communion? On the other hand, if 'in, under and with' describe the relation of identity involved in *Hoc est corpus meum*, then we are thrown back upon a conception of the Church as utterly hidden and invisible,⁶ and of the outward form of the Church as mere *larva*. That is perhaps mitigated by the notion of consubstantiation, which, as against transubstantiation, would mean that the outer form of the Church could not, in

¹ W.A. 2, pp. 752f. Cf. W.A. 31/2, p. 696: '*Christiani signati verbo, Baptismo et Sacramento altaris, quibus discernimur ab omnibus aliis gentibus, non solum coram mundo, sed verius in iudicio Dei.*
² W.A. 1, p. 639: '*Est autem fidelium communio duplex: una interna et spiritualis, alia externa et corporalis: spiritualis est una fides, spes, charitas in deum. corporalis est participatio earundem sacramentorum, i.e. signorum fidei, spei, charitatis, quae tamen ulterius extenditur usque ad communionem rerum, usus, colloquii, habitationis aliarumque corporalium conversationum.*'
³ W.A. 3, p. 150; 39/2, pp. 149, 161.   ⁴ W.A. 2, 240; 42, p. 187.
⁵ '*Duplex ecclesia*' is a common expression, especially in the Exposition of Genesis, e.g. on Chs. 4, 21 and 25 (Cf. W.A. 43, p. 159). Another expression here is *gemina ecclesia, vera et hypocritica* (W.A. 42, pp. 184f). '*Usque ad finem mundi adjuncta erit falsa ecclesia verae ecclesiae*' (W.A. 44, p. 23; 51, p. 477).
⁶ On one of the few occasions Luther appears to have used the expression '*ecclesia visibilis*' it is applied to the Papacy as the false Church (W.A. 7, p. 710), much like the term '*larvalis ecclesia*' (W.A. 4, pp. 715f). Cf W.A. 31/2, p. 550; and Erlangen edition 31, p. 304.

Luther's view, be consistently interpreted in terms of mere *species* or *accidents* as the Roman doctrine analogically would demand. On the one hand, then, the 'in, under and with' might be interpreted eschatologically of the nature and form of the Church which are concealed under the Sacraments, for the Sacraments are '*res sacrae non propter praesentem vitam institutae, sed ideo, ut sint praeparatio quaedam sacra rerum futurarum*'.¹ On the other hand, the element of identity involved in the sacramental relation between the spiritual and the corporal would seem to demand in the polity of the Church a form and order in which there is already manifest something of the future reality. What has Luther to say about that?

Here we have to bear in mind that for him the Sacraments are subordinate to the Word, so that whatever the Sacraments reveal of the form and order of the Church, they are to be interpreted in terms of the action of the Word of God, in terms primarily of *praedicatio* and *ordinatio*.

The whole purpose of the preaching of the Gospel is to collect us and include us 'within the unique revelation of God' given in Word and Sacrament. That is how Luther interpreted the final commands of Christ as recorded at the end of Matthew and Mark. '*Vult nos colligi in verbo et baptismo, tanquam certo et infallibili signo, quod velit nos salvare et adiuvare.... Ideoque collegit et conclusit nos intra limites verbi.*'² This compacting to the Church within the limits of the Word is what Luther called '*bona politia*'. '*Ubi verbum dei est, ordinatio dei et deus vult bonam politiam.*'³ It is in this sense that Luther seemed to think of the form of the Church. '*Si quaeris ubi sit Ecclesia? nusquam ea apparet At vero non ad externam formam respiciendum est, sed ad verbum, ad baptismum, et ibi quaerenda est Ecclesia, ubi Sacramenta integre administrantur, ubi sunt auditores, doctores, confessores verbi.*'⁴

Luther thought of the form of the Church, then, in two senses. '*Forma autem haec posita est primum in verbo et donis Spiritus Sancti*' (and he called that '*forma spiritualis*'⁵). '*Deinde in externa administratione seu politia pulcherrimis legibus divinitus instituta.*'⁶

---

¹ W.A. 43, p. 424. Luther continues a little later: '*Sed ita utor donis spiritualibus, ut, cum cessant corporalia, ex hac vita ad aeternam et immortalitatem deducar.*' See also pp. 425 and 427. ² W.A. 44, pp. 95f.
³ W.A. 31/2, p. 614. But this must not be a *humana politia* (W.A. 39/2, p. 147). ⁴ W.A. 44, p. 111. ⁵ W.A. 31/2, p. 657. ⁶ W.A. 31/2, p. 658.

Of the latter Luther did not speak very much,[1] and here the contrast between the Lutheran and the Reformed Churches is marked. In the Lutheran view all forms of Church life and order on earth are *adiaphora*, and will come under judgment at the Advent of Christ as part of the *schema mundi*. The Reformed Church laid greater emphasis upon shaping the Church here and now in accordance with the divine commands, and in building up its structure on the Word. For Luther, on the other hand, Reformation meant primarily letting the Word of God act critically upon the existing order and liturgy of the Church.[2] It meant, in fact, such eschatological suspension of order and liturgy as to leave room and freedom in the present for the preaching of the Gospel and the calling out of the community of the faithful.[3] In so far as the Word of God is already the bearer of the final judgment, it interrupts the closed systems of the Church's order and liturgy and keeps them in essentially imperfect condition, in order that they may be open to continual modification, and open towards the new creation that is yet to be revealed.[4] The Church's citizenship is in heaven. It may use the forms of this passing world, but only as garments to be flung aside like Adam's leather jacket when the time for their use is past.[5] Luther's doctrine of the Church is ultimately clear, therefore, only in his negative dialectical idea, in his mighty protest against the tendency of the Roman Church to identify the forms of the Church's historical existence with the pattern of the Kingdom of God.

Luther was mostly concerned with the *forma spiritualis* which is posited in the Word and Sacraments—and here one would expect him to say something of the true and ultimate form of the Church

[1] 'It is to be remembered that for Luther the word of God means primarily Christ Himself, Christ through the Scriptures, but primarily Christ over against the Scriptures, so that if necessary we have to urge the authority of Christ against the authority of the Bible' (W.A. 39/1, p. 47). The Bible cannot be used legalistically to provide the laws of the Church.

[2] Certain elements clearly had to be abolished, such as Papal supremacy, celibacy of clergy, and the sacrifice of the Mass, which he called the '*cauda draconis*' (Mass prayer for the dead). See W.A., *Briefe*, 1528, 1822; W.A. 38, p. 584, etc.

[3] This carried with it an element of freedom in liturgical and ceremonial usage (W.A. 6, p. 447; 10/3, pp. 5f; 12, p. 194).

[4] Luther's opposition to the uniformity of any liturgy is seen in regard to the Liturgy of Wittenberg as well as in regard to the Roman Mass (W.A. 19, pp. 44ff; 72; 26, pp. 175, 222f; W.A., *Briefe*, 1036).

[5] Cf. W.A. 19, pp. 113; 26, pp. 222ff.

as disclosed by Word and Sacrament, but he hesitates to do so. If the Word reveals Christ to us, does not the form of Christ thus revealed tell us anything about the essential form of the Church? Is there not even in the Word made visible in the holy Sacraments a glimpse of the future structure of the Church? But for Luther the real humanity of Christ is concealed *in* and *under* the sacramental elements, so that even there the real form of the Church lies hidden behind the *larva dei*. That is the point where Luther's tendency towards a docetic view of the risen humanity of Christ proves to be a real weakness in his doctrine of the Church, so that even when he thinks of the *forma ecclesiae* in terms of the Word and Sacraments, it is only to define the Church on earth functionally in terms of its marks or activities, rather than in terms of its essence as the risen Body of Christ within history; the mediaeval notion of *corpus mysticum* still bulks too largely in his thought, though it is combined with the mission of the Church in a new way.

The Church under the Cross

There are, however, other lines of Luther's thought which we must gather up into this discussion, for they contribute to his full doctrine of the Church as eschatological community.

In 1541 Luther published in *Wider Hans Worst*[1] a defence of the Reformation in Germany against the accusation that instead of the ancient Catholic Church Luther had founded a new Church. The argument that Luther developed in his reply was remarkably like that advanced by Calvin earlier in his reply to Cardinal Sadoleto, and may well have been dependent on it, but the interesting thing is that here towards the end of his life Luther propounds a view of the Church not unlike Calvin's view of the Reformed Church as the restoration of the face of the ancient Catholic Church. While admitting that the Church is always *zweyerley* and will be until the end of the world,[2] Luther repudiated the notion of novelty or *neuerey* and claimed *das wir die rechte alte Kirche sind*, demonstrating that along seven lines, with regard to Baptism, the Sacrament of the Altar, the Keys, proclamation of God's Word and the singing of the Psalms, the Apostle's Creed, the *Vater unser*, and finally the ancient Church's respect for the

---

[1] W.A. 51, pp. 469-572.   [2] W.A. 51, p. 477.

THE ESCHATOLOGY OF FAITH: MARTIN LUTHER 65

State and its refusal to kiss the feet of the Pope. Before throwing back upon the Papal Church the accusation of novelty and adulteration of the ancient faith, Luther went on to show that through the Reformation '*die vorige alte Kirche*' had begun to shine again, like the sun reappearing from behind the clouds.[1] That is the '*rechte alte Kirche*' which, says Luther, we are who 'with the whole holy Christian Church are one Body and one communion of saints'.[2] What the Reformation has done is to repudiate the devilish adulteration of the Apostolic faith and all the strange novelties that it brought with it, and to restore to the Church its virginity as the pure Bride of Christ.[3] By the purity of the Church Luther means that the Church has returned to the pure Word and Sacraments and is ready to be guided by the Word of God which is the only Way, Truth and Life. The Church of the Reformation acknowledges that before God it is sinful, and that its life lags behind the Reformation in Word and Sacrament,[4] so that though here there are the marks of the true Church, the Church itself remains '*ein hoch tieff verborgen ding*'[5] which faith knows to be holy before God but which before the world appears otherwise.[6] As Luther had said elsewhere, *coram deo* the Church is '*gloria et decor*', but *coram mundo* it is '*opprobrium et abjectio plebis*'.[7]

There seem to be three ideas involved here, which though distinguishable do not represent distinctions in actual fact:

(a) The Church is at once *justa et peccatrix*, and therefore presents a double front.[8] Externally the Church is still involved in the unredeemed world of the old man, but according to its inner aspect the Church is holy and justified. These two aspects can no more be separated in the Church than they can in the individual believer. 'It is not that a man is two things. So far as we believe we are new, so far as we do not believe, we are old.'[9] It is in that way then that we are to think of the true form of the Church, for the Church is not to be judged by what it is in its wavering life but by Him in whom it believes and by whom it is purified. '*Non sumus sancti formaliter intrinsece, sed extrinsece ab ipso Christo.*

---

[1] W.A. 51, p. 486. This is also interpreted in terms of 'the little horn of' Daniel 7. 1541 was the year of the publication of the *Supputatio annorum mundi*.
[2] W.A. 51, p. 487. [3] W.A. 51, p. 498. [4] W.A. 51, pp. 529f, 536f.
[5] W.A. 51, p. 507. [6] W.A. 9, pp. 566f. [7] W.A. 4, p. 242.
[8] W.A. 40/2, pp. 196, 558, 560; 8, p. 224; 50, p. 238; 49, p. 40; 30/3, p. 409.
[9] W.A. 24, p. 557.

Sophistae dicunt aliquem sanctum, quod omnia membra et cor sint sancta, a forma inherente dicunt sanctos, sed iusti et sancti a Christo, qui est nostra iustitia, sanctitas, weil wir sein verbum haben, facit nos sanctos, non obstante, quod concupiscentiae manent in carne, illae obscurantur a claritate Christi. Sicut sol obscurat omnem foetorem, quae est in aere, aqua.'[1] If therefore the Church is said to have a form it is a *forma extrinseca*, and that means that we must believe that the Church, all too visible in its sin and unrighteousness, is yet forgiven and justified and formed in Christ. '*Ecclesia vera est, quae orat ex fide, et serio orat: remitte nobis debita nostra, sicut nos remittimus debitoribus nostris. Ecclesia est, quae de die in diem proficit, quae de die in diem induitur novum hominem et exuit veterem. Ecclesia est, quae primitias Spiritus, non decimas, multo minus plenitudinem in hac accipit. Nondum sumus plane exuti carne, et nudi, sed sumus in exuendo et promovendo seu proficiendo.*'[2] In other words, the *forma*, or the *species*, or the *facies* of the Church has to be interpreted in terms of the eschatological *reputatio*. The Church cannot be thought of as *invisibilis ecclesiola*[3] but in terms of a *Christenheit* with a dual aspect as *justa et peccatrix*.

(*b*) The Church is a '*hoch tieff verborgen ding*' because '*ecclesia non habet externas notas, nisi valde contemptibiles, scilicet verbum, remissionem peccatorum, baptismum in mortem Christi, et coenam domini*'.[4] The Church presents a visible form in this world but of the kind that the world will accept by its standards, for to it the Church presents a contrary picture as weak and deserted and without sign of power of worth. But that, says Luther, is the '*stulticia dei sub cruce latens*'.[5] Thus whenever we pass judgment upon the Church 'we must not look where there are no offences, but where there is the pure Word, pure administration of the sacraments, where there are men who love the Word and confess the Word before the world. *Haec ubi invenies, ibi statue ecclesiam esse*, whether there are few or many who have and do these things.'[6] It is in the Word and Sacraments that God's *facies* is to be seen.

[1] W.A. 31/2, p. 689.
[2] Jena edition 4, p. 525 (*Enarr. in Ps. xc*, 1541).
[3] Cf. W.A. 7, p. 683; 12, p. 485; 19, p. 75. Luther does sometimes use the expression '*ecclesiola*' (W.A. 42, p. 241).
[4] Jena edition 4, p. 586b (*Comm. in Cap. VII Michae Prophetae*, 1542).
[5] W.A. 31/2, p. 506. Cf. 40/2, p. 558: '*Ideo nullus visus apparet in facie ecclesiae quam ea, quae dicuntur: vocatur sponsa diaboli, deserta a Christo.*'
[6] Jena edition 4, p. 525 (*Enarr. in Ps. xc*).

THE ESCHATOLOGY OF FAITH: MARTIN LUTHER 67

and it is there that the Church receives its true form,[1] but like the face of God it is discernible only by faith, for the Church lies '*pro aenigmate et obscuro verbo per baptismum*'.[2] The point that Luther emphasises again and again here is that the Church is *sacramentally* related to external and corporal things, and that the Sacraments by their very nature tell us that the Church exists on earth only '*sub contraria*'.[3] Where that relation is perverted as in the Papacy the Church only presents a '*falsa species*'.[4] Thus the Papal Church which Luther speaks of as the '*ecclesia diaboli*' also appears in a contrary form. '*Licet foris in speciem Ecclesia diaboli appareat sancta, et velit pro Christo contra diabolum agere videri. Econtra, Ecclesia Christi apparet haeretica, et velut pro diabolo contra Christum agere. Ideo benefacit Christus, qui verbo definit, et fide comprehendi docet, Ecclesiam veram esse contra Ecclesiam diaboli, Nam sensu et specie longe contrarium apparet.*'[5]

(c) The Church is always the Church militant under the Cross (*sub cruce*) and therefore 'according to its external aspect' it appears as afflicted by God (*percussa a domino*).[6] Because the Church in this world always lives '*in medio regni sathanae et in media cruce*',[7] it always presents a '*scandalosa facies*'.[8] That may be due to its contemptible smallness in the eyes of the world, but is mostly due to the fact that it suffers and is persecuted and is maligned. God hides the Church, therefore, '*sub obscuro et horribili tegumento*'.[9] The Church lives in the flesh and in the world but lives there in no other way than by faith in Christ the Son of God who suffered for the Church. The Church for Christ's sake suffers continuous abuse and vilification, is confounded and rejected by men, is mortified and dies, but it lives in Christ, and therefore all these opprobrious experiences and scandals which

---

[1] W.A. 42, p. 227; 44, p. 129; 31/2, p. 658. Cf. de Wette, *Luthers Briefe* 5, p. 431: '*Oportet enim Ecclesiam in mundo apparere: sed apparere non potest, nisi in larva, persona, testa, putamine et vestitu aliquo, in quo possit audiri, videri, comprehendi: alioque nusquam possit inveniri.*'
[2] W.A. 36, pp. 570f.   [3] W.A. 18, p. 652.
[4] W.A. 43, pp. 600f: '*Quanquam nostra quoque Ecclesia habet corporalia et externa multa, ut est panis, aqua, terra, etc., sed magna diversitas est inter ea, quae iactant Papistae, et quae nos habemus corporalia. Illa enim sunt contra Deum suscepta et usurpata, non pro Deo aut secundum Dei verbum: ideo tantum inanis fucus, imaginatio et falsa species est Ecclesia ipsorum.... Ecclesia autem Papistica non est regnum coelorum: quia quaerit aurum, argentum, regna, coronas mundi. Hae sunt claves ipsorum,*' etc.
[5] W.A. 38, p. 545.   [6] W.A. 31/2, p. 506.
[7] W.A. 24, p. 466.   [8] W.A. 38, p. 563.   [9] W.A. 44, p. 109.

the Church has in the World are the precious gems with which God ornaments the Church.[1] This way of regarding the form and order of the Church in this world, as essentially *sub cruce*, is well expounded in Luther's exposition of the Song of Songs, for example, in comments on 1.5: The Church is '*nigra coram mundo, coram deo quia ornata verbo et donis spiritus sancti, habet veritatem, sapientiam divinam, charitatem, patientiam et omnia ornamenta spiritualia, deinde habet externam administrationem divinitus ordinatam, optimis legibus instructam, oportet ein schone ordinatio sey, quam Deus immediate gestelt.*'[2] It is in persecution and suffering for Christ that these spiritual ornaments are bestowed upon the Church and that they shine out revealed and seen in the Word and Sacraments.[3] '*Quanquam sim politia divinitus instituta et ornata verbo Dei, Tamen in speciem miserrima esse videor, Nusquam succedit, paucissimi sunt, qui pacem publicam ament et tueantur. Videor non Politia, sed quaedam seditiosorum hominum colluvies esse. Nolite hac forma offendi. Figite oculos non in nigredinem sed in osculum, quod mihi Deus offert, et suum propter verbum, fidem. Sic Ecclesia Speciem habet meretricis omnium ludibrio expositae, lacerata. Ps. 22. ... opprobrium hominum, sed formosissima intus propter verbum, modo hoc adsit, es gehe denn externe, wie es wolle.*'[4] 'In the School of Christ we learn this hard lesson: *Deducit ad inferos et reducit, mortificat et vivificat.*'[5] That is Luther's constant theme that it is only through *agones* and *tentationes* that the Church exists and fulfils its mission, and therefore he insists on interpreting the whole idea of the essential form of the Church in history in terms of the Cross.[6]

This is precisely the way in which the Church grows and increases until the end of the world, so that 'the world is converted to faith, *scandaloso et miraculoso modo, scilicet per infirmitatem contra omnem potentiam, sapientiam, iusticiam etc., quae manifeste sunt divini miraculi.* For the kingdoms of the world are established not by infirmity but by power against the weak. *Ideo alia ratio est regni Dei propagandi et regni mundi.* This argument convinces us that the Church is the Kingdom of God; all the other kingdoms of the world fight against the one weak and despised Church but do not prevail at all. But the Church itself conquers at last all king-

---

[1] W.A. 44, p. 110. Cf. W.A. 57, p. 107.   [2] W.A. 31/2, pp. 657f.
[3] W.A. 44, p. 110.   [4] W.A. 31/2, pp. 610f.
[5] W.A. 38, p. 653.   [6] W.A. 44, pp. 111f; 50, p. 642.

doms and converts them to itself, by the very power of God. But before it increases like that its weakness and humility is scandalous.'[1] That comes from Luther's exposition of the parable of the mustard seed, but when he goes on to expound the parable of the leaven which a woman took and hid in three measures of meal, it is essentially the same thought that he sets forth. The Gospel preached by the Church is the *'novum fermentum'* which once mixed into humanity does not desist until the end of the world but penetrates the whole mass of those that need to be saved.[2] Here then in the midst of the world Christians and Christ are baked together into *'ein kuche, ein brod'*, for Christ as *fermentum* is incorporated into them to become one body with them, and can no more be separated from them than the leaven from the paste. In vain does the devil seek to separate Christ from the Church. *'Der teyg ist geseurt, der teufel wird die seure nicht sondern vom teyge. Er koche oder brate sie, oder röste und börne sie da zu, so ist der sauerteig Christus drinnen, Und sol drinnen bleiben bis an den iungsten tag, das alles durch seuret werde et nihil de pasta infermentatum maneat.'*[3] 'So long as Christ remains Christ and the Church remains the Church, the world will abound in scandals and evils',[4] but all this only serves to further the fermentation of the world through the Church until it is brought under the purpose of God or reduced to faith.

It belongs therefore to the very nature and mission of the Church that it should be hidden in this world and mixed up with hypocrites and unbelievers, and indeed, as we have already noted, it could not exist in the flesh without being so involved in humanity. There were times when Luther rather yearned for a separate Church of the pure and faithful to whom he could preach and minister[5]—though true Christians were too few for that purpose —but he did not wish to withdraw them out of their context in the social structure of the world by setting up a special ecclesiastical structure and so organising a clear-cut, separatist Church, a visible society of the saints, but preferred to allow the Church to

[1] W.A. 38, p. 563.
[2] Luther also applies this thought of fermentation to the operation of Baptism in the individual believer. Cf. especially *Rationis Latomianae Confutatio*, W.A. 8, p. 107.
[3] W.A. 38, p. 564.   [4] W.A. 38, p. 566. Cf. W.A. 8, p. 379.
[5] W.A. 19, pp. 73ff. Cf. W.A., *Briefe*, 1071; W.A. 12, pp. 169f; 11, pp. 408f; 12, pp. 11f.

work as a leavening *Christenheit* in the social hierarchies of the world, of family, worship and the state.¹ Certainly the Church was to be visibly marked out by the Word and Sacrament, by confession, from the world² but it was to be compacted by the Word within the authority and protection provided by the State. This did not mean that the Church was the tool of the State. How could it be if the Church was ruled by the majestic Word of God³ and was the instrument of that Word as it exercised its authority over all the kingdoms of the world? The very mixing of the Church as *Christenheit* within the hierarchies, even under persecution, would mean at once the preservation of the world for the sake of the Church and the Gospel,⁴ and at the same time the bringing of the world and its institutions under the reign of Christ so that He could use them as His *larvae* for the purpose of the Gospel and the growth of the Church.⁵

As a community of those who confess Christ, who are marked out by the Word and Sacraments, the Church is *visibilis in mundo*',⁶ but it is *in mundo* and until the day of judgment will always be the Church of hypocrites as well as of true believers, an external *Gemeinschaft*.⁷ For that very reason it will always be covered *sub cruce*, discernible only to faith—but that is because of its eschatological and teleological mission until the end of the world. The Church is joined to Christ, who has made it His Body, and as such it is the *Regnum Christi*. '*Idem regnum Christi hic et in futuro : hic per fidem incoatum, in futuro consummandum per gloriam.*'⁸ The Church is involved in the world and as such it is involved in its social structures and forms and is given shape within them by Word and Sacrament so that as *ferment* it may pervade and rule over the world and bring it under the *Regnum Christi*. It is only within this double involvement that the Church in Christ wearing the new humanity is to be interpreted—that is, it can be interpreted

---

¹ W.A. 26, pp. 504f; W.A. 30/2, p. 117.   ² W.A. 39/2, pp. 146-149.
³ Cf. W.A. 51, p. 519: '*Gottes wort sey so ein herrlich maiestetisch ding.*' See also W.A. 12, p. 192.
⁴ W.A. 42, p. 310: '*Etsi Ecclesia est exigua : tamen est rectrix orbis terrarum, et conservatur propter eam mundus.*'
⁵ W.A. 21, p. 432. Vide supra on *larva dei*. Cf. W.A. 31/2, pp. 688f: '*Nam verbum publice praedicatum cives domum reportant et ex verbo discunt se et suos gubernare. Ita ut ubique experiamur, in templo, in republica, in oeconomia certos verbi fructus, quod ceu fermentum omnes reipublicae partes, officia et status omnes pervadit.*'   ⁶ W.A. 39/2, p. 149.   ⁷ W.A. 22, p. 344.
⁸ *Luthers Briefe*, de Wette edition 2, p. 492.

THE ESCHATOLOGY OF FAITH: MARTIN LUTHER

only dialectically. It is not that Luther does not think of the Church as a *tertium datur* proleptically participant in the new creation, but this is only known to faith in crucifixion and mortification: it is concealed under the Cross and held forth in hope.

In other language, used by Luther early in his theological career, the Church as the *Regnum Christi* is the *Regnum gratiae* or the *Regnum in fide* and remains such *'usque ad iudicium extremum'* until the *'Regnum in quo Christus inquantum homo regnat'*, passes over into the *Regnum gloriae* when Christ will hand over the Kingdom to the Father. Now He rules *'in fide per humanitatem Christi, tunc in specie per revelationem essentiae dei.'*[1] Everything that Luther has to say about the Church in history, its form and polity, its face and visibility, its work and suffering and victory, is said in the context of that eschatological movement from *Regnum gratiae* to *Regnum gloriae*, from enigmatic concealment in grace to the revelation of glory. On the one hand it is the *theologia crucis*, but on the other hand it is the pressure of the *Regnum gloriae* and its imminent revelation, that demand eschatological suspension of form and order in the Church on earth.[2] That does not mean that the Church can do without form and order. On the contrary, but form and order have to be used eschatologically so that they leave room, as it were, for the breaking in of the *Regnum Dei* from above.[3]

In the Book of Revelation liturgy and apocalyptic belong together. The Eucharistic liturgy is part of the great apocalyptic conflict between the Kingdom of God and the kingdoms of this world, and so liturgical forms are understood as an engagement, if only by way of echo, in the conflict that took place on the Cross and from the Cross has been inserted into history. That is the way in which Luther seems to link up his apocalyptic intensity with the eschatological suspension of form and order in the Church and its life on earth. The believer within the Church is caught up in warfare, into the mighty and blessed battle of the Word of God, and his whole life is lived in tension. There can be no doubt that Luther's dialectical eschatology, the tension between *having* and

---

[1] *Luthers Vorlesung über den Galaterbrief*, 1516/17, edited by Schubert, p. 32.
[2] Cf. W.A. 19, p. 73; 21, p. 432. Luther opposed therefore the use of the Bible as a document to provide the Church with laws for worship and orders. W.A., *Briefe*, 1524; de Wette edition, 6, pp. 379f.
[3] See the important letter to Amsdorf, de Wette, *Briefe*, 5, pp. 431f and cf. his attitude to the Mass in this respect, W.A. 10/3, pp. 1ff; 12, pp. 205ff; 18, pp. 62f and p. 123; 19, pp. 14f, 72f.

not-having, created in him an insatiable hunger for the objective assurance of forgiveness, and threw him at times into great anxiety, an anxiety which he interpreted as real participation in the apocalyptic strife of the Kingdom of God. The term he employed to describe that was *'Anfechtung'* or *'tentatio'*.[1] The sharpness of that strife and the realisation, inherent in the *justus et peccator* dialectic, that before God the believer is always in the wrong,[2] helped him at times to lose sight of the new creation in Christ as already accomplished fact, as a *'perfectum praesens'*. It was not that Luther had no sense of the new creation either as regards the Church or as regards the individual believer, but that his weak stress on the renewal of the whole creation tended to rob it of temporal relevance and force. In the end Luther's doctrine of *Anfechtung*, which corresponds so well to his view of faith, means that the believer does not really learn to live on the resurrection side of the Cross. So far as Luther entered into the triumphant eschatology of the New Testament, it was employed rather as consolation in *Anfechtung*[3] than as actual anticipation of the final victory of the Son of Man. *'Ein feste Burg'* will ever remain one of the great hymns of the Church, but it expresses only one side of the eschatology of the Reformation.

[1] Cf. especially Luther's exposition of the 22nd Psalm (W.A. 5, pp. 620ff).
[2] Cf. W.A. 8, pp. 59ff, 73ff.
[3] Cf., for example, the sermon for the Second of Advent, 1544 (W.A. 52, pp. 16ff, and W.A. 7, pp. 784ff).

III

THE ESCHATOLOGY OF LOVE: MARTIN BUTZER

HISTORY has not yet taken its full measure of Martin Butzer, who must be adjudged as standing within the sphere of Reformed rather than Lutheran theology, not only because of his masterful influence on Calvin or Calvin's considerable influence on him,[1] but because his pioneer work in Biblical hermeneutics[2] and patristic study helped to shape the whole Reformed Church.[3] If Luther's theology is to be interpreted over against the development of Western thought, particularly in its mediaeval form, that of Butzer is to be understood in terms of the Catholic Church and patristic theology of the first six centuries,[4] for here we have a great attempt to get behind mediaevalism and, as Calvin put it, writing from Strasbourg, to restore the face of the ancient Catholic Church.[5] In further contrast to the Lutheran position, Butzer's theology is more broadly based on the teaching of Scripture. Ephesians, Galatians and the Johannine writings, for example, are interpreted together,[6] and so the Biblical ideas of election and adoption into the Body of Christ are placed alongside

---

[1] See, for example, Butzer's *Praelectiones on the Epistle to the Ephesians*, delivered in Cambridge in 1550 and 1551 (published at Heidelberg in 1561); in it Butzer apparently follows Calvin's Commentary (published in 1548) on the same Epistle, in which Christ is spoken of as the *cause of election* in all four senses of cause, *final, formal, efficient, material*. Butzer, *Enarr. in Eph.*, pp. 19ff.
[2] See the *In sacra quattuor Evangelia enarrationes perpetuae*, 1536, 1553.
[3] This is particularly clear in regard to the all-important little work, *Von der waren Seelsorge unnd dem rechten Hirtendienst, wie der selbige inn der Kirchen Christi bestellet unnd verichtet werden solle*, 1538. A Latin edition, *De vera animarum cura*, is found in the *Scripta Anglicana*, 1577, pp. 260-356, where the purpose of the work is described as '*ad ipsius gloriam sempiternam, sanctique regni sui incrementum*', p. 264.
[4] *Scripta Anglicana*, pp. 262f.   [5] *Vide infra*, pp. 98f.
[6] See again *Von der waren Seelsorge*, and also the *Explicatio in dictum Apost. Eph.* 4, *Scripta Anglicana*, pp. 504-538. It is this chapter in the Epistle to the Ephesians which became dominant in the Reformed doctrine of the Church, as taught by Calvin, Peter Martyr and John Knox. There is no doubt that it was Butzer's influence which was paramount there.

73

the doctrines of rebirth and justification by faith,[1] and they are thought into each other, while the ministry of the Gospel, as well as the Gospel itself, becomes a *de fide* matter.[2] It was in line with this that, while Luther laid all the stress upon the Word of God, Butzer (to be followed by Calvin) came to lay the stress upon the Word and Spirit in their inseparable conjunction.[3]

In contrast to Luther and Calvin there is a strong charismatic element in Butzer's theology apparent in his emphasis upon the love that is shed into our hearts by the Spirit. That is no doubt due in part to his religious inheritance in Strasbourg, to Tauler, for example, but it is also due to his Biblical studies. This is apparent already in his earliest published work, *Das ym selb niemant leben soll sonderen anderen* (1523),[4] in which he expounded the life of the Church in terms of a communion of love having its source in the activity of the divine love both in creation and in redemption. Though the actual programme he set forth was to be modified and enriched, the characteristic traits of Butzer's theology stand out clearly.

God has created a world distinct from Himself, with creatures utterly unlike Him in being and as unable to take part in His divine activity as the pot in the activity of the potter.[5] But in their humble sphere these creatures are made by God to be used in the purpose of His divine glory and so to participate in His service. It is this supreme purpose which makes all creatures dependent on each other, for they are interrelated in God's creative activity. That is specially true of man, who crowns the creaturely world, and who has been made in the image of God to reflect His glory, that is to say, he has been 'implanted with love and the desire to serve and do good'.[6] With the sin and fall of man, however, the whole creation became disordered and perverted. Man lost the

---

[1] *De Regno Christi, Op. Lat.*, XV, pp. 53f; *Scripta Anglicana*, pp. 517, 533, 556, etc.; *Enarr. in quatt. Evangelia*, pp. 671, 770, etc.; *Ein Summarischer vergriff der Christlichen lehre und Religion*, 1548, edited by F. Wendel in *Revue d'Histoire et de Philosophie Religieuses*, 1953/1. Cf. e.g., pp. 34f, 44f.

[2] *Ecclesiae Regnum* is the equivalent of *Evangelium Regni, Enarr. in Matt.* 4.23. See also *De vi et usu sacri ministerii explicatio, Scripta Anglicana*, pp. 553-610.

[3] *Enarr. in Johannem* 1.1; 5.39, 46; *De Regno Christi, Op. Lat*, XV, pp. 5f, 24f, etc.; *Scripta Anglicana*, p. 260; *Enarr. in Ps.*, p. 122; *Metaphrasis et Enarr. in Rom.*, 1562, p. vi, etc.

[4] Edited by H. Strohl, in *Revue d'Historie et de Phil. Relig.*, 1947, 3/4, pp. 141-213.   [5] Op. cit., pp. 156f.   [6] Op. cit., p. 162.

knowledge of the Creator and so of His creatures, which turned against each other in enmity.[1]

It was into this perverted and disordered world that the Son of God descended to restore creation to its true *Ordnung*, to renew the Kingdom of God, and to bring back all things, physical and spiritual, to their true being and usefulness in the praise of God. This is what God does in the Incarnation, for in Christ He has given a Head to all things to bring reconciliation, rehabilitation and renewal. That is being realised now in and through the Church, where God's Kingdom is set up in the midst of the fallen world, where men are brought back to the divine purpose of love and learn to live for God and for one another. It is only through faith in Christ that they participate again in the divine love and only in the activity of love that they participate again in the Kingdom of God.[2]

Regnum Christi

Between this work and the publication of his epoch-making *Von der wahren Seelsorge, unnd dem rechten Hirtendienst* in 1538,[3] Butzer's theology became more Christologically orientated, and the conception of the *Regnum Christi* became dominant. It is highly significant that it was under this essentially eschatological conception that Butzer brought his theological and ecclesiastical teaching together, while in 1557 it was under the title of *De Regno Christi*[4] that he set forth his counsels for the 'solid restitution' of the Kingdom of God in England, that is, for the reorganisation of the public and national life in obedience to the Gospel of Christ.[5]

At the outset of this work[6] Butzer notes that there are three Biblical terms for Kingdom: the *Kingdom of God*, the *Kingdom of His Beloved Son* and the *Kingdom of Heaven*. When we use the word 'kingdom', he says, we think of the government or administration of a people or state which is undertaken by one who is

---

[1] Op. cit., p. 168. [2] Op. cit., pp. 170f, 194f, 204f.
[3] A Latin edition was published in the *Scripta Anglicana* in 1577.
[4] This was published also in the *Scripta Anglicana*. A modern edition of the Latin text of 1550 and the French translation of 1558 has recently been published by François Wendel, Presses Universitaires de France, 1954.
[5] *De Regno Christi*, Op. Lat. XV, pp. 90, 293f; see also the preface to the *Metaphrasis et Enarr. in Rom.*, p. iv. It was Butzer's hope that through England the re-establishment of the *Regnum Christi* would spread all over Europe.
[6] *De Regno Christi*, Op. Lat. XV, pp. 3f.

pre-eminent in wisdom and virtue and whose concern it is to provide in every way for the good of all citizens, so that each from childhood is formed and guided into every virtue, into a blessed way of life and real felicity. We expect the Kingdom of God, therefore, to be supreme in all these ways and to exhibit the character of a true kingdom in the fullest and most perfect way. But the Kingdom of God we read of in Holy Scripture is unique, as unique as God, who alone is good and wise and mighty.[1] *Regnum Dei* thus expresses the Kingdom in its transcendent and eternal nature, and that is uniquely expressed in the *Regnum Christi dilecti Filii Dei*. This is the eternal Kingdom of God which has moved into this world (*in hoc seculo, in mundo*),[2] in the Son of the Father, and is administered throughout the world until its very end,[3] and then reaches out into the full Kingdom of God when Christ will hand it over to the Father.[4] That provides all history with its perspective. The day of the Kingdom of God has already dawned in the advent of Christ, the Light of the World, and through the preaching of the Gospel the Sun of Righteousness ascending on high increasingly sheds righteous rays over all the earth, but the *meridies* will not be reached until Christ comes again in the majesty of God. Before then, clouds of darkness and error will seek to oppose themselves to His light but He will shine all the more brightly. Thus the night is already passing and the day when Christ the Light of the World will be fully enjoyed approaches, even though no one *in hoc seculo* may yet expect it.[5]

On the one hand, then, the Kingdom is spoken of as *Regnum caelorum*, for though it has moved into the world and is already operative within this age, it is not of this world (*non de hoc mundo*), but of Heaven, where the citizenship of its true members is lodged.[6]

---

[1] *Scripta Anglicana*, p. 270, from the *De vera animarum cura*.

[2] This does not mean a *Münsterisch* view of the Kingdom, which Butzer explicitly repudiates; see *Ein Summarischer vergriff der Christlichen lehre und Religion*, p. 72: 'Reich Christi das sie ins zeitlich gesetzit.' This has to be balanced by the conception of the Kingdom as *Regnum caelorum*.

[3] *Scripta Anglicana*, p. 296: 'Pater Christo Domino nostro potestatem dedit super omnem carnem: ut redintegret omnia in coelo et in terra: ut ei flectatur omne genu omnesque linguae Dominum glorificent ac praedicent: denique ut regnet usque ad fines terrae, omnesque populos haereditate possideat.'

[4] *De Regno Christi, Op. Lat.* XV, p. 53. This is a very frequent and dominant concept which also plays a similar rôle in Calvin's thought.

[5] *In Prophetam Sophoniam explanatio* (published along with *Enarr. in Ps.*, 1554), p. 568.

[6] Cf. *Enarr. in Matt.* 3.2; *De Regno Christi, Op. Lat.* XV, p. 34.

On the other hand, however, Butzer thinks of the Church as the sphere where that Kingdom is progressively realised by a *'mirificum incrementum'* and is more and more apparent in this world, though in the nature of the case, until Christ comes again, that is only in part in accordance with our capacity in this life. That is the aspect of the glorious Kingdom of God so often predicted by the prophets, 'that Christ should have a *regnum et civitatem sanctam in terris: hoc est, Ecclesiam, eamque omni pietate et virtute exornatam.* This Church is called the place of God's feet in the earth for it is only in the Church that God exhibits Himself as truly present *pro modo nostrae capacitatis in hac vita*. In another way Heaven is regarded as God's seat where He reveals Himself fully. But the *terra sanctorum* is His footstool *in quo nobis se ex parte repraesentat: et ea parte, cuius percipiendae sumus hic eius dono compotes.*'[1]

The important concept here is the *Regnum Christi*, by means of which Butzer expresses very powerfully the idea that the eternal Kingdom of God has entered into the midst of our life on earth,[2] and overlaps this present age here and now.[3] This conception reposes on the analogy of the Incarnation. Christ, our King, has now ascended to the throne of God and is not subject to anyone, but when He was in the world, He subjected Himself to the powers that are entrusted with the sword, even to the most shameful death. In the same way the *Regnum Christi* submits to the kingdoms of the world, but every true *regnum mundi*, on the other hand (*'regnum dico'*, adds Butzer, *'non tyrannidem'*), subjects itself to the Kingdom of Christ, and especially the kings, as *Dei administratores*,[4] that they may cultivate godliness not so much for themselves as for their subjects.[5] Within this mutual relationship of subjection and purpose the *Regnum Christi* is a unique expression of the *Regnum Dei* of which it is a *'vera communio et administratio'*, but the form that it takes is the *Regnum Crucifixi*.[6] Within

---

[1] *De Regno Christi, Op. Lat.* XV, p. 33.
[2] Ibid. *'Regnum et civitatem sanctam in terris, hoc est Ecclesiam.'*
[3] *De Regno Christo, Op. Lat.* XV, pp. 6-20. As such it is *the Kingdom of God and Christ, Enarr. in Ps.*, pp. 147, 313, 361, etc.; *De Regno Christi, Op. Lat.* XV, p. 44.   [4] *Enarr. in Ps.*, p. 132.
[5] *De Regno Christi, Op. Lat.* XV, pp. 14f. The subjection of the *regnum mundi* to the *Regnum Christi* is on the ground that *'sacro baptismate omnes regno Christi incorporantur et in obedientiam eius sese addicunt'* (p. 14). Cf. p. 33.
[6] Or the *Regnum Mediatoris*, as he calls it elsewhere (*Enarr. in Ps.*, 11, p. 22).

this age or world the Kingdom of Christ is engaged in battle with the realm of evil and it flourishes in that warfare, but throughout 'Christ rules solely by His Word and Spirit'; 'not by external power', but 'by a marvellous power'.[1] Above all it is the expression of the divine love and grace and its supreme purpose is to lead men back to that love in God.[2] Meanwhile 'the Kingdom of Christ is properly the same as His Priesthood (*Sacerdotium*) and consists in the justification of the ungodly and intercession for the sanctified'.[3] The evangelical aspect of this Butzer is not concerned to expound fully in the *De Regno Christi*,[4] the opening section of which we have been expounding—that side is fully given in his other works and is concerned above all with the Church as the living Body of Christ.[5] It is precisely because the *Regnum Christi* involves this understanding of the Church as the Body of Christ within actual history that the *Regnum Christi* involves the overlap between the Kingdom of Heaven and the kingdoms of this world, so that it is at once '*temporarium et aeternum*'.[6] Although we must distinguish between the Kingdom of God and that of this world (*Regni Dei et mundi discrimen*),[7] and understand what is *proper* to each, it is also important to see 'how they are conjoined, and how they mutually subject themselves to each other and serve each other'.[8] One aspect of that duality is apparent in the fact that within the Kingdom of Christ there are believers and hypocrites,[9]

---

[1] *De Regno Christi, Op. Lat.* XV, pp. 5, 9, 14f, 24f, etc.
[2] *Enarr. in Lucam.* 2.33, where the Kingdom is spoken of as 'the sign of all grace and benevolence toward the *genus humanum*'.
[3] *Enarr. in Matt.* 13.20: '*Proprie regnum Christi est quod sacerdotium eius, et situm in justificatione et intercessione pro sanctificatis.*' It is the *regnum salvificum* (*De Regno Christi, Op. Lat.* XV, p. 44).
[4] But cf. p. 16: '*Omnis Christi Ecclesia debet esse evangelizatrix ita ut in omni sanctorum coetu sonet vox Evangelii assidue, fiducia maxima et studio ardentissimo. Summa Evangelii est nobis exhibere filium Dei, et ceu praesentem offerre et dicere, Ecce Deum Vestrum: hoc est, peccatorum condonatorem atque bonorum omnium Vitaeque aeternae largitorem. Hoc debet quaelibet vera Christi Ecclesia, non suis tantum hominibus, verum etiam quibuscunque possit populis et hominibus indefinenter, et quam clarissime praedicare atque adclamare, Ecce Deus Vester.*'
[5] See especially, *De vera animarum cura*, *De vi et usu sacri ministerii explicatio* and *Explicatio in Eph.* 4. The Reformed Churches had to fight for this doctrine against the Roman conceptions of the Church as absolute institution and *corpus mysticum*. See *Scripta Anglicana*, pp. 358, 508, 556f, etc.
[6] *Enarr. in Matt.* 13.24.   [7] *Enarr. in Matt.* 5.3.
[8] *De Regno Christi, Op. Lat.* XV, p. 20; '*Das ym selb niemant leben soll, vorred*', p. 154.
[9] *De Regno Christi, Op. Lat.* XV, p. 50; *Scripta Anglicana*, p. 287; *Enarr. in Matt.* 5.1f; *in Matt.* 5.18f. '*Ecclesia praesens aedificatur ex bonis et malis, sed caelestis ex electis solum*' (*Enarr. in Ps.*, p. 95).

those who adore Christ as Lord and King and those who speak against Him, the elect and the reprobate who contradict Christ and shatter themselves in judgment against His grace, and so fight against themselves.[1] This, then, is one of the great characteristics of Butzer's teaching, that the Kingdom of Christ stretches both over those who believe and are compacted into a *communion of love* by the Word and Spirit, and over those who are without the Church, for it concerns salvation temporal and eternal,[2] spans the whole life and activity of men and society and involves their reorganisation as a *regnum externum* in the service of the *Regnum Christi*.[3] A favourite term Butzer employs to speak of this is '*Respublica*', which is applied both to the Church and to the State, for if the Church has a State-character, the State has a Church-character in so far as it is the instrument of the Kingdom of Christ, who dwells in the midst of His Church and rules from there.

The Kingdom and the Church

When Butzer thinks of the Church before God, in terms of the Gospel, he regularly speaks of it as the Body of Christ, the Bride of Christ or the flock of the Good Shepherd; when he thinks of the Church in relation to the daily temporal affairs of men, he tends to use expressions such as '*societas Christiana*'; but when he thinks of the Church *vis-à-vis* the State he generally adopts the word '*communio*', adding to it '*sanctorum*', '*fidelium*', '*electorum*', '*renatorum*', etc.[4] As such it is often spoken of as identical with the *Regnum Christi* because it is its truest expression,[5] for there above all 'Christ reigns here and now in the midst of His people'.[6]

---

[1] *Enarr. in Matt.* 5.19; *Enarr. in Matt.* 12.31f; *Enarr. in Lucam* 2.23; *De Regno Christi, Op. Lat.* XV, p. 34, p. 53f. 'The Lord does not wish to make known to us the mysteries of election, but commands us to go into all the world and preach the Gospel to every creature—in all the world *and* to every creature', *Scripta Anglicana*, p. 296; cf. *De Regno Christi, Op. Lat.* XV, pp. 45f, 50f.
[2] *Ein Summarischer vergriff der Christlichen lehre und Religion*, p. 38.
[3] *De Regno Christi, Op. Lat.* XV, pp. 293f. The *universum Regnum* requires an *Ecclesiam universam, Met. et Enarr. in Rom.*, p. iv.
[4] E.g. *Scripta Anglicana*, pp. 556f. Although the Church is *communio par excellence*, Butzer recognises that it has *aliqua communio* in common with society in general on the ground of the *charitas* required by the law of all men in their relationships of life and work. See *Enarr. in Eph.*, pp. 29f.
[5] *Enarr. in Ps.*, p. 240.
[6] *De Regno Christi, Op. Lat.* XV, pp. 17f; 27f; the Church is therefore the *verus Israel*, the *terra Domini* (*Enarr. in Ps.*, p. 335); *Scripta Anglicana*, p. 271: '*Hoc regimen gerit et exercet Dominus in domo Jacob, id est, in Ecclesia, perpetuo est et habitat apud suos usque ad finem mundi: non quidem sensibiliter aut more*

That is particularly manifest in the sacramental life of the Church: *'darinn unser Herre Christus sein reich und Majestät uns gewaltigsten fürbringt'*.[1] Because this Kingdom is supremely the Kingdom of the Beloved Son who was crucified in order to redeem us from sin and restore us to the love of God, the Church is the sphere of reconciliation,[2] and is regarded mainly in terms of grace and its work in terms of brotherly love.[3] Butzer's favourite way of expressing that was by using the Biblical terms of compassion and mercy, such as 'shepherd and flock', 'bridegroom and bride', 'physician and the sick', etc. The clearest definition of that is to be found in the *Von der waren Seelsorge*, which from beginning to end is built up on this conception. *'Dis regiment inn seiner Kirchen hat und fueret unser Herre Christus, durch sich selb und seinen Geist, Darum dann die schrift in heisset den Koenig der himel, in den Meister, die Christen seine junger unnd schuler, in den hirten, die Kirch seine herd, in das haupt, die Christen seine glider, in den breütgam, die Kirch die braut, welche er im reinigt und seübert, bis er im selb darstelle ein herliche Gemeinde, die weder flecken noch runtzeln habe, in den artzet, die Christen die krancken, in den richter und zuchtiger, die Christen die so gerichtet und gezüchtiget werden.'*[4] This activity of the *Regnum Christi* results in the Church which can be spoken of in these terms: *'Die Kirch Christi, ist die versamlung und Gemeinde deren, die inn Christo unserem Herren, durch seinen Geist und wort, also von der welt versamlet und vereinbaret sind, das sie ein leib sind, und glider durch einander, deren jedes sein amt und werck hat zu gemeiner besserung des gantzen leibes und aller glider.'*[5]

---

huius mundi, quem reliquit, at vere tamen et efficaciter.' Cf. *Enarr. perpet. in quatt. Evang.*, pp. 332f.

[1] *Ein Summarischer vergriff*, p. 20.
[2] *Scripta Anglicana*, pp. 322f. It is the *archa foederis* (*Enarr. in Ps.*, p. 388).
[3] *Scripta Anglicana*, pp. 306f; cf. p. 7: 'vera fraterna charitas'.
[4] 1538 edition, p. 4. Similar definitions of the *Regnum Christi* are given in the *De Regno Christi*, *Op. Lat.* XV, pp. 54f: 'Regnum Servatoris nostri Jesu Christi, administratio est et procuratio salutis aeternae electorum Dei, qua hic ipse Dominus et Rex coelorum, doctrina et disciplina sua, per idoneos et ab ipso delectos ad hoc ipsum ministros administratis, electos suos (quos habet in mundo dispersos, et vult nihilominus mundi potestatibus esse subjectos) colligit ad se, sibique et Ecclesiae suae incorporat atque in ea sic gubernat, ut purgati indies plenius peccatis, bene beateque vivant et hic et in futuro.' An alternative definition follows on pp. 55f which stresses more the work of the Holy Spirit and the Sacraments. see also *Scripta Anglicana*, p. 271.
[5] *Op. cit.*, p. 1; cf. pp. 39, 47f, etc. and also *Scripta Anglicana*, pp. 267, 304f, 521f, 556ff.

THE ESCHATOLOGY OF LOVE: MARTIN BUTZER 81

This Church is the *Regnum Christi* because the *Rex* dwells in her midst, is governed through *minsitri et dispensatores mysteriorum eius*, pastors and doctors, bishops, presbyters and deacons.[1] They act as servants of Christ and through their 'subministration'[2] the whole flock is compacted and built up in Christ in a communion of love[3] as His Body,[4] so that within it all members are ordered to each other in *iunctura*, in mutual love and service as priests in the service of Christ.[5] '*Et hoc regni Christi esse proprium, quod qui vere eius cives sunt, iidem sint omnes veri sacerdotes Dei: id est, qui oris et totius vitae confessione adnuncient virtutes eius, qui vocavit eos ex tenebris in admirabilem suam lucem.*'[6] Butzer goes on to point out in this passage that the citizens of the Kingdom of Christ should devote themselves to their daily duties[7]: those who are able, to spiritual matters, and those who are so gifted, to the necessities of daily life; but the whole of life is understood as coming under the priesthood of the believer, and every believer must bear witness to his faith.[8]

Here undoubtedly we see the distinction between his teaching and that of Luther. Butzer insists that Christians must translate their faith into '*a true faithful and active love to all men*',[9] for they are to live out among men the communion of love to which they belong in Christ.[10] *Charitas* conditioned by *spes* is the ground and source of *solida virtus*.[11] The Kingdom of Christ is a *Communio* or *Respublica* of those who are moderated by the Spirit of Christ[12]

[1] *Scripta Anglicana*, p. 273; *Ein Summarischer vergriff der Christlichen lehre und Religion*, p. 44; *Met. et Enarr. in Rom.*, p. iv; *De Regno Christi, Op. Lat.* XV, pp. 6of, 118ff.
[2] *Scripta Anglicana*, pp. 177, 559. The old Latin translation of Eph. 4 is followed rather closely.
[3] This is supremely evident in the Lord's Supper, op. cit., pp. 321f.
[4] *Vide supra*, note 5 on p. 80.
[5] *De Regno Christi, Op. Lat.* XV, pp. 35, 89f; *Scripta Anglicana*, pp. 288, 559. Because Christ dwells in all Christians, all are needed to heal the wounds of the people (op. cit., pp. 304f, 533f). See also the *Formula brevis visitandi aegroti, Scripta Anglicana*, pp. 356-359.
[6] *De Regno Christi, Op. Lat.* XV, p. 35. Cf. p. 33, where *evangelizare* is spoken of as '*omnis Christiani hominis proprium et praecipuum munus*'.
[7] Cf. *Scripta Anglicana*, p. 268: '*Christiani communionem suam habent non solum in spiritualibus sed etiam in temporalibus.*' See also pp. 56of.
[8] Cf. *De Regno Christi, Op. Lat.* XV, pp. 21 (cf. 33f, 46): '*Quicunque vere credit Christo, is non potest regnum eius non praedicare, et ad illud, quos queat, invitare.*'
[9] *Ein Summarischer vergriff der Christlichen lehre und Religion*, p. 38: '*ein ware treue thetige liebe*'; *Das ym selb*, p. 154.
[10] *De Regno Christi, Op. Lat.* XV, pp. 34f, 55f, etc.
[11] *Enarr. in Eph.*, pp. 26f.
[12] *Enarr. in Matt.* 5.19; *in Matt.* 4.23.

and in whose hearts there is begotten a divine love which grows and increases, reaching out to the perfection of the resurrected life.¹ It is this amazingly eschatological conception of *love* that is the most moving and characteristic element in Butzer's theology. This insistence upon *true, faithful and active love* and upon the works of love, without which faith is dead, is not reached by any kind of legalism or moralism. We are unprofitable servants even after we have done all our duty, and therefore the whole of our life, even in our deeds of love on earth, is seen under the impact of the coming Kingdom, so that we must daily pray for forgiveness and daily put our trust and hope in Christ alone, for He only is our sanctification and redemption.²

Considered in itself the Church as an expression of the Kingdom of Christ combines eternal election and incorporation into the Body of Christ: '*ad colligendum et cooptandum in corpore suo electos suos.*'³ Here the Kingdom of God is thought of as eternal and transcendent on the one hand (*regnum*) and as the realisation of the Will of God in history on the other hand (*regnare*).⁴ Election is essentially corporate in nature, and operates through incorporation (*incorporatio, coaptatio, collocatio, consociatio, coniunctio*) into the Body of Christ through the Spirit, or respectively, through faith in Christ.⁵ The building up of the elect into the Body of Christ, that is of those who do not deny Christ but believe in Him and obey His Word, involves the translation of their faith into *virtus*, 'for the Kingdom of God does not consist in speech but in *virtue*'.⁶ That means for Butzer not morality, in the modern sense, but act of God, 'the crucifixion and the abolishing of the old man', and the reshaping of the new man for the Kingdom that is to come.⁷

---

¹ *De Regno Christi, Op. Lat.* XV, pp. 53f.
² *Ein Summarischer vergriff der Christlichen lehre und Religion*, pp. 40f.
³ *De Regno Christi, Op. Lat.* XV, p. 56.
⁴ See the recurring expressions in *Ein Summarischer vergriff der Christlichen lehre und Religion*: 'in geistlichen oder weltlichen sachen' (p. 16), 'durch sein h. Evangeli unnd auch in eüsseren zeitlichen thun' (p. 18), 'zu irem zeitlichen unnd ewigen heil' (p. 38), 'mit zeitlichen unnd ewigen gueteren' (p. 42), 'zu diesem unnd dem ewigen leben' (p. 84).
⁵ *De Regno Christi, Op. Lat.* XV, pp. 53f, 56 etc.; cf. also *Scripta Anglicana*, pp. 295f, 509f, 521f, 527f, 558, etc.
⁶ *De Regno Christi, Op. Lat.* XV, pp. 34, 52; *Scripta Anglicana*, p. 364; *Das ym selb.*, p. 154. In this context *virtus* means power, but it means more than that. Cf. *De Regno Christi, Op. Lat.* XV, p. 28: '*Ubi vox Christi non sonat cum virtute, ibi ecclesia Christi non est.*' Hence the Church itself can be called a '*viva vox*' (*Scripta Anglicana*, p. 739).   ⁷ *De Regno Christi, Op. Lat.* XV, p. 52.

Butzer's whole conception of the Christian life is well summed up in these words: '*Unde scandalum erit, quicquid omnino vel dixerimus, vel fecerimus, quod non ex solida fide natum et iuxta synceram dilectionem moderatum, ad gloriam Dei salutemque proximorum promovendam fecerit.*'[1] That means that we must love Christ and keep His commandments,[2] for they are '*verba et praecepta vitae, salutisque aeternae.*'[3] It is thus that we begin to manifest the nature of the *vita futura*, which already begins in us through faith, but which will be perfected by Christ at His advent.[4] Thus through the faith that works by love we have a taste here and now of the future life,[5] and of that fuller knowledge which will succeed faith through the operation of the Spirit.[6] If we have 'the Spirit of the reigning Christ' dwelling in us, He works in us efficaciously so that we daily die in Him and rise again, and are 'continuously reformed into His image and justified.'[7] But the *plena regeneratio* will only be perfected in the future '*per beatam resurrectionem*'.[8] Butzer's thought is very Biblical in that he thinks primarily of the whole Body of the Church in Christ in these terms, and within that one Body of the individual members.[9] The *incrementum* of the *corpus Christi* is discussed in great fulness and with remarkable power in the discussion of Ephesians 4,[10] as well as in the *De vi et usu sacri ministerii*.[11] The Church as the *Regnum Christi*, inhabited by the *Rex* and participating in His quickening Spirit, becomes more and more the *Regnum Christi* reaching out to the full *Regnum Dei*.[12]

The Eternal Kingdom

The Kingdom of Christ, however, has a much wider application in the teaching of Butzer. As *Sacerdotium* the *Regnum Christi* is concerned with the *Evangelium Regni*[13] and the Church

---

[1] *Enarr. in Matt.* 18.7f.   [2] *Ein Summarischer vergriff*, p. 238.
[3] *Scripta Anglicana*, pp. 167f.
[4] *Enarr. in Matt.* 8.11; *in Johannem* 3.15f, 21f.
[5] *Enarr. in Johannem* 17.1; *Scripta Anglicana*, p. 557.
[6] Cf. *Enarr. in Matt.* 9.2: '*Salus enim et vita est fides ipsa, hoc est certa futurae salutis et vitae persuasio: qua interea iustus vivit, accepto arrabone Spiritus, qui ad iustitiam inclinat quae Spiritus primitiae dicuntur.*' See *Enarr. in Matt.* 23.1.
[7] *Enarr. in Matt.* 28.1f. See also *Ein Summarischer vergriff der Christlichen lehre und Religion*, pp. 38, 70.   [8] *De Regno Christi, Op. Lat.* XV, p. 53.
[9] See especially *Ein Summarischer vergriff der Christlichen lehre und Religion*, section on *Die Christliche gemeinde*, XI, p. 44.
[10] See *Scripta Anglicana*, pp. 504ff.
[11] *Op. cit.*, pp. 556ff, and *Enarratio Epistolae D. Pauli ad Ephesios*, pp. 108ff.
[12] *Enarr. in Ps.*, pp. 312f, 373f.   [13] *Enarr. in Matt.* 4.23.

which the preaching of that Gospel calls out of the world, but the *Regnum Christi* also reaches out to include the whole *regnum externum* of human life on earth.[1] In so far as the Church participates in the *Regnum Christi* it is also involved in the whole *regnum externum*, so that the Church lays claim to all things in the reign of her Head and King.[2] The significance of the *Regnum Christi*, however, and its distinction from the *Regnum Dei* is that the reign of Christ over the whole human life is not implemented by the exercise of external power. Christ reigns over all things in the mode of Priesthood. Through the Gospel of the Cross, He rules in a marvellous manner[3] over all and claims allegiance from all. That rule is exercised from the Church, where Christ dwells as Lord and King, but because He has renounced external power for priestly mediation and intercession,[4] the Church which is His Body cannot and must not try to exercise force. Until the Kingdom of Christ is handed over to the Father, omnipotence and grace, so to speak, are held apart, so that temporal *sig, reich und hoffnung* are not promised.[5] Meanwhile the *Regnum Christi* lays claim over the whole of human life through the preaching of '*Christi verba et mysteria, verba et mysteria vitae aeternae*',[6] and the teaching of the precepts of the future life and salvation of men.[7]

Butzer regards Christ's Kingdom as set up and *solide* established[8] over men whenever and wherever they obey His will as proclaimed through the Church. In this way the Church serves the King by its *subministration*, but through that subministration Jesus Christ

---

[1] *De Regno Christi, Op. Lat.* XV, pp. 293f.
[2] *Scripta Anglicana*, p. 287: '*Ecclesiae autem a Christo Domino nostro per pretiosum eius sanguinem redemptae sunt, ut sint regnum eius sanctum ac liberum. Harum igitur sunt omnia, ipsae autem solius Christi.*' See also pp. 558f, where Butzer discusses Paul's ideas of the Church as $\pi\lambda\acute{\eta}\rho\omega\mu\alpha$.
[3] *De Regno Christi, Op. Lat.* XV, p. 5. Similarly the *Regnum Christi* is said to exercise its own *coaction* or *compulsion* but in a way *contra carnem* (*Scripta Anglicana*, p. 297).
[4] '*Munus proprium Christi praedicare Evangelium, non dare leges*' (*Enarr. in Matt.* 4.23).
[5] '*Wir verheissen auch den unseren/ so bei dem Euangelio bleiben/ nit zeitlichen sig/ reich unnd herschung/ wie die falschen Propheten zu Münster gethon/ sonder das der Herre verheissen hat/ ewige gnad und hilffe Gottes zu disem unnd dem ewigen leben/ damit wir hie/ so lang er uns will auff erden haben/ seinen Namen heiligen/ sein reich befordern/ und seinem willen geleben moegen*' (*Ein Summarischer vergriff der Christlichen lehre und Religion*, p. 84).
[6] *De Regno Christi, Op. Lat.* XV, p. 16. Of the ministry of the Church Butzer says: '*ut mundum ad verbum suum regnumque excitant*' (*Scripta Anglicana*, p. 275). [7] *De Regno Christi, Op. Lat.* XV, pp. 293f.
[8] Op. cit., pp. 90, 118, 293f, etc.

THE ESCHATOLOGY OF LOVE: MARTIN BUTZER

administers the whole *Regnum Christi* over men's life and work as well as in their faith and worship.[1] That was indeed the purpose of the *De Regno Christi*, which was addressed particularly to England, that the *Regnum Christi totum*, or the *Regnum Dei*, might be established or renewed there.[2] Because the Church is the sphere in this age and in this world in which the Kingdom has come, the Church must create room for itself and shape the context of its life and worship. That is very clear in the conclusion of Butzer's work. He declares that he has given 'an account of those ways and means by which Christian Kings and Princes (in order that we may be taught by the eternal and only saving Word of God) can and ought firmly to establish among their peoples the blessed Kingdom of the Son of God and of our Saviour: *hoc est, cum religionis tum reliquae reipublicae universae administrationem, ex Christi servatoris nostri, et regis summi sententia evocare, instaurare, atque confirmare.*'[3] Then he goes on to say that he beseeches and prays '*per regnum et adventum Domini nostri Jesu Christi, et communem omnium nostrorum salutem*', that they will consider what he has put before them, not according to the judgment of men either of today or of an earlier age, '*sed ex aeterno et immutabili Dei verbo*'.[4] Here we have concentrated the most intense eschatological urgency, for these matters apparently mundane, are really of the utmost moment for salvation and the future life. If the Church was to be all that Butzer held and hoped, then it was necessary that the conditions for obedience should be provided, that room should be created for it, an environment in which the *Regnum Christi* would exercise its mighty sway for the good of all. That is what the *Regnum Christi* and the *regnum mundi* have in common, to make their citizens godly and just, so that they acknowledge and worship God aright. The ultimate end of both should be the same, although they differ in *ratio* and *natura*.[5]

The significance of this can be seen from Butzer's insistence that true knowledge of God must be expressed in a godly life,[6] that faith

---

[1] *De Regno Christi, Op. Lat.* XV, pp. 10f, 87f, 241f; *Scripta Anglicana*, pp. 353ff.   [2] *De Regno Christi, Praefatio, Op. Lat.* XV, p. 1.
[3] Op. cit., p. 293.   [4] Op. cit., p. 295.
[5] *De Regno Christi, Op. Lat.* XV, pp. 7f. This involves the idea that the '*Oberkeit ein heilig Goettlich ampt ist*' (*Ein Summarischer vergriff der Christlichen lehre und Religion*, p. 72).
[6] '*In vera theologia tantum quisque rite novit quantum vita exprimit*'; cited from W. Pauck, *The Heritage of the Reformation*, p. 302. Cf. also '*Vera theologia*

operates by love (*ex fide et secundum dilectionem*),¹ and that this godliness and love are the characteristics of the future life already reflected, or which should be reflected, here and now, in the Church on earth. Room (*libertas rerum externorum*)² must be made for faith to take the field as active love, room for doctrine and discipline through which we are being prepared for the life to come with Christ in God. The Kingdom means that the whole of our life is to be embraced in the love of God³ and to be made serve the purpose of that love.⁴ To be sure, Butzer does not think of the general life of people or of the state as identifiable with the *Regnum Christi*,⁵ as he does of the Church,⁶ but the wider life of the people beyond the immediate bounds of the Church is no less under that Kingdom and has a concrete function to perform in daily life and work for the spiritual Kingdom.⁷ It does that by taking on itself 'the yoke of Christ'⁸ and acting '*ex instinctu Spiritus Sancti*'.⁹ God has given precepts for the life of His people, but they are meant for ends that are ultimately eternal and are to be understood as commandments of love and in terms of the law of love.¹⁰ Apart from the deeds of love and mercy which these inculcate 'no true communion of saints can exist',¹¹ for there would then be no Christians, for faith without the deeds of love is dead.¹²

non theoretica et speculativa, sed activa et practica est. Finis sequidem eius agere est, hoc est vitam vivere deiformem'; from *Enarr. in quat. Ev.* (Basel, 1536; cited from Pauck, ibid.). Cf. *Enarr. in Lucam* 2.50: '*Vera theologia scientia est pie et beate vivendi: sine quo multa nosse, et variis de rebus posse differere, etiam daemonum est.*'

[1] *Enarr. in Matt.* 18.7f. Cf. *De Regno Christi, Op. Lat.* XV, p. 25: '*Explicat vim suam fides per charitatem, quae ut benefaciat hominibus oblaedat neminem, semper elaborat.*'
[2] *Enarr. in Matt.* 18.7f; 15.1f. *De Regno Christi, Op. Lat.* XV, p. 52.
[3] *De Regno Christi, Op. Lat.* XV, p. 1.
[4] *Enarr. in Matt.* 13.30   [5] *Enarr. in Matt.* 5.3.
[6] *De Regno Christi, Op. Lat.* XV, p. 57; *Scripta Anglicana*, p. 556, etc.
[7] *Enarr. in Matt.* 24.27; in *Matt.* 5.38; in *Matt.* 22.41. 'Spiritual' usually refers to the priestly or mediatorial mode of the *Regnum Christi*, as distinct from the kingdoms of this world. He also speaks of *Regnum Christi* as '*Regnum cognitionis atque revelationis, Regnum Spiritus*' (*Enarr. in Iohann.* 1.34).
[8] *De Regno Christi, Op. Lat.* XV, pp. 100f.   [9] *Op. cit.*, p. 104.
[10] *Op. cit.*, pp. 25, 94f, 264f; *Scripta Anglicana*, pp. 347f. Cf. *Enarr. in Matt.* 7.12; 8.10; 5.19, etc. Even as *Respublica Christiana* the State is not to impose spiritual matters upon the people by edict but rather by persuasion (*De Regno Christi, Op. Lat.* XV, pp. 101f). No one is therefore to be compelled against his will in matters spiritual, e.g. in going to the Lord's Table (*Scripta Anglicana*, pp. 298f). '*Charitatis enim Christianae proprium est, ut quisque alterum praestantiorem habeat, et fidei libertatem circumscribere vult nemo.*' (*Enarr. Epistolae D. Pauli ad Ephesios*, p. 13.)   [11] *De Regno Christi, Op. Lat.* XV, pp. 143f.
[12] *Ein Summarischer vergriff*, pp. 28f.

The Christian Community

Thus in contrast to Luther's sharp distinction between the *Regnum spirituale* and the *Regnum corporale*, the *Regnum Christi* in Butzer's theology constitutes a third dimension, the *Communio Christiana*, which, through the Word and the Spirit, is visibly and actively realised on earth, and through obedience to the Church's preaching of the Word and daily witness also in the State.[1] The relations of the Church and State are mutual. The Word of God is communicated to the State through the Church, and in obedience to that Word the State creates within the world a sphere of liberty, setting bounds to the kingdom of Satan, so that the life of the Church protected by the State may freely grow in obedience to God's Word and in the exercise of love, and so assume the character of a *Respublica* or *Societas Christiana*.[2] This is the reason why *disciplina* must be added to *doctrina*,[3] to the true preaching of the Word and the right administration of the Sacraments, as a third mark of the true Church, for it is through the godly exercise of discipline (*disciplina vitae communis*)[4] in matters of faith and life that the Church assumes public as well as private form as the Kingdom of Christ promoted on earth. For Butzer the Kingdom of Christ in its relation to this world is not merely a *Hörreich* but also a *Sehreich* (to use Luther's terms), and it comes not simply *audiendo*, as Luther taught, but whenever by the power of the Spirit the Word is effectively translated into love and obedience, into life and action.[5]

Thus the *Regnum Christi* reaches out primarily through the Church, but also through the Commonwealth that is obedient to the Will of God, to the final advent of Christ and the manifestation of the Kingdom of God in glory and power. 'That will be an end of the *Regnum Christi*, when there will be an end of mediation and intercession, when the last enemy, death, will be extinct, when Christ by His mighty Kingdom repairs in His own the *love* in

---

[1] The State is also responsible for encouraging widespread preaching of the Word, and evangelism (*De Regno Christi, Op. Lat.* XV, pp. 110f).
[2] *De Regno Christi, Op. Lat.* XV, pp. 6-20.
[3] See, for example, *De Regno Christi, Op. Lat.* XV, pp. 42f, 45, 70ff, 111f, etc.; *Scripta Anglicana*, pp. 324f, etc.; *Von der waren Seelsorge*, pp. 13f: 'von dienst der Lere und geistlicher zucht'.
[4] *De Regno Christi, Op. Lat.* XV, pp. 70f.
[5] See above pp. 22ff.

which is lodged the consummation of all justice.'¹ 'So long as the Kingdom of Christ is in the world it battles against sin and flourishes, but when that battle is over, it is properly the Kingdom of God.'²

This means that at last the eschatological reserve between the *Regnum Dei* and the *Regnum Christi* will disappear, and God will be all in all.³ That does not mean, however, that all ends up in sheer monism, for the Kingdom of Heaven remains,⁴ the Kingdom in which men are given to participate in a heavenly Commonwealth and to be partakers of the divine nature. The centre of that will be the glorified Son of God. 'Now all things are ruled and established through the *Man* Christ who is exalted above all, but only because *this Man* has been assumed by the Word and He, Christ, is at once God and Man.'⁵ It is the hypostatic union in the person of Christ which eternally secures the relation of man to God and is the guarantee that at last the two realms, the Kingdom of God and creation, will be brought together in perfect unity and love. When that happens there will be a new heaven and a new earth, and the whole form of our life will change with the humble form of the *Regnum Christi*. All *principatus*, for example, whether of men or of spirits, will be abolished, and all *potestas* and *virtus* will be subjected to God.⁶ In a remark concerning the prophecy in Isaiah 65.17 about the new heavens and the new earth, Butzer claims that this is to be understood '*magis de Ecclesiae innovatione et foelicitate spiritali, quam de futuro mundi statu, immutationeque corporali*'.⁷ Is this just a statement of comparison, or does it imply that in the ultimate resort the physical creation will disappear or be transfigured in some 'spiritual', that is to say, empyrean, heaven? The place sometimes given by Butzer to the *covenant*⁸ may indicate that this is not the case, and that creation in the most realistic sense

---

¹ *Enarr. in Matt.* 13.30. Sometimes Butzer uses *humanitas* as a synonym for *charitas* (*De Regno Christi, Op. Lat.* XV, p. 25). *Humanitas* was more frequently used by Calvin. ² *Enarr. in Iohann.* 17.10.
³ *Enarr. in Iohann.* 17-10f; *De Regno Christi, Op. Lat.* XV, pp. 52f.
⁴ Cf. *Enarr. in Matt.* 4.23: '*Sola enim Christianorum Respublica Regnum et Dei et caeleste vocari meretur. Et Evangelium Christi, vere Evangelium Regni, nimirum praeconium Regis caelestis, hoc est aeternum iustificantis et salvantis omnes in se credentes.*' ⁵ *Enarr. in Iohann.* 17.10.
⁶ *De Regno Christi, Op. Lat.* XV, p. 53. ⁷ *Enarr. in Matt.* 5.18.
⁸ *De Regno Christi, Op. Lat.* XV, pp. 10, 57f, 67, 105, 113, etc.; *Enarr. in Matt.* 23.1. The Covenant is realised through holy Baptism and it is on this ground that the *regnum mundi* and *Regnum Christi* are seen to involve each other. Compare pp. 14f and 53f of the *De Regno Christi, Op. Lat.* XV.

THE ESCHATOLOGY OF LOVE: MARTIN BUTZER

will be restored in the Kingdom of God. That was the emphasis in Butzer's first work, *Das ym selb niemant leben soll sonderen anderer*, and there is no sufficient reason to indicate that he departed from it. The whole creation belongs to the Kingdom of God and will be renewed in the eternal purpose of His divine love.

Butzer's position may best be judged with reference to that of Calvin, to which we are now about to turn. Like Butzer, Calvin had a bi-polar eschatology, but he laid greater stress upon both poles of the whole eschatological relation, eternal predestination and final consummation. He also laid greater stress than Butzer upon the abiding relation here and now to the new creation in Christ, because Christology occupied a firmer and more central place. But their positions are not essentially different. Butzer tended to stress more than Calvin the concept of the Church as *Communio renatorum* on the one hand,[1] and on the other, the concept of the *Regnum Christi* as also *regnum externum* in the State. For Butzer, however, it is a profoundly Pauline and moving understanding of *love* as the eschatological reality that abides, when faith and hope have passed away,[2] that helps him hold the two sides of his thought together, whereas for Calvin it was a more powerful Christology, and a more precise doctrine of the Church. If Luther's eschatology can be described as the eschatology of faith, and Calvin's as the eschatology of hope, Butzer's is certainly to be described as the eschatology of love.

---

[1] This is apparent particularly in the *De vi et usu s. ministerii explicatio*. The theme of the new birth is found also throughout the *De Regno Christi*. See, for example, p. 17: 'Nam regignit nos Rex noster verbo et spiritu suo, ut semen, eius simus: et regignit in vitam aeternam.'

[2] *Enarr. in Matt.* 7.12.

IV

THE ESCHATOLOGY OF HOPE: JOHN CALVIN

WHEN Calvin first came to Strasbourg he had already published the first edition of the *Institute of the Christian Religion* (1536), in which the main substance of his theological position was set forth so maturely that he never had occasion to retract anything, but he had also published the *Psychopannychia* (1534 and 1536), a significant work on eschatology which was to see its third edition in Strasbourg (1542). This was Calvin's first theological work and from its appearance in 1534 to his death his exposition of Biblical eschatology characterised all his preaching and writing, while the prayers with which he regularly concluded his sermons and lectures indicate how profoundly eschatology had penetrated into the very heart of his faith. In his great commentary on the Epistle to the Hebrews published in 1549, which gives us Calvin's full discussion of eschatology in connexion with the death, resurrection and heavenly session of Christ, and which more than any other of his works represents his characteristic position, Calvin wrote of the last things: 'These are of the highest mysteries of celestial wisdom, nay the very end (*scopum*) of all our religion, to which we ought to direct our attention throughout the whole of life.'[1]

Early Views

The *Psychopannychia* was directed primarily against the Anabaptist idea of the sleep of the soul between death and final judgment, and was designed to expound the Biblical teaching that the souls of believers after death are in a state of alertness with and in Christ, actively praising Him and waiting for the resurrection of the body. That marked out even at this early stage the difference between the eschatology of Calvin and that of Luther,

[1] *Comm. on Heb.* 6.1. C.R. 83, p. 68.

who also held the notion of soul-sleep, an ingredient in his theology which helped to explain the deep element of quietism in Luther's whole position. In contrast Calvin's eschatology was activist, stressing the mighty acts of God in Christ and *therefore* the work of the Church in obedience and joy, in thankful assurance of victory waiting for the final act of redemption. In the same work Calvin expounded at length the eschatological nature of εἰρήνη as grounded upon the accomplished work of Christ in death and resurrection and ascension, and as an anticipation of the heavenly rest to come. Peace means not only the assurance of victory, not simply consolation in *tentatio*, but the positive experience of the Church which already lives on the side of the resurrection, for through faith the Church is made to sit in heavenly places with the triumphant Christ in His Kingdom, even though it is still engaged in the tribulations of the Cross on earth. It is because of this participation in the Kingdom of Christ, in the heavenly peace, that the Church can engage in its arduous task of extending that Kingdom on earth. And so throughout all his works Calvin made it a point of prime importance to teach the combination of the *meditatio vitae futurae* with the unceasing activity of the Church on earth in the growth and extension of the Kingdom of Christ.

Several other features of the *Psychopannychia* are worth noting for they indicate even at this early stage those elements which came to be so prominent in his mature exposition of eschatology.

(*a*) Like the early Fathers[1] Calvin can use the pattern of events in the experience of Israel from the Exodus and the crossing of the Red Sea to the crossing of the Jordan and entry into the Promised Land as supplying the essential schema for the eschatological life of the Christian Church. Thus in reference to 1 Cor. 10.1 he writes: 'We may be permitted to say that in Baptism our Pharaoh is drowned, our old man is crucified, and our members are mortified, we are buried with Christ, and emigrate from the captivity of the devil and the dominion of death, but we only migrate into the desert, a land arid and poor, unless the Lord rains manna from heaven and causes water to gush forth from the rock. For our

---

[1] In this work Calvin cites Melito of Sardis, Irenaeus, Tertullian, Augustine, Chrysostom, Origen, Cyprian, Jerome, Cyril of Alexandria, Ambrose, Gregory the Great, Eusebius of Caesarea, Hilary and Bernard.

soul, like that land without water, is in want of all things till He by the grace of His Spirit rains upon it. Afterwards we pass into the land of promise under the guidance of Joshua the son of Nun, into a land flowing with milk and honey; that is, the grace of God frees us from the body of death, by our Lord Jesus Christ, not without sweat and blood, since the flesh is then most repugnant and exerts its utmost force in warring against the Spirit. After we take up our residence in the land we feed in abundance. White robes and rest are given to us. But Jerusalem, the capital and seat of the kingdom, has not yet been erected; nor yet does Solomon, the Prince of Peace, hold the sceptre and rule over all. The souls of the saints therefore, which have escaped the hands of the enemy, are after death in peace. They are amply supplied with all things, for it is said of them, "they shall go from abundance to abundance". But when the heavenly Jerusalem shall have arisen up in its glory, and Christ, the true Solomon, the Prince of Peace, shall be seated sublime upon His tribunal, the true Israelites shall reign with their king.'[1]

(*b*) It will be noted that in this passage Calvin speaks of liberation from the body of death. Elsewhere in the same work Calvin uses similar language. Thus in a comment upon 2 Cor. 5.1f he says: 'We desire indeed to depart from this prison of the body (*ex hoc corporis ergastulo*), but not to wander uncertain without a home: there is a better home which the Lord has prepared for us; clothed with it, we shall not be found naked. Christ is our clothing.'[2] Or again: 'The body which decays weighs down the soul, and confining it within an earthly habitation, greatly limits its perceptions. If the body is the prison of the soul (*si corpus animae est carcer*), what is the state of the soul when set free from this prison, when loosed from these fetters?'[3] It is sometimes held that here we have the essentially Greek idea of $\sigma\hat{\omega}\mu\alpha$, $\sigma\hat{\eta}\mu\alpha$, and that this is evidence of the fact that Calvin has not shaken off the influence of Stoic philosophy, but that cannot be substantiated. Calvin is thinking of the Pauline expressions 'the body of sin', 'the body of death', 'the body of the flesh' or 'the body of the flesh of sin', and of such verses as Rom. 8.10: 'If the Spirit of Christ dwell in us, the body is dead because of sin, but the Spirit is life because of righteousness.'[4] So long as we still wait for the redemption of the

[1] C.R. 34, p. 214. [2] C.R. 34, p. 195. [3] Ibid. [4] C.R. 34, pp. 202ff.

body the eyes of our mind are dull because they are buried in the flesh of sin,[1] but it will be otherwise when that is 'fulfilled in the body which has now been begun in the soul'.[2] The discussion in the *Psychopannychia* makes it abundantly clear that deliverance from the prison of the body or the flesh means the resurrection of the body to a *better nature*,[3] i.e. to a new life in which the body with the whole man will be emancipated from the thraldom of evil which now reigns in the flesh and has changed the nature of man. That is the very antithesis of Stoic thought. 'When Christ shall have received us into His own glory, not only will the animal body be quickened by the soul but made spiritual in a manner which our mind can neither comprehend nor our tongue express (see Tertullian, and Augustine, Epist. 3, *ad Fortunat.*). You see, then, that in the resurrection we shall not be a different thing, but different nevertheless (pardon the expression). These things have been said of the body, to which the soul ministers life under the elements of this world; but when the fashion of this world shall have passed away, participation in the glory of God will exalt it above nature.'[4] 'Above nature' is to be interpreted in the sense of a *better nature which transcends that of Adam*. 'Everything that has fallen in Adam is renewed in Christ, but inasmuch as the power of grace was stronger than that of sin, so much has Christ been more powerful in restoring than Adam in destroying. The Apostle distinctly declares that the gift is not as the sin but is much more exuberant: *"non quidem in plures homines, sed abundatius, in quibus exuberavit"*.'[5]

(c) The real clue to Calvin's eschatology is to be found in the expression, 'Christ is our clothing'. That is to say, his eschatology, and all his language about the prison of the body and the resurrection of the body, are to be interpreted in terms of Christology.

---

[1] C.R. 34, p. 214.   [2] C.R. 34, p. 205.
[3] C.R. 34, p. 206: *'qui per Christum* in meliorem naturam *recreati sunt'*. For a full statement see Calvin's *Comm. on I. Cor.* 15.49f, where he speaks of our 'flesh' as 'participant in the glory of God', and 15.53, where he says: 'Mark how we shall live in the Kingdom of God both in body and in soul, while at the same time "flesh and blood cannot inherit the Kingdom of God"—for they shall previously be delivered from corruption. Our nature, then, as being now corruptible and mortal, is not admissible into the Kingdom of God, but when it shall have put off corruption, it will then make its way into it. This passage distinctly proves that we shall rise again in that same flesh that we now carry about with us, as the Apostle assigns a new quality to it which will serve as a garment' (C.R. 77, pp. 560f, 562f).   [4] C.R. 34, p. 202.   [5] C.R. 34, pp. 205f.

That is in fact the central argument of the *Psychopannychia*[1]: the death and resurrection of the believer are to be understood on the analogy of, or in conformity to, the death and resurrection of Christ, for the believer is given to participate in His death and resurrection. Thus the heart of Calvin's eschatology is to be found in his doctrine of the new humanity in Jesus Christ. It is *as Man* that Jesus Christ is given to have life in Himself. 'Seeing that Jesus Christ is Son of God and Man, that which He is by nature as God He is also by grace as Man, that thus we may all receive of His fulness, and grace for grace.... The Man Christ has received from the Father gifts for men, so that we may be able to find life in our nature.... Christ has life in Himself, i.e. fulness of life, by which He both lives Himself and quickens others; yet He has it not of Himself, as He elsewhere declares that He lives by the Father. And though as God He had life in Himself, yet when He assumed human nature, He received from the Father the gift of having life in Himself in that nature also.'[2] It is through union with Christ in His death and resurrection that the life residing in His human nature is given to us, so that we are given new humanity in Him, with new life residing in our human nature.[3]

Calvin's argument here derives from such pregnant texts as the following, cited in this very context: 'I live yet not I but Christ in me' (Gal. 2.20); 'Your life is hid with Christ in God' (Col. 3.3); 'Because I live, ye shall live also' (John 14.19). In his later language Christ is not only the agent but the matter and the substance of our new life and our justification, for in Him, through union with Him, we are given a new human righteousness which is the righteous humanity of the risen Jesus. This clothing with Christ, this concrete righteousness of the new Man who dwells in our heart by faith, is hidden and veiled from sight, or rather it still awaits the full manifestation of its glory, and therefore can be expressed only in terms of eschatology.

(*d*) Because the new life in Christ is a new human life it involves time-relations. Union with Christ in His human nature means *increase* and *growth*, the growing up into the perfect manhood of

---

[1] This new turn in the argument begins with the words: '*Nunc paulisper, o somniatores, redeatis ad cor et vobiscum cogitetis, quemadmodum Christus mortuus est*' (C.R. 34, p. 191).   [2] Ibid.   [3] C.R. 34, p. 191.

Christ of which St Paul speaks in Ephesians 4. That Calvin speaks of as '*profectus*',[1] by which he means eschatological growth in Christ. 'For our blessedness is always *in cursu usque ad diem illum qui omnem cursum claudet et terminabit: ita electorum gloriam et ultimae spei finem ad eum ipsum diem spectare ut impleatur.*'[2] Because it is growth or advance of an eschatological character, Calvin can lay the emphasis so much on the divine action as to speak of God as '*velut nascentem in electis suis et de die in diem crescentem*'.[3]

Calvin does not, however, think primarily in terms of individuals but in terms of the Church as the Body of Christ growing up into Him, and therefore in terms of His reign or Kingdom as it is manifested in the growth and extension of the Church. It is generally characteristic of Calvin that when he thinks of the Kingdom in terms of God's eternal majesty and reign he speaks of it as the *Regnum Dei*, but when he thinks of it in terms of the Incarnation and the death and resurrection of Christ, and of His reigning over the world until the manifestation of the new heaven and the new earth, he speaks of it as the *Regnum Christi*. 'God in Himself cannot reign otherwise than He reigned from the beginning. Of His majesty there cannot be increase or diminution. But it is called His Kingdom because it will be manifested to all. When we pray that His Kingdom may come, do we imagine that previously it has no existence? ... He reigns even now when we pray that His Kingdom may come. He reigns, indeed, while He performs miracles in His servants and gives the law to Satan. But His Kingdom will properly come when it will be completed. And it will be completed when He will plainly manifest the glory of His majesty to His elect for salvation and to the reprobate for confusion. What else is to be said or believed of the elect whose kingdom and glory it is to be in the glorious Kingdom of God and as it were reign with God and glory in Him—in short to be partakers of the divine glory? This Kingdom, though it is said not yet to have come, may yet be in some measure beheld. For those who in a manner have the Kingdom of God within them and reign with God begin to be in the Kingdom of God—the gates of hell cannot prevail against them. They are justified in God, it being said of them, "In the Lord will all the seed of Israel be justified and

---

[1] C.R. 34, pp. 197, 212, etc.   [2] C.R. 34, pp. 210f.   [3] C.R. 34, p. 197.

praised" (Is. 45.25). That Kingdom wholly consists in the building up of the Church (*aedificatio ecclesiae*), or the progress of believers (*profectus fidelium*).'[1]

On the one hand, then, Calvin can speak of the Church in terms of *aedificatio, profectus* and *incrementa*, but on the other hand he insists that this is to be understood in terms of the ultimate manifestation of the divine *gloria*, so that the progress of the Church is to be spoken of in terms of eschatological fulfilment, in terms of hiddenness and final unveiling. He quotes the Apostle, therefore, 'Ye are dead and your life is hid with Christ in God. When Christ your life shall appear, then shall ye also appear with him in glory' (Col. 3.4), and adds: 'He indeed attributes to us a hidden life with Christ our Head beside God. He delays the glory to the day of the glory of Christ who as the Head of the Church will bring His members with Him (*gloriam differt in diem gloriae Christi, qui ut caput est ecclesiae trahet secum sua membra*). The very same thing is expressed by John, though in different terms,—"Beloved, now are we the sons of God; but it doth not yet appear what we shall be, but we know that when he shall appear we shall be like him, for we shall see him as he is and be like him" (1 John 3.2). He says not that meanwhile, for some length of time, we shall be nothing; but, seeing we are the sons of God, who wait for the inheritance of the Father, He *sustains and suspends our expectation* till that day on which the glory of God will be manifest in all and we shall be glorified in Him (*sustinet et suspendit expectationem nostram in diem illum quo in omnibus gloria Dei manifestabitur et nos in eo gloriabimur.*'[2] That '*sustinet et suspendit expectationem nostram in diem illum*' continued to be one of Calvin's most characteristic ways of expressing the eschatological life and hope of the Church in Christ.

(*e*) One further feature of the *Psychopannychia* should be noted, its stress upon the sheer *joy* of the Christian life. 'The Lord creates a people for Himself who sing and celebrate the praise of His goodness when He delivers and restores the hopes of those who were afflicted, bruised and in despair.'[3] It was in Strasbourg that Calvin began to introduce congregational singing into the liturgy and in 1543, the year following the publication of this edition of

---

[1] C.R., p. 212.   [2] C.R. 34, p. 213.
[3] C.R. 34, p. 227.

THE ESCHATOLOGY OF HOPE: JOHN CALVIN   97

the *Psychopannychia*, he prepared *La Forme des Prieres et Chantz Ecclesiastiques*[1] for the Church in Geneva. It is difficult for us to appreciate today what a startling change in the worship of the Church the introduction of this music meant—it was that which above all enshrined the eucharistic eschatology that inspired the worship of the Reformed Churches as they lifted up their hearts to God and mingled their voices with those of the angels.[2] A few years later, in the *Commentary on the Epistle to the Hebrews*, Calvin was to say: 'Christ leads our songs and is the chief composer of our hymns.'[3]

The Word and the Spirit

During this early period Calvin published another important little work which must be placed side by side with the *Psychopannychia*, the *Responsio ad Sadoleti Epistolam* of 1539. These two publications make it clear that Calvin felt constrained to champion the Reformed position by doing battle on two fronts: against the Anabaptists on the one hand, and against the Papacy on the other. The issues involved were the form and continuity of the Church and the relation between the Church and the Kingdom of God. Against the Anabaptists he fought for a doctrine of the continuity of the Church and defended infant Baptism, but against the Roman Church he fought against a false notion of the continuity of the Church and opposed the docetic violence to history enshrined in the doctrine of transubstantiation in the Mass. Against both Calvin insisted that the true Christian position maintains *the unity of the Word and the Spirit*. And so he wrote to Cardinal Sadoleto: 'We are assailed by two sects which seem to differ most widely from each other. For what similitude is there in appearance between the Pope and the Anabaptists? And yet that you may see that Satan never transforms himself so cunningly, as not in some measure to betray himself, the principal weapon with which they both assail us is the same. For when they boast extravagantly of the Spirit, the tendency certainly is to sink and bury the Word of God that they make room for their own falsehoods.... It is no less unreasonable to boast of the Spirit without the Word, that it

---

[1] See *Opera Selecta*, vol. II, pp. iiff.
[2] This understanding of Church music Calvin owes mainly to Chrysostom and Augustine (O.S. II, p. 15ff). [3] *Comm. on Heb.* 2.12, C.R. 83, p. 29.

would be absurd to bring forward the Word itself without the Spirit.'[1]

The unity and inseparability of Word and Spirit is one of the characteristic doctrines of Calvin, for it was in terms of it that he came to work out so fully, in the fourth book of the *Institutes* particularly, the relation between the historical Church as the Body of Christ and the Kingdom of Christ. Through the Word and the Spirit the Church on earth is given continuous participation in the *Regnum Christi*, and is shaped and reformed in conformity to the Christological pattern of the Kingdom. In a comment upon 'Thy Kingdom come' Calvin writes: 'This is done partly by the preaching of the Word and partly by the secret power of the Spirit. It is His will to govern men by His Word, but as the small Voice, if the inward power of the Spirit be not added, does not pierce to the hearts of men, *both must be joined together in order that the Kingdom of God may be established.*'[2] Against the Anabaptists this meant the emphasis upon the progress and growth of the Church in history, its growth through Word and Spirit in union with Christ, and therefore its abhorrence of all schism, but against the Church of Rome it meant not the creation of a new Church but the reform of the Church according to the Head of the Church, whose Body the Church is, and therefore the renewal through Word and Spirit of 'the ancient form of the Church'[3] against the schismatic innovations which had disrupted the continuity of the Catholic Church and defaced its true form. Because the Church grows in history Calvin appeals not simply to the Church as it is seen in the New Testament, but to the Church of the Early Catholic Fathers and the ancient canons.[4] 'I will not press you so closely as to call you back to that form which the Apostles instituted (though in it we have the only model of a true Church, and whosoever deviates from it in the smallest degree is in error) but to indulge you so far, place before your eyes, I pray, that ancient form of the Church such as their writings prove it to have been in the age of Chrysostom and Basil among the

---

[1] O.S. I, p. 465.
[2] *Comm. on Luke* 11.10, C.R. 73, p. 197; cf. *Comm. on Acts* 16.14, C.R. 76, pp. 377f.   [3] O.S. I, p. 466.
[4] O.S. I, p. 479: 'We have not the least objection,' Calvin says to Sadoleto, 'that the discipline which was sanctioned by the ancient canons should be in force at the present day and be carefully and faithfully preserved.'

Greeks, and of Cyprian, Ambrose, and Augustine among the Latins; after so doing contemplate the ruins of that Church as now surviving among yourselves.'[1] Or, as Calvin says later in the same work: 'In attacking, breaking down and destroying your kingdom, we are armed not only with the energy of the divine Word, but with the aid of the holy Fathers also.... The ancient Church is clearly on our side and opposes you not less than we do ourselves.'[2] However, while Calvin lays the greatest possible stress upon the historical continuity of the Church,[3] it is historical continuity under the eschatological impact of the Word of God as it is preached in the Gospel. 'When you describe the Church as that which in all parts, as well as at the present time, in every region of the earth, being united and consenting in Christ, has been always and everywhere directed by the one Spirit of Christ, what comes of the Word of the Lord, that clearest of all marks, which the Lord Himself in designating the Church so often recommends to us? For seeing how dangerous it would be to boast of the Spirit without the Word, He declared that the Church is indeed governed by the Holy Spirit but in order that the government might not be vague and unstable, He bound it to the Word.'[4] That is indeed 'why the preaching of the Gospel is so often called the Kingdom of God, because it is the sceptre by which the heavenly King rules His people. Nor will you find this in the Apostolic writings only but whenever the Prophets foretell the renewal of the Church or its extension over the whole globe, they always assign the first place to the Word.'[5]

It was while Calvin was engaged in this double debate, during his ministry at Strasbourg, that he began a series of new editions of the *Institutio* in which the positions adopted in the *Psychopannychia* and the *Responsio ad Sadoleti Epistolam* are elaborated in full, and in which all the doctrines of the faith are closely integrated

---

[1] O.S. I, p. 466. [2] O.S. I, pp. 474f.
[3] Calvin felt this so keenly that he wished wherever possible to preserve the historical succession of the ministry. Cf. his letter to the King of Poland: 'I confess it were desirable that an uninterrupted succession lent us its sanction, that the function itself were transmitted as it were from hand to hand. (*Hic, fateor, optandum esset, ut valeret continua successio, ut functio ipsa quasi per manus traderetur.*) But because by the tyranny of the Pope, the continuous line of ordination has been broken a new expedient is requisite for the restoration of the Church' (*Quia autem papae tyrannide abrupta fuit vera ordinationis series, novo subsidio nunc opus est ad ecclesiae instaurationem*). C.R. 43, p. 335.
[4] O.S. I, pp. 464f. [5] Ibid.

with eschatology. It was during this period that Calvin spent the happiest and most peaceful years of his life, with leisure to continue his patristic studies and in discussion with Butzer to engage in the Biblical work which produced his commentaries. From Butzer Calvin learned much about election, the Kingdom of Christ, the ministry of the Church, and the place and function of discipline, while his controversies already mentioned and his discussions with Lutherans helped him to clarify his understanding of the Reformation as the movement restoring the face of the Catholic Church, which he came also to speak of as the restoration of the Kingdom of Christ. All this had its impact upon his rewriting of the *Institutes*, which were now given shape according to the articles of the Apostles' Creed. Final shape came only after Calvin had more or less completed his Biblical commentaries, two of the most significant for his eschatology being the **Commentary on the Harmony of the Gospels**, in which, as he says in the foreword, he had made Butzer especially his model, and the **Commentary on the Epistle to the Hebrews**, already mentioned, in which Calvin's divergence from Luther appears at its widest, for in spite of his early superb lectures on the Epistle Luther came to dislike Hebrews as a rather Jewish book.

Union with Christ

It is significant that eschatology received treatment mainly in connexion with the third member of the Creed in book 3, on the doctrine of the Holy Spirit, where Calvin expounded his central idea of *union with Christ*, while in book 4 eschatology is woven into the doctrines of the Church and the ministry, the Sacraments, and the relation between Church and State. It is worth while studying carefully here the actual procedure of Calvin's exposition. He begins in book 3 with the doctrine of the Holy Spirit and faith as union with Christ through the operation of the Spirit. But this union with Christ involves us in His death and resurrection, for we cannot become one with Him without participating in His death and resurrection, that is, without mortification and regeneration. It is only after a long discussion of regeneration as an actualisation in the believer of the risen life of Christ, and as an anticipation in conditions of time of the final resurrection, that Calvin feels he can go on to discuss justification, for then he is in a position to show that justification entails all this at its heart and as its substance. Justification is thus expounded only in strictly Christological terms and on the analogy of Christ's death and resurrection. That is followed up at the end of the third book by two corollary doctrines, election and the last resurrection, which are doctrines emphasising the eternal foundation of our union with Christ and its future blessedness when its full reality will be revealed. Then in book 4 Calvin goes on to expound the same teaching in terms of Baptism and Eucharist, for justification and baptismal incorporation into Christ are essentially counterparts, and sanctification and Holy Communion as our continuing and deepening union with Christ are essentially counterparts. As he who is sacramentally incorporated into the Body of Christ is in Holy Communion continually nourished and maintained in the Body of Christ, so sanctification is the continual unfolding and maintaining of our justification. Sanctification is not a response of man that must be added to justification, but the continual renewing and re-enacting in the believer of a justification that is made once and for all. The experience of sanctification is such an exercise in Word and Sacrament that the believer is ever being nourished with the new humanity of Christ, and being clothed with His divine-human righteousness, which is the fundamental reality of his Christian being.

Apart from this setting Calvin's mature teaching about eschatology cannot be understood, but in this setting it is very clear that eschatology is the analogical transposition of Christology to the whole understanding of the Church. In His birth, life, death, resurrection and ascension Christ is our only way to understanding the celestial mystery of the last things. He is the Alpha and the Omega, the Elect One and the Final Goal of the Kingdom, but through union with Christ the Church becomes the Body of which He is the Head, so that whatever happens to the Head happens also to the members. Or, to put it otherwise, eschatology is the doctrine of the Spirit and all that *union with Christ through the Spirit* involves.

Faith itself is eschatological because it is Christologically determined, for 'Christ is both the aim and the object of faith'.[1]

---

[1] *Comm. on Eph.* 1.15: '*Fidem dicit in Christo, quia proprius fidei scopus, et obiectum (ut vulgo dicunt) ipse est*' (C.R. 79, p. 155).

Commenting upon the words of Paul and Silas, 'Believe on the Lord Jesus' (Acts 16.31), Calvin writes: 'This is but a short and apparently jejune but in fact a complete definition of salvation, that we are to have faith in Christ. For Christ alone has all the parts of blessedness and eternal life included in Him, which He offers us by the Gospel. And by faith we receive them. Here let us note that Christ is the unique goal (*unicum scopum*) of faith, and therefore men's minds do nothing but wander when they turn away from Him.'[1] Faith has its eyes which penetrate into the invisible Kingdom of God and keep Christ before them,[2] but faith involves more than the turning of our eyes on Christ; it involves union with Christ and incorporation into Him. 'Faith does not look at Christ as though He were far off, but it embraces Him, that He may become ours and dwell in us. It causes us to be incorporated into His Body, to have life in common with Him and to become one with Him.'[3] 'The nature of faith is to be estimated from Christ, for that which God offers to us in Christ we receive only by faith. *Hence whatever Christ is to us is transferred to faith which makes us capable of seeing both Christ and all His blessings.* There would be no truth in the words of John that faith is the victory by which we overcome the world (1 John 5.4) did it not ingraft us into Christ (John 16.33) who is the only conqueror of the world.'[4] Such union with Christ immediately gives those who believe actual participation in His death and resurrection. He did not die and rise again 'for Himself alone', but for 'the whole human race', so that His resurrection is the 'substance and pledge' (*hypostasis et pignus*) of ours.[5] But after His resurrection Christ ascended and is enthroned at the right hand of the Father in the heavenly places. Nor did that happen to Christ for Himself alone but for us also. We are 'sharers of His ascension'.[6] Thus because faith involves union with Christ *faith is made to participate in the motion of*

---

[1] *Comm. on Acts* 16.31, C.R. 76, pp. 388f.

[2] *Comm. on I Peter* 1.8. C.R. 83, p. 214: '*Habet quidem et fides oculos suos, sed qui in regnum Dei invisibile penetrant ... sed Christum pro scopo habet.*'

[3] *Comm. on John* 6.35, C.R. 75, p. 145; cf. *Instit.* 3.2.35; *Comm. on Matt.* 12.48, C.R. 73, p. 350; on *I John* 3.5, C.R. 83, p. 334. See *Comm. on Rom.* 11.19, where Calvin speaks of a threefold ingrafting into Christ (C.R. 76, p. 222).

[4] *Antidote to the Sixth Session of the Council of Trent*, C.R. 35, p. 451.

[5] *Comm. on I Cor.* 15.21, C.R. 76, p. 546. '*Resurrexit ergo Christus ut nos haberet socios futurae vitae*' (*Instit.* 3.25.3).

[6] *Serm. on Acts* 1.9-11, C.R. 76, p. 620.

Christ's resurrection and ascension.[1] 'The only way in which we are conjoined to Christ is by raising our minds above the world. Accordingly, the bond of our union is faith, which raises us upwards, and casts its anchor in heaven, so that instead of subjecting Christ to the inventions of our reason, we seek Him above in His glory.'[2]

This is a point of supreme importance in all Calvin's theology. 'By His ascension into heaven the Lord has opened up access to the heavenly Kingdom which Adam has shut. For having entered it in our flesh, as it were in our name, it follows that we are in a manner now seated in the heavenly places, not entertaining a mere hope of heaven, but possessing it in our Head.'[3] But Christ is yet to come again, so that faith is made not only to rise above this world to find its substance in the heavenlies, but is stretched out beyond the ages into the world to come in eager anticipation of the advent of Christ.[4] 'Faith cannot stand otherwise than by looking to the coming of Christ.'[5] The reason for that is that faith involves union with the advent Christ and so merges with *hope*. We have already discussed faith, so that it will be sufficient here to note the essential relation between faith and hope in Calvin's thought. 'Wherever living faith exists it must have hope of eternal life as its inseparable comparison or rather must of itself beget and manifest hope.'[6] The reason for that is that 'faith by its very nature has to stretch out beyond itself, beyond the whole course of this life, to a future immortality'.[7] That is clearly stated in a comment on Titus 3.5: 'He speaks of faith and teaches us that we have *already* obtained salvation. Although, involved in sin, we

---

[1] Cf. *Comm. on Heb.* 6.1: 'So he would have our faith so founded as afterwards to ascend upwards until by daily progress it be at length completed' (C.R. 83, p. 76). See *Instit.* 2.16.14f; *Comm. on Matt.* 27.27, C.R. 73, p. 761; on Luke 24.31, C.R. 73, p. 809.

[2] '*Optima ineundae concordiae ratio*', O.S. II, p. 295: '*Non aliter Christo coniungimur, quam si mentes nostrae mundum transscendant. Nostrae itaque cum Christo coniunctionis vinculum est fides, quae sursum nos tollit, et anchoram suam iacit in caelo, ut in sua gloria potius quaeratur a nobis Christus, quam ut rationis nostrae figmentis subiaceat.*'

[3] *Instit.* 2.16.16; 3.25.1-4; cf. *Comm. on Heb.* 6.19, C.R. 83, pp. 80f.

[4] 'There remains no other support of our faith and patience but this, that we keep out of view the conditions of the present life, and apply our minds and senses to the last day and pass through the obstructions of this world until the fruit of our faith at length appear' (*Comm. on John* 6.39, C.R. 75, p. 147).

[5] *Comm. on I John* 3.2: '*Neque enim aliter stare fides nostra potest, quam dum in Christi adventum respicit*' (C.R. 83, p. 330).

[6] *Instit.* 3.2.42; 3.18.8.   [7] *Instit.* 3.2.40.

carry about a body of death, yet we are certain of our salvation, provided that we are ingrafted into Christ by faith, according to that word, "He who believes in the Son of God has passed from death to life" (John 5.24). Yet shortly afterwards by introducing the word *faith*, he shows that we have not yet actually attained what Christ procured for us by His death. Hence it follows that, on the part of God, our salvation is completed, while the enjoyment of it is delayed till the end of our warfare. And that is what the same Apostle teaches on another passage, that we are saved by hope (Rom. 8.24).'[1] Thus faith is such incorporation into Christ and such knowledge of Him that from our point of view on earth we are still in eschatological arrears in relation to the full reality of the divine fulfilment.[2] 'As we are ingrafted by faith into the body of Christ, we are adopted by God as His children, and of this adoption the Spirit is the *witness, seal, earnest* and *pledge*, so that with this assurance we may freely cry *Abba Father* (Rom. 8.15; Gal. 4.6). Now we know that we are the children of God, but it does not yet appear that we shall be, till, transformed into His glory, we shall see Him as He is (1 John 3.2); we are not yet actually reckoned to be His children. And though we are renewed by the Spirit of God, yet as our life is still hidden (Col. 3.3) the manifestation of it will truly and perfectly distinguish us from strangers. In this sense our adoption is said by Paul to be delayed till the last day (Rom. 8.21).'[3] This relation between faith and the ascension and advent of Christ is so important that Calvin devoted a whole chapter of the *Institutes* to it, entitled the 'Meditation of the Future Life'[4] as part of the life and exercise of daily faith.[5] 'Faith is a kind of transition from eternal predestination to future glory.'[6]

Election

How does this bearing of eschatology upon faith relate to

---

[1] *Comm. on Tit.* 3.5, C.R. 80, p. 430.
[2] *Comm. on I Cor.* 13.12: 'Faith and hope belong to a state of imperfection: love will abide on into a state of perfection', C.R. 77, p. 514. Ibid. cf. *Instit.* 3.18.8, O.S. IV, p. 279.
[3] *Comm. on Matt.* 22.30, C.R. 73, p. 606; for another typical passage see *Comm. on Titus* 3.5, C.R. 80, p. 430.
[4] *Instit.* 3.10.
[5] It is in this way also that Calvin speaks of prayer (*Instit.* 3.20).
[6] *Instit.* 3.13.4; cf. 3.11.11.

Calvin's doctrine of predestination?[1] That question is very rarely discussed either by those who support Calvin's doctrine of predestination or by those who combat it, but there can be no doubt that for Calvin election and eschatology are twin doctrines (*predestination* and *post-destination*) which must not be separated. 'If God has elected us to this end that we may believe, take away faith and election will be imperfect'[2]—as indeed the very order of exposition in the 1559 *Institutes* demands, for there the Last Resurrection is expounded immediately after the section on Election. Jesus Christ is not only the '*speculum resurrectionis*', but the '*speculum predestinationis*'.[3]

A study of Calvin's *Commentary on the Harmony of the Gospels* seems to indicate that Calvin took over the bi-polar eschatology of Martin Butzer, in which he spoke of the Kingdom in terms of eternal election and yet of the Kingdom coming as the Will of God on earth. Commenting on the words of the Lord's Prayer: 'Thy Kingdom come, thy will be done on earth as it is in heaven', Calvin discussed the two ways in which God reigns, and added: 'Although the will of God, viewed in itself is one and simple, it is presented to us under a twofold aspect.'[4] That understanding of the dual aspect of the Kingdom as the Kingdom prepared for the elect from the beginning, and as the Kingdom that is continually growing and advancing to the end of the world, played a part of great importance in Calvin's theology. It was in this way, for example, that he met the problem of particular predestination in regard to both election unto salvation and to reprobation. 'Although to our apprehension the will of God is manifold, yet He does not in Himself will opposites, but according to His manifold

---

[1] In a remark about Rom. 8.23f Calvin says: '*Ergo videmus transitum non fieri intempestive a doctrina illa quae praecessit de salute electi populi ad ultimum Christi adventum* (*Comm. on Daniel* 12.2, C.R. 69, p. 290).
[2] *Comm. on John* 6.40: '*Si nos in hunc finem elegit Deus ut credamus, tolle fidem, et mutila erit electio* (C.R. 75, p. 147).
[3] *Instit.* 2.17.1; 3.22.1; 3.24.5; 3.25.3. It is significant that Calvin first speaks of election particularly at the end of Book 2 of the *Institutes* (2.17.1f), to indicate that our salvation does not begin in the historical Jesus; though it is grounded in Him it goes back to eternity. Because Christ was eternally chosen on our behalf we are chosen in Him. This is all Calvin has to say about election as a *saving* doctrine; when he discusses it later it is as a *corollary* of faith, a *guard* against error, and a *confirmation* of our trust, but as such it is secondary, not primary.
[4] *Comm. on Matt.* 6.10, C.R. 83, p. 198; *Serm. on I Tim.* 2.3f, C.R. 81, pp. 147f.

wisdom (so Paul calls it, Eph. 3.10), transcends our senses, until such time as it shall be given us to know how He mysteriously wills what now seems to be adverse to His will.'[1] Calvin is careful to point out that the will of God is that all men should be saved,[2] that it is the nature of the Gospel to bring light and life, and that therefore judgment is an *accidental* characteristic of God's action. Commenting on Mark 4.12, he writes: 'The doctrine is not, strictly speaking or by itself, or in its own nature, but by accident (*per accidens*), the cause of blindness.... When the Word of God blinds or hardens the reprobate, it belongs truly and naturally to themselves, but it is accidental as respects the Word.'[3] Or again, speaking of the *binding* power of the Gospel in contrast to its *loosing* power, he says: 'This does not belong to the nature of the Gospel, but is *accidental* (*accidentale*).'[4] And in a similar vein he writes a comment on 2 Cor. 2.15: 'The Gospel is preached for salvation. This is what properly belongs to it, but believers alone are partakers of that salvation. In the meantime, its being an occasion of condemnation to unbelievers—that arises from their own fault. Thus Christ came not into the world to condemn the world (John 3.17), for what need was there of this, inasmuch as without Him we are all condemned? Yet he sends His Apostles to bind, as well as to loose, and to retain sins as well as to remit them (Matt. 18.18; John 20.23). He is the light of the world (John 8.12) but He blinds unbelievers (John 9.39). He is a rock, for a foundation, but He is also to many a stone of stumbling (Isaiah 8.14). We must always therefore distinguish between the proper office of the Gospel and the *accidental* one (so to speak), which must be imputed to the depravity of mankind, to which it is owing that life to them is turned into death.'[5] It is for this reason, Calvin points out, that reprobation and destruction can have no place in

---

[1] *Instit.* 3.24.17; cf. 1.18.3; 3.20.43.
[2] Cf. *Comm. on I Tim., Introd. Argument*: 'By exhibiting to all the Gospel and Christ the Mediator God shows that He wishes all men to be saved' (C.R. 80, p. 246). See also *Comm. on I Tim.* 2.4f: 'The fruit of the sacrifice by which He made atonement for sins, extends to all' (C.R. 80, p. 268). 'The mystery is that "souls" perish who are bought by the blood of Christ' (*Serm. on 2 Tim.* 2.19, C.R. 82, p. 165).
[3] *Comm. on Mark* 4.12, C.R. 83, p. 361.
[4] *Comm. on Matt.* 16.19, C.R. 83, p. 475.
[5] *Comm. on 2 Cor.* 2.15, C.R. 78, p. 34; later on he writes on 3.7: 'It happens *accidentally* that the Gospel is the source of death, and accordingly is the occasion of it rather than the cause, inasmuch as it is in its own nature salutary to all' (C.R. 78, p. 42). Such passages could be multiplied *ad lib*.

the Creed. Scripture certainly speaks of a resurrection to judgment as well as to life, and tells us that Christ will separate the kids from the goats, 'but Scripture more frequently sets forth the resurrection, as intended, along with celestial glory, for the children of God only: because properly speaking, Christ comes not for the destruction but for the salvation of the world: and therefore in the Creed the life of blessedness only is mentioned'.[1]

Calvin makes it quite clear, therefore, that he will not regard election and reprobation on the same level as making a double decree. 'We fully believe that God's will is simple and one; but as our minds do not fathom the deep abyss of secret election, in accommodation to the capacity of our weakness, the will of God is exhibited to us in two ways.'[2] The advent of Christ will reveal however the impropriety of this language and that throughout God has one will of grace to save mankind. In other words, if Calvin's doctrine of predestination is divorced from eschatology, then it falls a prey to merciless logic which demands a double decree. But that is just what Calvin will not do.[3] Predestination and eschatology are two doctrines, but neither can be expounded without the other. Because predestination is essentially an eschatological event, its full accomplishment reaches out to future judgment and glory,[4] but because it lies hidden thus at God's 'inaccessible tribunal',[5] we must raise up our minds above ourselves[6] and rest them in Christ alone.[7] Because He alone is 'the fountain of life', and 'the anchor of salvation', and 'the Heir of the Kingdom of heaven', and 'our final goal', it would be infatuation to understand election 'out of Him'.[8]

In other words, Calvin's conception of the *arcanum consilium* that lies behind and above predestination is to be understood in terms of the ascension, which means that Christ as Cause[9] of our

---

[1] *Instit.* 3.25.9. Cf. also *Catechism of Geneva*, 1545, O.S. II, pp. 92f.
[2] *Comm. on Matt.* 23.37, C.R. 83, p. 644.
[3] It is for this reason that we must expound election and reprobation differently. In regard to election we must lay all the weight upon the hidden act, the ultimate cause hid with Christ in God, and not upon the manifest cause which is faith; but with regard to reprobation we must lay all the weight upon the manifest cause, which is unbelief, and not upon the hidden judgment of God. *Instit.* 3.22.5f; 3.24.1f; 3.23.8; 3.24.1f, etc.   [4] *Instit.* 3.21.7.   [5] *Instit.* 3.22.6.
[6] *Instit.* 3.23.4. Unless we ascend higher the effect will bury the cause (*Instit.* 3.24.3).   [7] *Instit.* 3.24.5.   [8] Ibid.
[9] Calvin speaks of Christ as cause of our election in all four senses of cause, the efficient, the material, the final and the formal cause (*Comm. on Eph.* 1.5-8, C.R. 79, pp. 148f; *on Eph.* 1.12, C.R. 79, p. 152).

election transcends our reason and suspends our full understanding until He comes again,[1] and yet insists that we must lift up our minds to meditate upon His heavenly glory and advent. 'When we have made great progress in thus meditating, let us understand that if the conceptions of our minds be contrasted with the sublimity of the mystery, we are still halting at the very entrance.'[2] The conjunction of eschatology with predestination means that eternal election is more to be wondered at than expressed, and indeed it was thus that 'Paul found rest because he found wonder'.[3] The school of meditation upon the future life and the resurrection is the only place where we may learn to speak properly about election. '*Et ipsi dediscimus bene loqui ubi cum Deo loqui desinimus.*'[4]

The Ascension of Christ

There can be no doubt, then, that for Calvin predestination is the *prius*, eschatology the *posterius*, of the Christian faith, and between the two the whole life of the Church on earth is to be understood. The *prius* and the *posterius*, however, are not to be understood as terms of mere temporality, but in a transcendant fashion appropriate to the Kingdom of God, for the ascension of Christ means that we must lift up our minds in faith above and beyond the concepts of time and space which we have in this world of bondage and sin and decay.[5] For that very reason all our language about God has an element of impropriety about it,[6] but it is not for that reason false.[7] God has accommodated His Revelation to our weakness and capacity, for 'we cannot speak of the Kingdom of God without using our ordinary language'.[8] This

---

[1] 'Since Scripture uniformly teaches us to look with expectation to the advent of Christ and delays the crown of glory till that period, let us be contented with the limits divinely prescribed to us, viz. that the souls of the righteous, after their warfare is ended, obtain blessed rest where in joy they wait for the fruition of promised glory, and that thus the final result is suspended till Christ the Redeemer appear' (*Instit.* 3.25.6). [2] *Instit.* 3.25.10.
[3] *Instit.* 3.23.5: '*Requievit Paulus quia admirationem invenit.*'
[4] *Instit.* 3.23.5.
[5] See especially *Comm. on Eph.* 1.20, C.R. 79, p. 158; *on Eph.* 4.10, C.R. 79, p. 195; and *Instit.* 2.16.14f.
[6] *Comm. on Heb.* 1.3, C.R. 83, pp. 11f; *on Heb.* 7.12, C.R. 83, p. 89.
[7] *Instit.* 2.16.3; cf. *Instit.* 4.19.1: 'Christians are the masters of words as they are of all things, and therefore they may at pleasure adapt words to things, provided a pious meaning is retained though there should be some impropriety in the mode of expression—it is better to make words subordinate to things than things to words.'
[8] *Comm. on Eph.* 4.10, C.R. 79, p. 195; *Comm. on Jer.* 31.12, C.R. 66, p. 660.

THE ESCHATOLOGY OF HOPE: JOHN CALVIN   109

means, however, that the whole life of faith and union with Christ is exercised in eschatological tension (*suspensio*) between[1] the *prius* manifested in the calling of God, and the *posterius* of final revelation and redemption,[2] and in a wondrous anticipation or foretaste of the glorious consummation.[3] In other words, the eschatological relation involved in Christian faith is at once the relation between the heavenly and the earthly here and now, and the relation between the present and the future.[4] Two quotations may suffice to make that clear. Speaking of the ascension of Christ, he comments: 'He expressly calls Himself the Lord and King of *heaven and earth*, because, by constraining men to obey Him in the preaching of the Gospel, He establishes His throne *on the earth*; and, by regenerating His people to a new life, and inviting them to the hope of salvation, He opens *heaven* to admit to a blessed immortality with angels those who had formerly not only crawled on the earth but been plunged in the abyss of death.'[5] About the words of Matthew, 'Now when the Son of Man shall come in His glory', Calvin writes: 'He will then assume the title of King, for though He commenced His reign on the earth, and now sits at the right hand of the Father, so as to exercise the supreme government of heaven and earth; yet He has not yet erected before the eyes of men that throne from which His divine majesty will be far more fully displayed than it now is at the last day; for that glory, of which we

---

[1] For instances of *suspendere* see the following: *Instit.* 3.25.6: '*Interea quum Scriptura ubique iubeat pendere ab expectatione adventus Christi, et gloriae coronam eousque differat, contenti simus his finibus divinitus nobis praescriptis: animas piorum militiae labore perfunctas in beatam quietem concedere, ubi cum foelici laetitia fruitionem promissae gloriae expectant; atque ita omnia teneri suspensa donec Christus appareat Redemptor.*' C.R. 33, p. 407: '*diem illum cogitemus, cuius expectatione suspensi semper esse debent hominum animi.*' And *Instit.* 3.2.42; *Comm. on Matt.* 24.29, C.R. 73, p. 667; *on Matt.* 19.28, C.R. 73, p. 545; *on Matt.* 25.31, C.R. 73, p. 685; *Comm. on Col.* 2.14, C.R. 80, p. 108, etc.
[2] *Instit.* 3.21.7.
[3] The expression is '*gustare*' or '*gustus*'. See *Serm. on Matt.* 27.27f, C.R. 74, p. 914; *Comm. on Matt.* 17.2, C.R. 73, p. 485; *on Matt.* 24.4, C.R. 73, p. 650; *on Matt.* 25.31, C.R. 73, p. 686; *on Matt.* 16.28, C.R. 73, p. 483; *Comm. on* 1 *Tim.* 4.8, C.R. 80, p. 300, etc. Calvin also uses words like '*delibare*' (*Instit.* 3.9.3), and '*praeludium*' (*Instit.* 3.25.7, 12, etc.) to express eschatological expectation and anticipation.
[4] Calvin attacks Servetus for teaching what is now known as *realised eschatology*! 'From a wish or at least the pretence of a wish to extol the greatness of Christ, Servetus abolishes the promises entirely, as if they had come to an end at the same time with the law. He pretends that by the faith of the Gospel all the promises have been fulfilled, as if there is no distinction between us and Christ' (*Instit.* 2.9.3).
[5] *Comm. on Matt.* 28.18, C.R. 73, p. 821.

now obtain by faith nothing more than an anticipation (or taste) will then have its full effect. So then Christ now sits on His heavenly throne, as far as it is necessary that He shall reign for restraining His enemies and protecting the Church, but *then* He will appear openly to establish perfect order in heaven and earth, to crush His enemies under His feet, to assemble His believing people to partake of an everlasting and blessed life, to ascend His judgment seat; and, in a word, there will be a visible manifestation of the reason why the Kingdom was given to Him by the Father.'[1]

These two aspects of the eschatological relation Calvin speaks of in many ways, such as promise and fulfilment,[2] concealment and manifestation,[3] commencement and perfection,[4] accomplishment and final fruition,[5] expectation and delay,[6] grace and glory.[7] It is this tense relation between the present and the future that gives Calvin his characteristic *nuance* in eschatology: the eager straining of faith in hope intent upon the future revelation of our life in Christ—'*in spem manifestationis Christi intenti*',[8] '*in spem resurrectionis intenta*'[9]; '*salus in spe est reposita: proprium spei est, futuris et absentibus bonis intentam esse*'.[10] Thus although faith is the foundation of hope and love, faith has hope as its constant companion to nourish and sustain it,[11] for it is in hope that faith stretches out to its possession of glory in Christ.[12] All that belongs

---

[1] *Comm. on Matt.* 25.31, C.R. 73, p. 686.
[2] *Comm. on Matt.* 24.3f, C.R. 73, pp. 649f; *on Matt.* 13.43f, C.R. 73, p. 371; *Comm. on Mark* 15.43, C.R. 73, pp. 788f.
[3] *Comm. on Matt.* 22.30, C.R. 73, p. 606; *on Matt.* 24.26, C.R. 73, p. 664; *on Matt.* 24.29f, C.R. 73, pp. 666f; *on Matt.* 24.32, C.R. 73, p. 670; *on Matt.* 25.31, C.R. 73, pp. 685f; *on Matt.* 26.29, C.R. 73, pp. 708f.
[4] *Comm. on Matt.* 22.30, C.R. 73, p. 606; *on Matt.* 24.3f, C.R. 73, pp. 649f; *on Matt.* 25.31, C.R. 73, p. 685; *on Matt.* 27.52, C.R. 73, p. 783; *Comm. on Mark* 15.43, C.R. 73, p. 788.
[5] *Comm. on Matt.* 24.3f, C.R. 73, pp. 649f; *Comm. on Luke* 24.46, C.R. 73, p. 817; *on Matt.* 13.43, C.R. 73, p. 371.
[6] *Comm. on Matt.* 22.23, C.R. 73, pp. 604f; *on Matt.* 24.29f, C.R. 73, pp. 666f; *on Matt.* 24.32f, C.R. 73, p. 670.
[7] *Comm. on Luke* 1.74, C.R. 73, p. 49; *on Luke* 2.14, C.R. 73, pp. 76f.
[8] *Comm. on* 1 *Thess.* 1.3, C.R. 80, p. 141.
[9] *Comm. on Rom.* 8.19, C.R. 77, p. 152. Cf. *Comm. on Phil.* 1.6, C.R. 80, p. 9: '*Atque adeo quum de spe agitur, semper ad beatam resurrectionem, tanquam ad scopum referendi sunt oculi.*'
[10] *Comm. on Rom.* 8.25, C.R. 77, p. 156.
[11] O.S. I, p. 94: '*Fides fundamentum est, cui spes incumbit, spes fidem alit et sustinet.*' O.S. I, pp. 402f.
[12] *Comm. on Eph.* 2.6, C.R. 79, p. 164: '*Et certe, quamvis salus nostra in spe adhuc abscondita quantum ad nos spectat: in Christo nihilominus immortalitatem et gloriam.*'

to our salvation is already wrought and is contained in Christ,[1] so that because of the secret unity between the Head and the members[2] through hope we share in His resurrection,[3] and the whole of our life, and indeed the whole of creation, is stretched out eagerly towards its ultimate manifestation,[4] towards the 'universal redemption' when Christ will appear to restore all things.[5]

The *Commentary on the Harmony of the Gospels* particularly is full of discussion of the Kingdom as at once present and future in these ways. The question is raised at the very beginning in the introductory argument. 'Christ is not only the pledge of all the blessings that God has ever promised, but we have in Him a full and complete exhibition of them. As Paul declares elsewhere, "all the promises of God in him are yea and in him amen" (2 Cor. 1.20). ... The Gospel therefore is a public exhibition of the Son of God manifested in the flesh (1 Tim. 3.16) to deliver a ruined world and to restore men from life to death. It is justly called a good and joyful message for it contains perfect happiness. Its object is to commence the reign of God and by means of our deliverance from the corruption of the flesh and of our renewal by the Spirit, to conduct us to the heavenly glory. For this reason it is often called the Kingdom of Heaven, and the restoration to a blessed life which is brought to us by Christ is sometimes called the Kingdom of God: as when Mark says that Joseph waited for the Kingdom of God (15.43) he undoubtedly refers to the coming of the Messiah.'[6]

In a comment upon Matt. 19.27 and the parallel passages in Mark and Luke, Calvin points out that Christ warns the disciples 'that the glory of His Kingdom which at that time was still hidden was about to be revealed', and yet He also held the wishes of the disciples 'in suspense till the latest revelation of His Kingdom, when they will receive the fruit of their election. And though the Kingdom of Christ is in some respects manifested by the preaching

---

[1] *Comm. on Col.* 1.23, C.R. 80, p. 91; *Comm on Col.* 3.10, C.R. 80, p. 121.
[2] *Comm. on Eph.* 2.6, C.R. 79, p. 164. Cf. *Comm. on 1 Cor.* 6.15: '*Nota, unitatem spiritualem quae nobis cum Christo est, non animae tantum esse, sed pertinere etiam ad corpus: ut caro sumus de carne eius* (Eph. 5.30). *Alioqui infirma esset spes resurrectionis, nisi talis nostra coniunctio, hoc est plena et solida.*'
[3] *Comm. on 1 Thess.* 1.10, C.R. 80, p. 145.
[4] *Comm. on Rom.* 8.19, C.R. 77, p. 152.
[5] *Sermon on Acts* 1.9-11, C.R. 48, pp. 621f.
[6] *Commentary on the Harmony of the Gospels, Introd. Arg.*, C.R. 73, p. 2.

of the Gospel, there is no doubt that Christ here speaks of the last day'.[1] Referring to the expression 'in the regeneration', Calvin continues: 'I explain *regeneration* as referring to the first coming of Christ, for then the world began to be renewed and arose out of the darkness of death into the light of life. This way of speaking occurs frequently in the Prophets and is very well adapted to the connexion of this passage. For the renovation of the Church, which has been so frequently promised, had raised an expectation of wonderful happiness, as soon as the Messiah should appear. And therefore in order to guard against that error, Christ distinguishes between the beginning and the completion of His reign (*inter principium regni sui et complementum distinguit*).'[2] The same thought is expounded more fully in connexion with the parables of the pounds and the talents. 'In both Christ intended to show that the disciples were greatly mistaken in supposing that His royal authority was already established, and that He was coming to Jerusalem in order to commence immediately a course of prosperity. Thus by taking away the expectation of an immediate Kingdom, He exhorts them to hope and patience; for He tells them that they must long and steadily endure many toils before they enjoy the glory for which they pant too earnestly. . . . Christ must undertake a long journey in order to obtain the Kingdom. By the *distant country* I think that Christ expresses nothing more than His long absence, which would extend from the time of His death to His last coming. For though He sits at the right hand of the Father, and holds the government of heaven and earth, and though from the time that He ascended into heaven, all power was given to Him (Matt. 28.18) that every knee should bow before Him (Phil. 2.10), yet He has not yet subdued His enemies, has not yet appeared as Judge of the world, or revealed His Majesty; it is not without propriety that He is said to be absent from His people, till He return again clothed with a new sovreignty. It is true indeed that He now reigns while He regenerates His people to the heavenly life, forms them anew to the image of God, and associates them with angels; while He governs the Church by His Word, guards it by His protection, enriches it with the gifts of the Spirit, nourishes it by His grace, and maintains it by His power, and, in short, supplies it with all that is necessary for salvation,

---

[1] *Comm. on Matt.* 19.28, C.R. 73, pp. 544f.   [2] Ibid.

while He restrains the fury of Satan and of all the ungodly and defeats all their schemes. But as this way of reigning is concealed from the flesh, His manifestation is properly said to be delayed till the last day.'¹

In a characteristic passage from his commentary on the Fourth Gospel, which reminds us of Luther, Calvin puts it in quite another way. It is given with reference to Rom. 8.22f. 'Let us know that we too must groan until, having been delivered from the incessant afflictions of the present life, we obtain a full view of the fruit of our faith. To sum up the whole in a few words, believers are like women in labour, because, having been born again in Christ, they have not yet entered into the heavenly Kingdom of God and a blessed life; and they are like pregnant women who are in childbirth, because being held captive in the prison of the flesh, they long for that blessed state which lies hidden under hope.'²

Between the Advents

It is clear then that Calvin thinks of the Kingdom of God in terms of two great eschatological moments, the *initium* and the *complementum*, but what does he think of the *medium* between these moments? That is to be understood on the analogy of Christ Himself. Calvin frequently speaks of the relation between the crucifixion and the resurrection as the *initium* and the *complementum* of our salvation. 'This distinction must be carefully observed that we may know what we must look for from the death of Christ (that sin is done away), and what from His resurrection³ (that righteousness is procured). When, however, in other places the Scripture makes mention only of His death, let us understand that in those cases His resurrection is included in His death, but when they are mentioned separately the commencement of our salvation is in the one and the consummation of it in the other (*sed quum distincte nominantur, in illa salutis nostrae initium est, in hac complementum*).'⁴ Christ Himself is thus the *medium* in His humanity

---
¹ *Comm. on Luke* 19.12, C.R. 73, p. 568.
² *Comm. on John* 16.21, C.R. 75, p. 366.
³ Calvin speaks of the resurrection as the *hypostasis, fundamentum* and *caput* (*Comm. on 1 Cor.* 15.13, C.R. 77, p. 542). It is called 'the chief article of the faith'—'or the chief point of salvation' (*Comm. on Matt.* 28.7, C.R. 73, p. 796).
⁴ *Comm. on 1 Cor.* 15.4, C.R. 77, p. 538; 15.19, pp. 544f; 15.28, pp. 549f; 15.49; 15.54, pp. 563f, etc.

and will continue to be the *medium* until He hands over the Kingdom to the Father.[1] Here Calvin speaks of the *Regnum Christi* as leading up to the all-comprehensive *Regnum Dei* of which it is the anticipation. The *Regnum Christi* considered in itself is Christ in His own Person who died and rose again, but considered in its counterpart it is the Church which is His Body. Just as Calvin then thinks of the death and resurrection of Christ as the *initium* and the *complementum salutis*,[2] with Christ Himself as *medium*, so he thinks of the founding of the Church by Christ as *initium* and the consummation as *complementum*, with the *Regnum Christi*, in which the Church participates through the Holy Spirit, as *medium*. Or, more concretely, it is Christ Himself who is the '*medium inter nos et Patrem ut nos ad eum tandem adducat....*' 'Let us wait patiently until Christ shall vanquish all His enemies and bring us, along with Himself, under the *imperium Dei* that the *Regnum Dei* may in every respect be fulfilled in us.'[3]

Calvin lays great emphasis upon this, that in Christ all parts of our salvation have already been accomplished.[4] Thus in his *Commentary on John's Gospel*: 'In the Cross of Christ, as in a magnificent theatre, the inestimable goodness of God is displayed before the whole world. In all creatures, indeed, both high and low, the glory of God shines, but nowhere has it shone more brightly than in the Cross, in which there has been an astonishing change of things (*admirabilis rerum conversio*), the condemnation of all men has been manifested, sin has been blotted out, salvation has been restored to men, and, in short, the whole world has been renewed and everything restored to order (*toto denique mundo reparato omnia in ordinem restituta*).'[5] Even 'the last judgment will be nothing else than an approbation or ratification of the doctrine of the Gospel'.[6] And yet, without retracting such thoughts, for they are one aspect of the truth, Calvin insists that the two moments are

---

[1] *Comm. on* 1 *Cor.* 15.27 and 28; *Instit.* 2.15.5; *Comm. on Amos* 9.11, C.R. 71, pp. 170f.
[2] In another extension of the analogy Calvin can speak of the condition of the soul after death as the *initium* and the resurrection as the *consummatio* (*Comm. on* 2 *Cor.* 5.1f).
[3] *Comm. on* 1 *Cor.* 15.27, C.R. 77, pp. 548f.
[4] *Instit.* 3.25.1, 2; 2.9.3.
[5] *Comm. on John* 13.31, C.R. 75, p. 317.
[6] *Comm. on John* 12.48, C.R. 75, p. 303; *Serm. on* 2 *Thess.* 1.6-10, C.R. 80, p. 238: 'Our Lord Jesus Christ must appear from heaven.... This coming is to seal and ratify all He did and endured for our salvation.'

THE ESCHATOLOGY OF HOPE: JOHN CALVIN

not just in dialectical relation; there is a *medium* in which they are temporally and eschatologically related. This is the side that is stressed in the *Commentary on the Acts of the Apostles*. 'Regeneration is the beginning of this Kingdom and the end of it is blessed immortality, but in between there are advances in a more ample progress and increase of regeneration (*huius regni initium est regeneratio: finis ac complementum beata immortalitas: medii progressus sunt in ampliore regenerationis profectu et augmento*).'[1] As early as 1539 he had spoken of this as '*regni Christi amplitudo*'.[2] Here it is given fuller description: '*quatenus renovatur interior homo noster in spiritualis vitae profectum, ad perfectionem regni Dei magis accedimus, quae est divinae gloriae societas. Regnare ergo Deus nunc vult in nobis, ut tandem nos regni sui participes faciat.*'[3]

This has to be understood in a twofold sense. 'When we speak of the Kingdom of Christ, we must respect two things: the doctrine of the Gospel, whereby Christ doth gather unto Himself a Church, and whereby He governs it being gathered together; secondly, the society of the godly (*societas piorum*), who being joined together by the sincere faith of the Gospel are truly accounted the people of Christ (*populus Christi*).'[4] This means that in so far as we think of the *Regnum Christi* in terms of Christ Himself and His Gospel, the Kingdom is already complete, and in that sense Calvin can well say all things have already been accomplished and we await only the final revelation of Christ in glory; but in so far as we think of the *Regnum Christi* as the society of the godly, we cannot but think of it in a historical perspective in terms of growth and increase. In His own life, death, resurrection and ascension[5] Christ has in a manner already renewed the whole world,[6] and assumed the Kingdom at the right hand of the Father.[7] In a profound sense the Kingdom is wholly realised in Christ, realised in

---

[1] See page 115, note 6.
[2] *Responsio ad Sadoleti Epistolam*, O.S., I, p. 462.
[3] *Comm. on Acts* 1.3, C.R. 77, p. 4.
[4] *Comm. on Acts, Epistola Dedicatoria*, C.R. 42, p. 293.
[5] 'By this means the force and fruit of Christ's death and resurrection are sealed' (*Comm. on Acts* 2.33, C.R. 76, p. 47; *Serm. on Acts* 1.9-11, C.R. 76, pp. 613-622).
[6] *Comm. on Heb.* 7.17f, C.R. 83, pp. 91f; *on Matt.* 24.14, C.R. 73, pp. 656f; *on Luke* 12.47, C.R. 73, pp. 680f; *Comm. on Gen.* 17.7, 13, C.R. 50, pp. 237, 241f; *on John* 13.31, C.R. 75, pp. 316f.
[7] *Comm. on Matt.* 25.31, C.R. 73, pp. 685f; *on Matt* 28.18, C.R. 73, pp. 820f; *Serm. on Acts* 1.1-4, C.R. 48, pp. 585-96.

Him on behalf on the Church,[1] but 'this must be transferred to the whole body of the Church'.[2]

Historically, however, Calvin thought of the renovation of the Church as beginning, and therefore of the Kingdom of Christ as commencing, when God called His people out of Babylon,[3] and as established not simply when Jesus refounded the Israel of God in the twelve disciples, but when He Himself rose again from the dead as the Head of the Church, ascended His throne, and by pouring out His Spirit at Pentecost incorporated the Church once and for all into His resurrection-Body. Moreover, Calvin did not think of Christ only as the Author and Finisher of our faith but as Himself the whole substance or matter of regeneration or renewal,[4] so that by substantial union with Christ the Church actually and continuously participates in the new humanity of the resurrection and in the *Regnum Christi*. Calvin thinks of the Church as at once a completed structure,[5] the Body of Christ, the corporate election realised in Christ,[6] and yet as the new humanity reaching forward to the *societas divinae gloriae*.[7] Launched into history, it grows and increases until the advent of Christ.[8]

When Calvin thinks of the Church in this historical perspective he does not forget that there is a historical prelude in the Old Testament Church. He is careful to point out the historical relevance of the prophecies in Isaiah and Ezekiel, for example, to the restoration of the nation and kingdom in Jerusalem, but sees in them a wider reference to the *Regnum Christi* in which the whole world along with Judaea will be involved.[9] 'When the Prophets

---

[1] *Comm. on Heb.* 2.11, C.R. 83, pp. 28f; *on Heb.* 7.25, C.R. 83, p. 94; *Instit.* 2.9.3; *Serm. on 2 Tim.* 1.9, C.R. 82, pp. 54f; *Serm. on Isaiah* 53.7, C.R. 63, pp. 639f; *Serm. on Matt.* 27.45f, C.R. 74, pp. 924f; *Serm. on John* 1.1-5, C.R. 75, pp. 466f.   [2] *Comm. on Acts* 8.33, C.R. 76, p. 194.

[3] *Comm. on Heb.* 2.13: 'The restoration from the Babylonian exile was a sort of prelude to the great redemption obtained by Christ for us and the Fathers' (C.R. 83, p. 31).

[4] *Serm. on John* 1.1-5, C.R. 75, pp. 465f; *Serm. on Luke* 2.1-14, C.R. 74, pp. 955f.

[5] *Comm. on Acts* 2.17; *Comm. on Isaiah* 54.2; *Comm. on Heb.* 2.13.

[6] *Serm. on 2 Tim.* 1.9-10, C.R. 82, pp. 51f; O.S. I, pp. 86f; *Instit.* 3.21.5-7; *Comm. on Gal.* 3.16, C.R. 78, pp. 211f; *Comm. on Gen.* 17.7f, C.R. 50, pp. 237f.

[7] *Comm. on Acts* 1.3, C.R. 76, p. 5.

[8] Though 'Christ has already restored all things by His death the effect does not fully appear, for that restoration is yet *in cursu*', *Comm. on Acts* 3.21, C.R. 76, p. 73.

[9] *Comm. on Isaiah* 35.1. The whole of this chapter in Calvin's Commentary is a valuable discussion of eschatology (C.R. 64, pp. 590ff).

promise restoration to the Church, they do not restrict their discourse to the person of Christ, but begin with the return of the people: for that was the prelude (*praeludium*) of the full and solid liberty which was at length made manifest in Christ. . . . As often as the Prophets hold out the hope of liberty to the elect they embrace the whole time from the return of the people or from the end of their exile to the end of the Kingdom of Christ. When, therefore, the reign of Christ is treated we must date its commencement (*exordium*) from the period of the building of the temple after the people's return from their seventy years' captivity: and then we must take its boundary, not at the ascension of Christ, nor yet in the first or second centuries, but through the whole progress of His Kingdom until He shall appear at the last day.'[1] This Old Testament prelude with reference to the growth of the New Testament Church is well put in a comment upon Isaiah 54.2: 'This prophecy began to be fulfilled under Cyrus who gave the people liberty to return,[2] and afterwards extended to Christ in whom it has its full accomplishment. The Church therefore conceived, when the people returned to their native country, for the body of the people was gathered together from which Christ should proceed in order that the pure worship of God and true religion might again be revived. Hitherto, indeed, this fertility was not visible, for the conception was concealed, as it were, in the mother's womb, and no outward appearance of it could be seen. But afterwards the people were increased and after the birth of the Church grew in infancy to manhood, till the Gospel was preached. This was the actual youth of the Church, and next follows the age of manhood down to Christ's last coming, when all things will be fully accomplished.'[3]

As well as thinking of the Church growing up, into the mature manhood of Christ, Calvin also thinks of it as extending to the very ends of the earth. In this sense the preaching of the Gospel to all nations is itself the Kingdom of Christ, the stone of Daniel's

---

[1] *Comm. on Ezekiel* 17.22, C.R. 40, p. 417.
[2] Cf. *Comm. on Isaiah* 35.7: 'That deliverance was but a feeble representation of the accomplishment in Christ. And yet the full accomplishment of this promise ought not to be expected in the present life; for as it is through hope that we are blessed (Rom. 8.24) so our happiness, which is now in some respects concealed, must be an object of hope till the last day. And it is enough that some taste of it be enjoyed in this world, that we may more ardently long for that perfect happiness' (C.R. 64, p. 595).
[3] *Comm. on Isaiah* 54.2, C.R. 65, p. 270.

vision which smites the image of the kingdoms of this world and destroys them, until the Kingdom of Christ is extended over the whole earth.[1] It is significant that Calvin dedicated his *Commentary on Daniel* 'to all the godly worshippers of God who desire the Kingdom of Christ to be rightly constituted in France'. He recognised that 'when Christ goes forth with His Gospel serious commotions arise',[2] and he wished to strengthen the faith of the Church under trial and persecution by infusing into them the mighty apocalyptic hope of the Kingdom of Christ, which through the sceptre of the doctrine of the Gospel is constituted among men and nations, and by showing the 'perpetuity of the Kingdom' and of the Church.[3] 'God shows how all earthly power which is not founded on Christ must fall, and He threatens speedy destruction to all kingdoms which obscure Christ's glory by extending themselves too much.'[4]

All this, the advance of the Church between *initium* and *complementum* and the reign of Christ between His two advents, Calvin sees in the historical perspective of the two ages, the old world and the new world to come, but like the New Testament he thinks of them as overlapping.[5] The last times have already overtaken the Church in the resurrection of Christ and in the pouring out of the Holy Spirit,[6] so that the last day is to be looked for every

[1] *Comm. on Dan., Epist. Dedicatoria*, C.R. 46, pp. 620f; *on Dan.* 2.40-43, 44f, C.R. 68, pp. 599ff, 603f: 'The Stone by which those kingdoms were destroyed, which had made war on God, was not formed by the hand of man: and although it was rude and unpolished, yet it increased to a great mountain.'
[2] C.R. 68, pp. 533f. Cf. *De Scandalis*, O.S. II, p. 193: '*Si Christum in medio hostium dominari oportet, sicut Spiritus testimonio olim testatum est, regnum eius inter nos sine militia et continuis certaminibus esse non potest.*'
[3] *Comm. on Dan.* 2.44, C.R. 68, p. 603.
[4] *Epist. Dedic.* As in the case of the final judgment so here Calvin insists that 'the Kingdom of Christ is said to break up the empires of the world, not directly, but *accidentally*, as the phrase is'. *Comm. on Dan.* 2.40f, C.R. 68, p. 601. This is because the real purpose of the *Regnum Christi* is a positive structure of grace, so that the breaking up of the kingdoms of this world is but the sign of the edification and manifestation of the *Regnum Christi*.
[5] Cf. *Instit.* 3.7-10; 4.20.1f; *De Scandalis*, O.S. II, p. 159ff; *Sermons* 29 and 30 *on Gal.*, C.R. 88, pp. 633f, 643f; *Comm. on Eph.* 1.14, 22, C.R. 77, pp. 460f.
[6] *Comm. on Acts* 2.17, C.R. 76, p. 31; *Comm. on* 1 *Cor.* 15.52, C.R. 77, p. 562; *Comm. on* 1 *John* 2.18, C.R. 83, pp. 320f; *Comm. on* 1 *Cor.* 10.11, C.R. 77, pp. 460f; cf. *Serm. on Acts* 2.13-17, C.R. 76, pp. 643f, where, with ref. to Joel 2.30-31, Calvin says: 'By these words he indicates that great and marvellous things must happen when Jesus Christ will manifest Himself. And why? Because the world undergoes a change. Also those who would follow Jesus Christ must change entirely from their natural selves. That is also why the time of the coming of Jesus Christ is called the "last days." Besides this is not said of a day or a month, but the prophet applies all that is said here to all the time

hour.¹ This overlapping of the two ages is often expounded by Calvin in contrast with the eschatological expectation of the Old Testament Church. With reference to that, the Kingdom of God is to be seen in its consummation already accomplished once and for all in Christ, but with reference to the final advent of Christ, the Christian Church, while already in the Kingdom, also looks forward in eschatological expectation. '*Now once in the end of the world Christ has appeared.* That is the end of the world or the consummation of the ages, which Paul calls "the fulness of time" (Gal. 4.4) for it was the maturity of that time which God had determined in His eternal purpose. . . . Christ's death was in due time, as He was sent into the world for this end by the Father, in whose power is the lawful right to regulate all things as well as all times, and who ordains their succession with consummate wisdom, though often hid from us. This consummation is also set in opposition to the imperfection of past time; for God so held His ancient people in suspense that it might have been easily concluded that things had not yet reached a fixed state. Hence Paul declares that the end of the ages had come upon us (1 Cor. 10.11), by which He means that the Kingdom of Christ contains the accomplishment of all things (*regnum Christi omnibus rebus complementum attulisse*).'² Speaking in the next chapter of *futura bona*, Calvin continues: 'These, I think, are eternal things. *Fateor quidem, futurum Christi regnum, quod nobis praesens est, olim annuntiatum fuisse.* But the Apostle's words mean that we have a lively image of future blessings (*vivam nos habere futurorum bonorum effigiem*). He thus understands that spiritual pattern (*spirituale illud exemplum*) whose full fruition (*plena fruitio*) is deferred to the resurrection and the future world. At the same time I confess that these good things began to be revealed at the beginning of the Kingdom of Christ; but what he now treats of is this, that they are not only future blessings as to the Old Testament, but also with respect to us, who still hope for them.'³ In his *Commentary upon Micah* Calvin says:

between the coming of Jesus Christ and the Last Judgment: and we must include the wonders which will be done at the coming of Jesus Christ between the time when He has come and the last day.'
¹ *Comm. on* 1 *Cor.* 15.52, C.R. 77, p. 562.
² *Comm. on Heb.* 9.26, C.R. 83, p. 119; see *Comm. on Lev.* 26.3, C.R. 53, p. 14.
³ *Comm. on Heb.* 10.1, C.R. 83, p. 121; cf. *Comm. on Heb.* 9.11: 'As μέλλων καιρός, time to come, is set in opposition to τῷ ἐνεστηκότι, so future blessings are in opposition to the present' (C.R. 83, p. 109).

'The Last Days the Prophet no doubt calls the coming of Christ, for then it was that the Church of God was built anew. In short, since it was Christ that introduced the renovation of the world, His advent is rightly called a *new age*, and hence it is also said to be the extremity of days: and this mode of expression very frequently occurs in Scripture; and we know that the time of the Gospel is expressly called *the last days* and *the last time* by John (1 John 2.18) as well as by the author of the Epistle to the Hebrews (1.2) and also by Paul (2 Tim. 3.1) and this way of speaking they borrowed from the Prophets.¹ Paul gives us the reason for this mode of speaking in 1 Cor. 10.11: "Upon whom," he says, "the ends of the world are come."² As Christ then brought in the completion of all things at His coming, the Prophet rightly says that it would be the last days when God would restore His Church by the hand of the Redeemer.'³ Of the inevitable duality which this involves Calvin writes in a comment to 1 Cor. 15.57: '*Thanks be to God*. Christ *has* conquered sin and by conquering it *has* redeemed us from the curse of the law (Gal. 3.13). Hence it follows that we are no longer lying under the power of death. Hence although we have not yet a full revelation (*plena revelatio*) yet we may already with confidence glory in them because it is necessary that what has been accomplished in the Head must be accomplished also in the members. We may therefore triumph over death as subdued because Christ's victory is ours. When, therefore, he says, *that victory has been given to us*, you are to understand by this (1) that it is inasmuch as Christ *has* in His own person abolished sin, *has* satisfied the law, *has* endured the curse, *has* appeased the anger of God, and *has* procured life, and (2) because He *has* already begun to make us partakers of all these benefits.'⁴ 'As we are by nature impatient of delay, and soon succumb under weariness, he reminds us that *salvation is not deferred because it is not yet prepared but because the time of its revelation is not yet come.*⁵ This doctrine

---

¹ Cf. *Comm. on Joel* 2.28f, C.R. 70, pp. 564ff; *Comm. on Dan.* 10.14, C.R. 69, p. 208, C.R. 30, p. 852.
² *Comm. ad. loc. cit.*: 'He says, then, that the ends of all ages have come upon us, inasmuch as the fulness of all things is suitable to this age because it is now the last time' (C.R. 77, p. 461). *Comm. on Dan.* 8.24, C.R. 69, p. 121; *on Dan.* 9.25, C.R. 69, pp. 173f.   ³ *Comm. on Micah* 4.1f, C.R. 71, pp. 339f.
⁴ *Serm. on Matt.* 27.55-60, C.R. 74, pp. 941f; *Comm. on* 1 *Cor.* 15.57, C.R. 77, p. 565.
⁵ This does not mean that we are 'to expect any *new revelation*, for it was not a Word in part that Christ brought but the final conclusion. It is in this

is intended to nourish and sustain our hope. Moreover, he calls the day of judgment *the last time*, because the restitution of all things is not to be previously expected, for *the intervening time is still in progress*. What is elsewhere called *the last time, is the whole time from the coming of Christ*, and is so called from a comparison with the preceding ages. But Peter had a regard to the end of the world.'[1] Calvin takes this overlapping of the two ages so realistically that he speaks of this world *as already in a manner renovated by the coming of Christ*.[2] 'To make the matter clearer, let us suppose two worlds, the first the old, corrupted by Adam's sin, the other, later in time, as renewed by Christ. The state of the first creation has become wholly decayed, and with man has fallen as far as man himself is concerned. Until, then, a new restitution be made by Christ, this Psalm (8) will not be fulfilled. It hence now appears that here the renovated world is not that which we hope for after the resurrection but that which began at the beginning of Christ's Kingdom, but it will no doubt have its full accomplishment in our final redemption.'[3]

The very fact that the Church is involved in the overlap of the two worlds and the tension that they involve between 'the life that now is and is to come'[4] Calvin sees is to the advantage of the Church as it allures it on to desire the future world. 'Let us remember to distinguish between the good things of the present and of the future life, for God bestows kindness on us in this world in order that He may give us only a taste of His goodness, and by such a taste allure us to the desire of heavenly benefits, that in them we may find satisfaction. The consequence is that the good things of the present life are not only mingled with many afflictions, but, we may almost say, overwhelmed by them, for it is not expedient for us to have abundance in this world lest we should indulge in luxury.'[5] That applies to our common mercies day by day but it applies much more profoundly to the *Regnum Christi* and the

sense that the Apostle takes "the last times" and "the last days" ' (*Comm. on Heb.* 1.1, C.R. 83, p. 10).

[1] *Comm. on* 1 *Pet.* 1.5, C.R. 83, p. 211; cf. *on* 1 *Pet.* 1.14, C.R. 83, pp. 221f.
[2] *Comm. on Heb.* 7.17f, C.R. 83, pp. 91f; cf. *Comm. on Mark* 15.43 and *Luke* 23.51, C.R. 73, p. 788. In a *comment on Luke* 12.50 Calvin speaks of the renovation of the world as already consecrated in the death of Christ (C.R. 73, p. 681).
[3] *Comm. on Heb.* 2.6, C.R. 83, p. 24; cf. *Comm. on Eph.* 1.22, C.R. 79, p. 159; *on Heb.* 9.11, C.R. 83, pp. 11f.
[4] 1 Tim. 4.8.
[5] *Comm. on* 1 *Tim.* 4.8, C.R. 80, pp. 299f; *Instit.* 3.9.3.

Church. Because of the ascension, in which Christ has withdrawn His glory and delays its manifestation, 'His Kingdom is obscurely hidden under the cross and is violently assailed by enemies'.[1] Moreover, because 'it is in the Church that Christ holds the seat of His Kingdom',[2] the Church is also under the Cross,[3] although in another sense it already sits with Christ in heavenly glory.[4] Although Christ has set up His Kingdom, 'He has assigned to us a period of warfare to exercise our patience till He come again from heaven to complete His reign which He has commenced. It is therefore the virtue of believers to seek the things which are above (Col. 3.1) and especially since the grace of God has shone upon us through the Gospel teaching us that, denying ungodliness and worldly lusts, we should live soberly, justly and piously, *in the present world*, looking for the blessed hope and *manifestation of the glory* of the great God (Titus 2.11-13).'[5]

The Two Conditions of the Kingdom

This Biblical language leads Calvin to draw a distinction between what he calls the two conditions of the Kingdom, i.e. 'between the present condition of the Kingdom and its future glory (*discernit Christus praesentem regni sui statum a futura eius gloria*).'[6] This indeed is the main burden of Calvin's commentary on *the little Apocalypse*. The disciples tended to misinterpret the teaching of Jesus about the coming of His Kingdom, and 'they confounded the perfection of Christ's reign with the commencement of it and wished to enjoy on earth what they ought to seek in heaven'.[7] Christ sets out to correct that by teaching them that the Church must suffer 'scandals', though it must not be terrified by them, for it is only through tribulation that the Church, like the Son of Man, will enter into the glory of the Kingdom.[8] Thus 'whenever the question relates to the origin, restoration, condition, and the

---

[1] *Comm. on 2 Tim.* 4.1, C.R. 80, p. 385.
[2] *Comm. on 1 Tim.* 1.20, C.R. 80, p. 264.
[3] *Instit.* 3.8, *De crucis tolerantia.*
[4] *Comm. on Col.* 3.3, C.R. 80, p. 118; *on John* 5.24, C.R. 75, pp. 115f.
[5] *Comm. on Mark* 15.43 and *Luke* 23.51, C.R. 73, p. 789.
[6] *Comm. on Matt.* 24.30, C.R. 73, p. 667.
[7] *Comm. on Matt.* 24.4, C.R. 73, p. 650.
[8] *Comm. on Matt.* 24.3f, C.R. 73, pp. 649f; *on Matt.* 24.30, C.R. 73, pp. 667f; cf. *Instit.* 3.8.1.

whole salvation of the Church, we must remember not to stop at what our senses can comprehend but must honour the power of God by admiring His hidden work'.[1] 'For though the Church is now tormented by the malice of men, and even broken by the violence of the billows, and miserably torn in pieces, so as to have no stability in the world, yet we ought always to cherish confident hope, because it will not be by human means, but by heavenly power, which will be far superior to every obstacle, that the Lord will gather His Church.[2] This is what Calvin regularly means when he speaks of the Kingdom as 'spiritual'[3] or 'heavenly', because it is not to be judged according to the carnal reason.[4] The two conditions of the Kingdom or, correspondingly, of the Church, involve a contrast 'between a state of concealment and the extension of the Kingdom far and wide',[5] but that does not mean that even now God does not manifest His glory in the Church under the Cross.[6] 'It is not that the glory and majesty of the Kingdom will not appear till the last coming of Christ, but because till that time is delayed the accomplishment of those things which began to take place after His resurrection, and of which God gave His people nothing more than a taste that He might lead them further on in the path of hope and patience.'[7] 'The general instruction is conveyed that the weak and frail condition of the Church ought not to lead us to the conclusion that it is dying, but rather to expect the immortal glory for which the Lord prepares His People

---

[1] *Comm. on Matt.* 21.42, C.R. 73, p. 597.
[2] *Comm. on Matt.* 24.30, C.R. 73, pp. 667f.
[3] The Kingdom is spiritual also because it is gained through the priestly mediation of Christ. The outstanding thing about His Priesthood is that His Priesthood and Kingship *are* one. Because His Kingdom is gained by Priestly mediation and atonement, it is *spiritual*, not like the kingdoms of this world which repose on force. See *Comm. on Harm. of the Pentateuch,* on *Exod.* 19.6, C.R. 52, p. 196; on *Exod.* 28.1, 9, C.R. 52, pp. 426f, 431f; *Comm. on Heb.* 1.13f, C.R. 83, p. 19; on *Heb.* 7.7f, C.R. 83, pp. 86f; on *Heb.* 7.12f, C.R. 83, pp. 89f; on *Heb.* 8.1f, C.R. 83, pp..96f; *Comm. on Matt.* 16.17, C.R. 73, p. 473; *Comm. on Psalm* 2.6, C.R. 59, p. 45; on *Ps.* 20.1, C.R. 52, p. 207; on *Ps.* 78.70, C.R. 52, pp. 745f; on *Ps.* 110.4, C.R. 53, p. 164.
[4] *De Scandalis,* O.S. II, p. 179: Of the *universalis Ecclesiae conditio* Calvin says, '*nunquam ea specie nitet, in qua hominum sensus Dei regno agnoscant*'.
[5] *Comm. on Matt.* 24.26, C.R. 73, p. 664; *Serm. on Matt.* 27.55f, C.R. 74, pp. 941f.
[6] Cf. *de Scandalis,* O.S. II, p. 187: '*quo magis sub cruce oppressa fuit Ecclesia, eo clariorem in ea erigenda Dei virtutem exstitisse.*' And p. 190: '*ac quo gravior fuit crucis pressura, eo clarius ostendit Deus sua manu erigi Ecclesiam, erectamque sustineri: sub regno Christi longe clarior est huius rei conspectus.*'
[7] *Comm. on Matt.* 24.29, C.R. 73, p. 667.

by the cross and by afflictions, for what Paul maintains with reference to each of the members must be fulfilled in the whole body, that *if the outward man is decayed the inward man is renewed day by day* (2 Cor. 5.16).'[1]

It is to this idea that Calvin devotes a special section of his remarkable work *De Scandalis*, from which we may take this significant passage: 'Why is it that today many draw back from a sincere profession of the Gospel but because they see us to be few in number, of little authority and of no power, while, in the opposite camp everything is quite contrary? And in fact as things are today it is not surprising that the marred form of the Church[2] should deter them when the splendour that shines among our adversaries catches their eyes. None will stumble at this stone nor will this offence hinder any, except those who refuse to acknowledge the spiritual Kingdom of Christ. Those who are not put off by the stable in which He was born, nor by the cross on which Christ hung, from adoring Him as their King, will not in the least despise the humble fortune of His Church. They all confess with their mouth, as indeed they ought, that it is altogether reasonable that the living image of Christ should appear in the form of the Church as in a mirror (*ut in Ecclesiae forma, quasi in speculo, viva Christi effigies appareat*).[3] And when Paul speaks of a conformity between the Head and members in the bearing of the cross (Rom. 8.17) all agree. When he says that we must die with Him that we may participate in His life (2 Tim. 2.11), no one contradicts. When all Scripture compares our present life to hard warfare and teaches that it is full of various struggles, even this they agree to be true and right. And so the name of *Church Militant*, as it is commonly called, is even found on the lips of children. But when it comes down to actual practice all this is forgotten and they treat the

---

[1] *Comm. on Matt.* 24.32, C.R. 73, p. 670. Cf. *De Scandalis*, O.S. II, p. 191: '*inter mortes innumeras fatebitur continuam fuisse multarum resurrectionum seriem.*'

[2] Cf. *Serm. on Gal.* 4.26f: "The Church does not triumph in this world, nor does it shine with such pomp and splendour that men are ravished at the very sight of it and so submit themselves to it. Rather is it usually despised and disfigured' (C.R. 88, p. 648).

[3] Cf. *Comm. on Eph.* 1.20: 'Christ alone is the mirror in which we can contemplate that which the weakness of the Cross hinders from being clearly seen in ourselves: ... We shall find advantage in directing our views to Christ, that in Him, as in a mirror, we may see the glorious treasures of Divine grace, and the unmeasurable greatness of that power which has not yet been manifested in ourselves' (C.R. 79, p. 157).

image of Christ (*imaginem Christi*) as something quite unheard of and strange. But if they are granted what they desire, that the Church prospers in every way, that it abounds in wealth and power and enjoys continual peace and finally that nothing is lacking for its blessedness in anything one could desire, what would that be but *terreni imperii facies?* Then one would have to look elsewhere for the *spirituale Regnum Christi*. Then indeed the Church would be divided from its Head. We remember, however, that thus the outward appearance of the Church is contemptible that its beauty may shine within; it fluctuates on earth that it may have its fixed seat in heaven; before the world it lies lacerated and ruinous that before God and His angels it may stand whole and vigorous; it is miserable in the flesh that its felicity may repose in the Spirit.[1] Thus when Jesus Christ lay despised in the manger, angels hymned His excellence in the clouds, the stars in the sky gave their testimony to His glory, and wise men from a great distance perceived His greatness. When He hungered in the wilderness, when He struggled with the wiles of Satan even to sweating blood, the angels again ministered to Him. When His enemies came to take and bind Him He drove them back with His voice alone. While He was hanging on the Cross the sun hailed Him as king of the world by its own eclipse, the opened graves confessed Him Lord of death and life. If now we see Christ tormented in His own body by the arrogant outrages of the ungodly, oppressed by savage tyranny, exposed to shameful treatment, driven here and there by violence, let none of those things confound us. Rather let us remember this that it is appointed to the Church, as long as it has its pilgrimage in the world, to engage in warfare continually under the cross (*in hoc ordinatam esse Ecclesiam, ut quamdiu in mundo peregrinatur, militet sub perpetua cruce*).'[2]

The Ministry

It is within the context of this eschatological relation of the

---

[1] '*Nos vero meminerimus, sic contemptibilem esse externum Ecclesiae aspectum, ut decor eius intus splendeat: sic in terra fluctuari, ut fixam habeat in caelo sedem: sic coram mundo laceram et ruinosam iacere, ut coram Deo et eius angelis stet nihilominus in spiritu reposita sit felicitas.*' Cf. *Comm. on Rom.* 52, C.R. 77, p. 89: '*Quamvis nunc in terra peregrinentur fideles, fiducia tamen sua caelos transcendere ut futuram haereditatem tranquilli in sinu foveant.*'

[2] *De Scandalis*, O.S. II, pp. 179f; cf. *Serm. on 2 Tim.* 2.16-18, C.R. 82, pp. 163f.

Church between the two advents of Christ that Calvin understands the ministry of the Word and the Sacraments. The Word and Sacraments belong essentially to time and history as they are conditioned by the incarnation, death and resurrection of Christ on the one hand, and by the *Parousia* and the resurrection of the body on the other. They are the full union with Christ refracted in the overlap of the ages, or rather the way and measure in which Christ gives Himself to us here and now while we still wait for the redemption of the body and the final revelation of His glory. 'The ministry of the Word is like a looking-glass. For the angels have no need of preaching or other inferior helps nor of Sacraments, for they enjoy a vision of God of another kind, and God does not give them a view of His face merely in a mirror, but openly manifests Himself as present with them. We, who have not as yet reached that great height, behold the image of God as it is presented to us in *the Word*, in the *Sacraments*, and in fine, *in the whole service of the Church*.'[1] It is important to examine these three carefully in the light of Calvin's eschatology.

(1) *The Ministry of the Word.* Because of the setting of our knowledge in the overlap of the two ages we must speak of knowledge and faith dialectically. 'We do not see Christ and yet we see Him: we do not hear Christ and yet we hear Him.'[2] On the one hand a full revelation has been made in Christ. 'When the Wisdom of God was manifested in the flesh, He fully unfolded to us all that the human mind can comprehend or ought to think of the heavenly Father. Now therefore since Christ the Sun of righteousness has arisen we have the perfect refulgence of divine truth like the brightness of the noon-day, whereas light was previously dim. *God in these last days has spoken to us by His Son* (Heb. 1.1f). He will not henceforth speak by this one and that one; He will not add prophecy to prophecy or revelation to revelation, but has so completed all the parts of teaching in the Son, so that it is to be regarded as His last and eternal testimony. For this reason the whole period of the new dispensation, from the time when Christ appeared to us with the preaching of His Gospel, until the day of judgment, is designated by *the last hour, the last times, the last days*, that,

---

[1] *Comm. on Matt.* 13.16 C.R. 73, p. 362; cf. on 19.28, C.R. 73, pp. 544f.
[2] *Comm. on* 1 *Cor.* 13.12, C.R. 77, p. 514. Cf. *Instit.* 3.25.10.

contented with the perfection of Christ's doctrine, we may learn to frame no new doctrine for ourselves or admit any one devised by others.'[1] In giving us even in the Christian Gospel all that we can comprehend or ought as yet to know God has accommodated Himself to the weakness and littleness of our capacity.[2] 'God comes down to *earth* that He may raise us up to *heaven*. . . . He condescends to our ignorance. Therefore when God prattles (*balbutit*) to us in Scripture in a rough and ready style, let us know that this is done on account of the love He bears to us.'[3] 'It is not without an admirable arrangement of providence that the sublime mysteries of the Kingdom of Heaven have been delivered with a contemptible meanness of words.'[4] This clothing of the Word in our contemptible language is for Calvin part of the whole humiliation of the Word or the Son on the Cross, so that the preaching of this same Word, which is thus the Word of the Cross, makes foolish the wisdom of this world. 'It is the prerogative of the Gospel to bring down the wisdom of the world in such a way that stripped of our own understanding, we show ourselves to be simply docile, and do not think or even desire to know anything but what the Lord Himself teaches. . . . For the Lord admits none into His school but little children. Hence those alone are capable of heavenly wisdom who, contenting themselves with the preaching of the Cross, however contemptible it may be in appearance, feel no desire whatever to have Christ under a worldly form (*larvatum*).'[5]

This means that for Calvin all understanding of the Scripture and all preaching of the Scripture must have regard to its *scope*,

---

[1] *Instit.* 4.8.7; cf. O.S. I, p. 238.
[2] *Comm. on* 1 *Cor.* 13.12: 'The measure of knowledge that we now have is suitable to imperfection and childhood, as it were, for we do not as yet see clearly the mysteries of the heavenly Kingdom, and we do not as yet enjoy a distinct view of these' (C.R. 77, p. 514).
[3] *Comm. on John* 3.12, C.R. 75, p. 61; *Serm. on John* 1.1f, C.R. 75, pp. 469f; *Serm. on* 1 *Tim.* 2.3-5, C.R. 81, p. 155.
[4] *Instit.* 1.8.1.
[5] *Comm. on* 1 *Cor.* 1.17, C.R. 77, p. 321. It is for this reason that Calvin insists that the only way for true theology is the *a posteriori* way. 'God now presents Himself to be seen by us, not such as He is, but such as we can comprehend. Thus is fulfilled what is said by Moses, that we see only as it were *His back* (Exod. 33.23) for there is too much brightness in His face' (*Comm. on* 1 *John* 3.2, C.R. 83, p. 331). 'This is the rule of sound and legitimate and profitable knowledge to be content with the measure of revelation and willingly to be ignorant of what is deeper than this. We must indeed advance in the acquisition of divine instruction but we must so keep in the way as to follow the guidance of God' (*Comm. on Exod.* 33.18, C.R. 53, p. 108).

or its essential perspective in Christ to whom Holy Scripture leads us. 'Where all Scripture is not taken as referring to Christ as its one aim (*scopum*) it is mistakenly twisted and perverted.'[1] Like the Scripture, the ministry of the Word must point beyond the Word itself to the subject-matter, to Christ who died and rose again, ascended and will come again in glory.[2] But in that perspective we realise that 'the knowledge which we have of God for the present is obscure and slender in comparison with the glorious view which we shall have on the occasion of Christ's last coming'.[3] 'For many things are kept from us in this life, the perfect and full manifestation whereof is deferred until that day, wherein we shall see Him as He is with new eyes face to face.'[4] 'Then we shall see God—not in His image, but in Himself, so that there will be, in a manner, a mutual view.'[5]

(2) *The Sacraments*.[6] In a discussion of the significance of the Passover Calvin says that 'the use of this Sacrament was twofold, both to exercise the people in the recollection of their past deliverance and to nourish them in the hope of future redemption (*duplicem huius sacramenti fuisse usum: quia in recordatione praeteriti beneficii populum exercuerit, et spem aluerit redemptionis futurae*)'[7] and so he speaks of this ancient Sacrament as '*symbolum redemptionis futurae*'[8] or '*liberationis futurae*'.[9] To this, however, he says, corresponds the Holy Supper.[10] There is of course a very

---

[1] *Comm. on 2 Cor.* 3.16, C.R. 78, p. 45.
[2] Cf. *Comm. on 2 Tim.* 1.10: 'When he ascribes to the Gospel the manifestation of life he does not mean that we must begin with the word, leaving out of view the death and resurrection of Christ (*nam verbum potius in subjectam materiam recumbit*) but he only means that the fruit of this grace comes to men in no other way than by the Gospel' (C.R. 80, p. 353).
[3] *Comm. on 2 Cor.* 3.18, C.R. 78, p. 47.
[4] *Comm. on Acts* 20.26f, C.R. 76, p. 467.
[5] *Comm. on 1 Cor.* 13.12, C.R. 77, pp. 514f.
[6] Here too Calvin applies his doctrine of *accommodation*. Cf. *Catechism of the Church of Geneva* on the Sacraments: 'In this way God consults our weakness. If we were wholly spiritual we might, like the angels, spiritually behold both Him and His grace, but as we are surrounded with this body of clay, we need figures or mirrors to exhibit a view of spiritual and heavenly things in a kind of earthly manner; for we could not otherwise attain to them' (O.S. II, p. 131; cf. p. 41).
[7] *Comm. on Exod.* 12.5f, C.R. 52, p. 289.
[8] *Comm. on Exod.* 12.1: '*tam futurae quam praeteritae redemptionis fuit symbolum*' (C.R. 52, p. 286). [9] *Comm. on Exod.* 12.43, C.R. 52, p. 291.
[10] *Comm. on Exod.* 12.42, C.R. 52, p. 291. There is a similar correspondence between circumcision and Baptism (*Instit.* 4.16.3f). Cf. Calvin's quotation from the *Council of Mileois*: 'Let him who says that Baptism is given for the remission of sins only and not in aid of future grace, be anathema' (*Instit.* 4.19.8).

THE ESCHATOLOGY OF HOPE: JOHN CALVIN

big difference between the Sacraments of the Old Testament and the two Sacraments of the New Testament. They differ not in respect of significance but in respect of efficacy.[1] 'In both there is an exhibition of Christ but in ours it is more full and complete.'[2] Augustine is cited to support this view. ' "The sacraments of the Mosaic law foretold Christ, ours announce Him" (*Quaest. sup. Num.*, c. 33). "Those were promises of things to be fulfilled these indications of fulfilment" (*Contra Faustum, lib*, 19, 14), as if he had said, those figured Him when he was still expected, ours, now that He has arrived, exhibit Him as present. Moreover, with regard to the mode of signifying, he says, as he also elsewhere indicates, "The law and the Prophets had Sacraments foretelling a thing future, the Sacraments of our time attest that what they foretold was to come has come".'[3] Thus the Christian Sacraments are Sacraments of the fulness of time, filled with the presence of the Incarnate Christ. 'Christ is the matter or the substance of all the Sacraments, since in Him they have their whole solidity, and out of Him promise nothing.'[4] For that very reason, however, the Sacraments are involved in the ascension of Christ[5] and look toward His second advent,[6] in exactly the same way as faith, which also incorporates us into Christ.[7] The Christian Sacraments belong therefore to the time of the Church between the advents of Christ, and are the way in which Christ presents Himself to us until His full and glorious manifestation. '*Until He come*—as He is not present with us in a visible form, it is necessary for us to have some symbol of His presence, by which our minds may exercise themselves.'[8] And so Calvin says of the two Sacraments: 'They have been delivered to the Christian Church to be used from the beginning of the new dispensation to the end of the world, Baptism being a kind of entrance into the Church, an initiation into the faith, and the Lord's Supper the constant aliment by which Christ spiritually feeds His family of believers. . . . It be-

---

[1] *Instit.* 4.14.25. [2] *Instit.* 4.14.26. [3] *Instit.* 4.14.26. [4] *Instit.* 4.14.16.
[5] 'We teach that if believers would find Christ in heaven, they must begin with the Word and Sacraments. We turn this view to Baptism and the Supper, that in this way they may rise to the full height of celestial glory. Thus Jacob called Bethel the gate of heaven, because aided by vision he did not fix down his mind upon the earth, but learned to penetrate by faith to heaven' (*Sec. Def. c. Westphalum*, C.R. 37, p. 84).
[6] *Instit.* 4.17.26; 4.17.26; *Comm. on Matt.* 26.29f, C.R. 73, pp. 708f.
[7] Cf. *Comm. on John* 6.54f, C.R. 75, pp. 154f.
[8] *Comm. on 1 Cor.* 11.26, C.R. 77, p. 490.

hoves us to hunger after Christ only, to seek Him, look to Him, learn of Him, and learn again, until the arrival of the great day on which the Lord will fully manifest the glory of His Kingdom and exhibit Himself to our admiring eye (1 John 3.2). And for this reason this age of ours is designated in Scripture (1 John 2.18; 1 Pet. 1.20; Luke 10.22; Heb. 1.1; 1 Cor. 13.12) by the last hour, the last days, the last times, so that no one may deceive himself with the vain expectation of some new doctrine or revelation.'[1]

The crucial point for Calvin in a doctrine of the Sacraments is the ascension and all that the ascension implies. He speaks in the most realistic terms of union with Christ through the Sacraments, of eating His Body and drinking His Body,[2] but refuses to forget the fact that the withdrawal of Christ in Body from us in His ascension introduces an eschatological *distance* which must be observed. 'Only when we obtain Christ Himself do we come to be partakers of His benefits. He is obtained not only when we believe that He was made an offering for us, but when He dwells in us, when He is one with us, when we are members of His flesh, when we are incorporated with Him into one life and substance. I attend to the import of the words, for Christ does not simply present to us the benefit of His death and resurrection, but the very Body in which He suffered and rose again. Christ's Body is *really*, that is, *truly* given to us in the Supper, to be wholesome food for our souls. Our souls are nourished by the substance of the Body that we may be truly made one with Him, or what amounts to the same thing, that a life-giving virtue from Christ's flesh is poured into us by the Spirit, though it is at a great *distance* from us, and is not mixed with us.'[3] Therefore, Calvin goes on, 'in order that we may be capable of participating we must rise heavenwards'.[4] It is for this reason that the ancient liturgies have the *sursum corda*.[5] The Sacraments are the mode in which we are united to Christ in His death, resurrection and ascension, so that while we must speak of a real and substantial union with Him as 'members of His body, of His flesh and of His bones'[6] (Eph. 5.30), we must also speak of that without denying the ascension, and that

---

[1] *Instit.* 4.18.19f.
[2] See *Comm. on* 1 *Cor.* 11.24, C.R. 77, pp. 485f; *on Matt.* 16.26, C.R. 73, p. 481; as well as the *Institutes* and the replies to Westphal and Heshusen.
[3] *Comm. on* 1 *Cor.* 11.24, C.R. 77, p. 487.   [4] Ibid.
[5] *Instit.* 4.17.1f; 4.17.10; 4.17.24f; 4.17.26f; 4.17.36, etc.   [6] *Instit.* 4.17.9.

is the great mystery which the Sacraments enshrine.¹ 'The sum is, that the flesh and blood of Christ feed our souls just as bread and wine maintain and support our corporeal life. For there would be no analogy in the sign did not our souls find their nourishment in Christ. This could not be, did not Christ truly coalesce with us in one, and refresh us by the eating of His flesh and the drinking of His blood. But though it seems an incredible thing that the flesh of Christ, while at such a *distance* from us in respect of space, should be food to us, let us remember how far the secret virtue of the Holy Spirit far surpasses all our conceptions and how foolish it is to wish to measure its immensity by our feeble capacity. Therefore what our mind does not comprehend let faith conceive, *that the Spirit truly unites things separated by space.* That sacred communion of the flesh and blood by which Christ transfuses His life into us, just as if it penetrated into our bones and marrow, He testifies and seals in the Supper, and that not by presenting a vain and empty sign, but by there exerting an efficacy of the Spirit by which He fulfils what he promises.'² And so at the appropriate point Calvin inserted into the *Form for Administering the Lord's Supper* these words, to be spoken just before the actual communication in the Eucharist: '*Let us raise our hearts and minds on high where Jesus Christ is in the glory of His Father, and from which we look for Him at our redemption.*'³

(3) *The Church.* We have already seen that the Church as incorporated into Christ is so formed by Him to be His Body that it wears His image. 'God manifests Himself so familiarly in *the order of the Church* that the heavens, so to speak, are opened to us.' 'God has appeared to us by His Son, who is His living image, and in whose person He wishes to be known in perfection. But St Paul declares again and again that the Gospel is the mirror in which Jesus Christ is beheld (2 Cor. 4.4). The same thing may be affirmed of the general order which God has established in His Church.'⁴ 'That there is a universal Church, that there has been

---

¹ *Instit.* 4.17.9. ² *Instit.* 4.17.10.
³ O.S. II, p. 48; cf. also p. 44. The Sacrament also involves the redemption of the body, so that by the Sacrament 'the resurrection of the body is confirmed to us by a kind of pledge since the body also shares in the symbol of life' (*Cat. of the Ch. of Geneva*, O.S. II, p. 141).
⁴ *Serm. on Psalm* 27.8, C.R. 36, p. 426; see also *Serm. on Psalm* 27.4, C.R. 36, pp. 409ff.

from the beginning of the world, and will be even to the end, we all acknowledge. The appearance (*aspectus*) by which it may be recognised is the question. We place it in the Word of God, or (if anyone prefers to put it) since Christ is her Head, we maintain that, as a man is recognised by his face (*ex facie*), so she must be seen in Christ. Let us hold then that the Church is seen where Christ appears and where His Word is heard.'[1] It is in this way that Calvin understands the *order* of the Church.[2] 'God might indeed of Himself, without the agency of men, preserve His Church in good *order*, but He takes men for His ministers, and makes use of their hands.'[3] But 'while God appoints pastors over His Church, He does not convey His right to others, but acts in the same manner as if a proprietor were to let a vineyard or field to a husbandman, who would labour in the cultivation of it and make an annual return'.[4] The difficulty arises, however, as in the parable, when the tenants of the vineyard seek to usurp ownership of it and control over it. That was what happened in the Old Testament with the priests in whose hands was 'the regular and permanent government of the Church',[5] but God sent men of another order, the prophets, whose business it was to recall the priests to their proper function. 'The prophets were sent as an extraordinary supply to clear the vine from weeds, to lop off the superfluous wood, and in other ways to make up for the neglect of the priests; and at the same time, severely to reprove the people, to raise up decayed piety, to awaken drowsy souls, and to bring back the worship of God and a new life. And what else was this than to demand the revenue which was due to God from His vineyard? All this Christ applies justly and truly to His purpose, for the regular and permanent government of the Church was not in the hands of the prophets but always held by the priests.'[6]

It is in this direction that Calvin interprets the relation of the Kingdom of Christ to the ancient Church and its order. 'By the

---

[1] *Artic. Facult. S. Theol. Paris*, ad XVIII, C.R. 35, p. 31.
[2] C.R. 30, p. 750: '*Deus ipse in medium prodit, et quatenus huius ordinis auctor est, vult se praesentem in sua institutione agnosci.*'
[3] *Comm. on Matt.* 21.33, C.R. 73, p. 592. Cf. *Instit.* 4.5.5: 'It is the office of a presbyter (and this both the Word of God prescribes and the ancient canons enjoin) to feed the Church and administer the spiritual Kingdom of Christ.' Cf. C.R. 30, p. 750: '*nos hodie humanitus vult docere.*'
[4] *Comm. on Matt.* 21.23, C.R. 73, p. 592.   [5] Ibid.
[6] *Comm. on Matt.* 21.33f, C.R. 73, p. 593.

Kingdom we must understand the renovation (*instaurationem*) promised through Christ, for the perfection of order (*integritas ordinis*) which the prophets had everywhere promised would exist at the coming of Christ, cannot exist unless God assembles under His government (*imperium*) those men who had gone astray.'[1] 'Therefore Christ set up the Kingdom of God by restoring affairs from confusion and disorder to a regular and proper condition (*in rectum et legitimum statum*).'[2] That belongs therefore to 'the last days, the fulness of time, by which is meant the stable condition of the Church (*stabilis ecclesiae conditio*) in the manifestation of Christ.'[3]

But Jesus Christ has ascended and once more the Head of the Church is in the *far country*, as it were. 'Christ by His ascension took away His visible presence from us, and yet He ascended that He might fill all things: now, therefore, He is present in the Church, and always will be. When Paul would show the way in which He exhibits Himself he calls our attention to the ministerial offices which He employs (*rationem qua se exhibet dum vult Paulus ostendere, ad ministeria quibus utitur nos revocat*).'[4] This means that for Calvin the order of the Church has an essentially eschatological duality. In the supreme sense the order consists in the government exercised by the ascended Lord through His Word and Spirit,[5] so that the Church is brought into conformity with 'Christ speaking to us from the lofty throne of His heavenly glory'. 'He only is the Head, under whose government (*principatu*) we are all united to each other according to that order and form of polity (*secundum eum ordinem et eam politiae formam*) which He himself has prescribed.'[6] 'The perfection of grace and the supreme power of government reside only in Christ.'[7] 'But the Apostle teaches that the whole subministration is diffused through the members (*totam subministrationem per membra diffusam*), while the power flows from the one celestial Head.'[8] It is with that in mind that Calvin says

[1] *Comm. on Mark* 15.43 and *Luke* 23.51, C.R. 73, p. 788.   [2] Ibid.
[3] *Comm. on Acts* 2.17, C.R. 76, p. 31. '*Porro Ecclesiae reparatio quasi novum saeculum futura erat*' (ibid.).
[4] *Instit.* 4.6.10; 4.3.2.
[5] *Comm. on Matt.* 18.18, C.R. 73, pp. 515f.
[6] *Instit.* 4.6.9.   [7] *Instit.* 4.6.9.
[8] Ibid. Cf. O.S. II, p. 272: '*Non aliter vitam in nos suam diffundit, nisi dum caput nostrum est, ex quo totum corpus compactum et connexum per omnem iuncturam subministrationis secundum operationem in mensura cuiusque membri augmentum corporis faciat*' (Eph. 4.16).

that 'the Kingdom of Heaven and the Kingdom of God denote the *new condition of the Church*',[1] for the Church and the Kingdom are essentially correlative.

Order in the Kingdom

This correlativity between Church and Kingdom, however, is to be understood in terms of the eschatological tension and reserve involved in the overlap of the two ages, for here and now the Church is not so correlative to the Kingdom that it transcribes the perfect form of the Kingdom in earthly existence. Within history, therefore, the order of the Church is essentially ambiguous; the face of Christ is not always to be directly discerned. Calvin thinks of this in several ways.

(1) He insists that there must be a 'fixed form', 'a legitimate form', and a 'firm polity' (*stata forma, legitima forma, politia firma*).[2] 'So far are we from condemning laws which conduce to this that we hold that the removal of them would unnerve the Church, deface and dissipate it entirely.'[3] 'Christ has so ordered the ministry in His Church that if it is removed the whole edifice must fall.'[4] Calvin continues: 'Paul's injunction, that all things be done decently and in order, cannot be observed unless order and decency be secured by the additions of ordinances, as a kind of bond. In these ordinances, however, we must always attend to the exception, that they must not be thought necessary to salvation, nor lay the conscience under a religious obligation, they must not be compared to the worship of God, nor substituted for godliness.'[5] This *fixed form* of the Church order is not so rigid that it does not

---

[1] *Comm. on Matt.* 11.11: '*Regnum coelorum et Dei pro novo Ecclesiae statu capitur, quod Christi adventu promissa esset rerum omnium instauratio*' (C.R. 73, p. 303).

[2] *Instit.* 4.10.27; 4.2.12. Cf. the letter to the unknown Curé (1543?), C.R. 39, pp. 485f. 'It is rather an odious thing to alter what has been hitherto received. But the order which our Lord has once delivered ought to be for ever inviolable. Thus when it has been forsaken for a season, it ought to be renewed and set up again, even should heaven and earth commingle. There is no antiquity, no custom which can be set up or pleaded in prejudice of this doctrine, that the government of the Church established by the authority of God should be perpetual to the end of the world, since He has willed and determined that it should be so.'

[3] *Instit.* 4.10.27; 4.3.2. Calvin speaks of the orders of the Church as its *nerves*. C.R. 30, p. 905; O.S. I, p. 256. Cf. letter of 31st July 1563: '*Sic omnino anima ecclesiae verbi auditione constat, ita ut etiam nervorum locum obtineat ordo et politia constituta apposite, ad bonum corporis illius habitum conservandum*' (C.R. 48, p. 115). [4] *Instit.* 4.1.11. [5] *Instit.* 4.10.27.

allow of growth and development, for 'the Church cannot be so framed by and by, but that there remains somewhat to be amended; neither can so great a building be finished in one day, that there may not something be added to make it perfect.'[1] Indeed Christ 'has not been pleased to prescribe every particular that we ought to observe (He foresaw that this depended on the nature of the times and that one form would not suit all ages). We must have recourse to general rules, therefore, which He has given, employing them to test whatever the necessity of the Church may require to be enjoined for order and decency. As He has not delivered any express command, because things of this nature are not necessary to salvation, and, for the edification of the Church, should be accommodated to the varying circumstances of each age and nation, it will be proper as the interests of the Church may require, to change and abrogate the old, as well as to introduce new forms.'[2] It is within this freedom that Calvin regarded the traditions of the Fathers. 'I do not deny that there were certain traditions of the Apostles that were not committed to writing but I do not admit that they were parts of doctrine, or related to things necessary to salvation. What then? They were connected with order and government. For we know that every Church has liberty to frame for itself a form of government that is suitable and profitable for it, because the Lord has not prescribed anything definite.'[3]

(2) 'Furthermore, we learn that there is no ordinance of God so holy and laudable, which is not either corrupt or made unprofitable through the fault of men. We wonder that things are never so well ordered in the world, but there is always some evil mixed with the good; but it is the wickedness and corruption of our nature which causes this.'[4] It is the constant sin of men in the Church that 'they arrogate to themselves the power of Christ which He Himself while in the world refrained from using', and lord it over the Church, so forcing the hand of God as if they controlled His Kingdon. 'Men mount the throne of judgment and, as if they were gods, anticipate the day of Christ, who alone is appointed by the Father as Judge, allot to every one his station of honour, assign to some a high place, and degrade others to the

---

[1] *Comm. on Acts* 6.1, C.R. 76, pp. 117f.   [2] *Instit.* 4.10.30.
[3] *Comm. on 1 Cor.* 11.3, C.R. 77, p. 474.
[4] *Comm. on Acts* 6.1, C.R. 76, p. 118.

lowest seats.'[1] That makes it imperative that the Church should regard her form and order and her whole appearance in the world in the light of Christ 'whom the heavens must contain until the time of restoring'. And so 'We hope for the last restoring of all things. . . . Christ has already restored all things by His death but the effect does not yet fully appear, because that restoring is yet in course, and so consequently our redemption, for as much as we do yet groan under the burden of servitude. For as the Kingdom of Christ is only begun, and its perfection is deferred until the last day, so those things which are annexed thereunto do now appear only in part. Therefore, if at this day we see many things confused in the world, let this hope set us on foot and refresh us that Christ shall once come that He may restore all things.'[2] Until Christ comes the Church is engaged in warfare[3] and her weapon is the Word of God, for it is through the majesty of the Word[4] that disorder is subdued to order, and the deformed state of the Church is reformed to conformity with Christ.[5]

(3) Calvin has a deeper reason for seeing the order of the Church to be essentially ambiguous in history, for the constitution of the Church now under the Cross is designedly different from what it will be in the glory of the Kingdom. 'In that perfect glory the administration of the Kingdom will not be such as it now is.'[6] At present the Kingdom of Christ is to be understood in terms of Christ's humiliation as described by St Paul in Phil. 2.9-11, where Christ laid aside His power and glory for the way of the Cross. There 'God commends an order in the Kingdom of Christ (*in Christi regno ordinem*) which is necessary for our present infirmity'.[7] 'This is the order in which Christ interposes Himself (*intercedit*

---

[1] *Comm. on 1 Cor.* 4.3, C.R. 77, p. 364; cf. *on Matt.* 20.25, C.R. 73, pp. 556f.
[2] *Comm. on Acts* 3.21, C.R. 76, p. 73.
[3] 'And this is the reason why Christ does not immediately appear, because the warfare of the Church is not yet complete, the time of which, seeing it is appointed by God, it is not for us to anticipate (*antevertere*)' (*Comm. on Acts* 3.21, C.R. 76, p. 73).
[4] *Comm. on 1 Cor.* 4.20: 'The preaching of the Gospel is of such a nature that it is inwardly replete with a kind of solid majesty' (C.R. 77, p. 376). Cf. *Comm. on Matt.* 18.18, C.R. 73, p. 515.
[5] *Instit.* 2.15.5. Cf. C.R. 29, p. 212: '*Cum ecclesia regnum sit Christi, regnet autem non nisi per verbum suum, an ullis iam obscurum erit quin illa mendacii verba sint quibus Christi regnum absque eius sceptro, id est, sacrosancto eius verbo esse fingitur?*' Cf. also C.R. 30, p. 850.
[6] *Instit.* 2.15.15.
[7] Ibid. Cf. *Comm. on 1 Cor.* 15.27: 'We acknowledge, it is true, God as Ruler, but it is *in the face of the Man Christ*' (C.R. 77, p. 549).

medius) that He may gradually bring us to full communion with God.... For God is pleased mediately (*mediate, ut ita loquar*) in His person to rule and defend the Church.'[1] Thus through the Incarnation and the Cross the Kingdom assumes a mediatorial form which is humble and spiritual. As yet while the Gospel is preached, God deliberately holds apart—in eschatological reserve —the two conditions of the Kingdoms, and in that *intermediate condition* He uses the kingdoms of this world.[2]

Until Christ comes and restores all things and hands over the Kingdom to the Father, God has bestowed under the reign of Christ gifts and governments to conserve the existence of the world and for the fulfilment of His will on earth. But 'all earthly principalities and honours are connected exclusively with the keeping up of the present life and consequently are a part of the world. Hence it follows that they are temporary. As the world will have an end, so also will government, and magistracy, and laws, and distinctions of ranks, and different orders of dignities, and everything of that nature. There will be no more any distinction between servant and master, between king and peasant, between magistrate and private citizen. Nay more, there will be then an end put to angelic principalities in heaven, and to ministries and superiorities in the Church, that God may exercise His power and dominion by Himself alone, and not by the hands of men and angels. The angels, it is true, will continue to exist, and they will also retain their distinction. The righteous too will shine forth, every one according to the measure of grace, but the angels will have to resign the dominion which they now exercise in the name and by the commandment of God. Bishops, Teachers, and Prophets will cease to hold these distinctions, and will resign the office which they now discharge.'[3]

This vast change will be completed when Christ Himself will hand over the Kingdom to the Father 'that God may be all in

---

[1] *Instit.* 2.15.15; cf. 3.2.1.
[2] 'Though Christ's Kingdom is spiritual, still we must maintain that as He is the only Son of God, He is also the Heir of the whole world, so that all things ought to be subject to Him and to acknowledge His authority. God has not, therefore, appointed kings and established governments over mankind, in such a manner as to place Him who is the Son in the same rank indiscriminately with others, but yet that, of His own accord, He will be a servant along with others, till the glory of His kingdom be displayed' (*Comm. on Matt.* 27.25).
[3] *Comm. on* 1 *Cor.* 15.24, C.R. 77, pp. 546f.

all'.¹ 'Christ will then restore the Kingdom which He has received, that we may cleave wholly to God. Nor will He in this way resign the Kingdom, but will transfer it in a manner (*quodammodo*) from His humanity to His glorious Divinity, because a way of approach will then be opened up from which our infirmity now keeps us back. Thus then Christ will be subjected to the Father because the veil being then removed, we shall openly behold God reigning in His majesty, and Christ's humanity will no longer be interposed to keep us back from a closer view of God.'² Calvin is not always lucid in the language he uses at this point, though it is clear that while here Christ's kingdom continues *alio modo*, He continues to wear our humanity, but in such a way that we see Him in the full glory and majesty of Godhead.³ This Kingdom will involve the final perfection of heaven and earth, for both will be wholly renewed.⁴ Calvin thinks of that as of the resurrection of the flesh in the most realistic way.

What is said of the whole Kingdom of Christ, however, 'may be said also respecting powers that are sacred and lawful in their kind, for they in a manner hinder God's being seen aright by us in Himself'.⁵ This is why Calvin insists upon regarding all orders in the Church in terms of eschatological suspension, not that they are for that reason unnecessary—they are absolutely necessary, and without them the whole Church will collapse—but they are to be regarded rather as the scaffolding of the Church by means of which it is built up as the Body of Christ, so that even the face of Christ is already reflected in the Church. But it is only when the Church sees God face to face in His glory that she will become like Him and perfectly reflect His image and glory.⁶

Meanwhile the Church must so meet and so order itself in the

---

[1] *Comm. on 2 Peter* 3.12, C.R. 83, p. 477.
[2] *Comm. on 1 Cor.* 15.27, C.R. 77, p. 549.
[3] *Instit.* 3.25.2, 11. *Comm. on Amos* 9.11, C.R. 71, pp. 170f; Cf. *Comm. on Matt.* 25.31, C.R. 73, pp. 685f; *Comm. on Eph.* 1.21, C.R. 79, pp. 158f.
[4] *Comm. on Isaiah* 66.22, C.R. 65, p. 453; *on Rom.* 8.21, C.R. 77, p. 153; *2 Peter* 3.10, C.R. 83, p. 476; *Comm. on 1 Peter* 4.7, C.R. 83, pp. 274f; *Comm. on Heb.* 12.27, C.R. 83, p. 185.   [5] *Comm. on 1 Cor.* 15.28, C.R. 77, p. 550.
[6] That is why *imago Dei* in Calvin's thought is essentially an eschatological concept: cf. *Instit.* 2.1-2; 3.3.9; 1.54; *Comm. on 2 Cor.* 3.18; *Serm. on Job* 19.26f, C.R. 62, pp. 129f: 'God did not create me like a bull or an ass to live here a certain space of time, but He has formed me in His image in order that I may hope in His Kingdom to be a partaker of the glory of His Son....' *Imago Dei* and *meditatio vitae futurae* belong together. See *Serm. on Gal.* 1.3-5, C.R. 88, p. 299.

name of Christ and in obedience to His Word that it places itself under His judgment,[1] and waits for the final manifestation of His judgment when He will re-order all things. The Church that meets in the name of Christ already participates in that future judgment, and that is the way in which it is correlative even now to His Kingdom. 'Whenever believers meet in one place, in the name of Christ, there is already in their assembly a sort of image of the future judgment, which will be perfectly brought to light on the last day.'[2]

The Difference Between Calvin and Luther

We are now in a position to see more clearly the contrast between the eschatology of Calvin and that of Luther, and to note the chief respects in which they differ, though these several respects are but variations on the same theme—*the analogy of Christ*.

(1) The difference is apparent all along the line in the persistence with which Calvin applies Christology to the understanding of the whole life and work of the Church. What happened to Christ the Head of the Church happens also to the Church as His Body, so that eschatology, as we have noted, becomes analogically transposed to determine eschatology. In this the chief emphasis is laid by Calvin upon the doctrines of union with Christ and the resurrection. After dealing extensively with Christology in the second book of the *Institutes* Calvin began the third book by saying that 'the first thing to be attended to is this, that as long as we are without Christ and are separated from Him, nothing which He suffered and did for the salvation of the human race is of the least benefit to us. To communicate to us the blessings which He received from the Father, He must become ours and dwell in us. Accordingly, He is called our Head, and the first-born among many brethren, while, on the other hand, we are said to be ingrafted into Him and clothed with Him (Eph. 4.15; Rom. 6.5; 11.17; 8.29; Gal. 3.27), all which He possesses being, as I have said, nothing to us until we become one with Him.'[3] 'It will never do to separate Christ

---
[1] Cf. *Instit.* 3.12: 'On the Necessity of Contemplating the Judgment.'
[2] *Comm. on* 1 *Cor.* 6.2, C.R. 77, p. 388.
[3] *Instit.* 3.1.1. This involves, of course, a full doctrine of the Spirit, because it is 'the Holy Spirit which is the bond by which Christ effectually binds us to Himself' (ibid.). This He calls the '*sacrum coniugium*' (*Instit.* 3.1.3). Cf. *Comm. on Matt.* 22.2f, C.R. 73, p. 398.

from us, nor us from Christ, but we must with both hands keep a firm hold of that alliance by which He has rivetted us to Himself. ... Thus Christ is not external to us but dwells in us; and not only unites us to Himself by an undivided bond of fellowship but by a wondrous communion brings us daily into closer connexion, until He becomes altogether one with us.'[1]

This means that great weight must be thrown upon the resurrection of Christ in His humanity, for that new humanity is the very substance of our faith and hope.[2] And so Calvin speaks in the same way of the resurrection as of union with Christ, for 'without it all that has hitherto been said (of the death of Christ) would be defective. For seeing that in the Cross, death and burial of Christ nothing but weakness appears, faith must go beyond all these in order that it may be provided with full strength. Hence although in His death we have an effectual completion of salvation, because by it we are reconciled to God, satisfaction is given to His justice, the curse is removed, the penalty paid, still it is not by His death but by His *resurrection* that we are said to be begotten again to a lively hope because, as He, by rising again, became victorious over death, so the victory of faith consists *only* in His resurrection.'[3] 'The Cross of Christ *only then* triumphs in the breasts of believers over the devil and the flesh, sin and sinners, when their eyes are directed to the power of the resurrection.'[4] 'It is a surpassing joy that the Son of God allots to us the same course with Himself that He might lead us with Himself to a blessed participation in heavenly glory. For we must bear in mind this truth, that we have the dying of Christ in our flesh, that His life might be manifested in us. This then is the whole consolation of the godly that they are associates with Christ, that hereafter they may be partakers of His glory; *for we are always to bear in mind this transition from the cross to the resurrection.* The day of the revelation of Christ's glory is not to be overlooked but expected. There is a twofold joy, therefore: one which we now enjoy in hope, and the other the full fruition of which the coming of Christ shall bring to us.'[5]

---

[1] *Instit.* 3.2.24.
[2] Cf. *Instit.* 3.11.9: 'The materials of righteousness and salvation reside in His flesh.'
[3] *Instit.* 2.16.13. Cf. *Serm. on Matt.* 27.27f, C.R. 74, p. 908: 'Jesus Christ repaired everything by His resurrection.'
[4] *Instit.* 3.9.6. Cf. *Serm. on Acts* 2.22f, C.R. 76, pp. 658f; *Serm. on Matt.* 27.55f, C.R. 74, pp. 941f.   [5] *Comm. on* 1 *Pet.* 4.12f, C.R. 83, pp. 278f.

It was for this purpose that Calvin made meditation on the future life so integral a part of the Christian life, for the believer in Christ lives on the side of the resurrection, even though he only experiences a taste of it; but because he lives already within the resurrection life, his attitude to this world is expressed in terms of '*contemptus praesentis vitae*' and '*contemptus mundi*'.[1] That does not in any sense mean a depreciation of our earthly life—how could it, for it is God's *kindness*, His *good creation*, even though it is marred by our sin?[2]—but such handling of our present life that its future renewal or restoration is already made to govern the present. It is in this way that the Christian already risen with Christ is delivered through faith from the limitations and restrictions and from the vanity of the present world,[3] and it is in this way that the Christian life sanctifies the present which Christ has already consecrated by His death and resurrection unto its complete renewal. It is as we already learn to taste the life of the future laid up for us in Christ which is 'our native country'[4] that we can *descend again* to our earthly life and see it 'as a gift of the divine mercy'.[5] If God sends us troubles in the present life it is only in order to prepare us through the *tolerantia crucis* for the glory of the heavenly Kingdom.[6] 'No man has made much progress in the school of Christ who does not look forward with joy to the day of death and resurrection, for Paul distinguishes believers by this mark (2 Tim. 4.8; Tit. 2.13).'[7] He who does meditate on the resurrection will learn that though the glory of the new creation is only as yet exhibited fully in Christ the Head, the condition of our present world is only the obverse of the perfect reality which it already has before God.[8] The Church 'cannot be severed from Christ its Head', so that the Church must live already 'in the power

---

[1] *Instit.* 3.9.1; 3.9.3. This is the victory of faith over a *diseased* attitude to the world—the words are *stupiditas* and *malum*.

[2] *Instit.* 3.9.3f. We must not allow 'any hatred of it or ingratitude to God'.

[3] *Instit.* 3.9.2.

[4] *Instit.* 3.9.5. Cf. O.S. I, p. 117: 'Non enim levibus experimentis suos probat Dominus, nec molliter exercet, sed in extrema quaeque saepe adigit, et adactos diu in eo luto haerere sinit, antequam gustum suae dulcedinis aliquem illis praebeat, atque (ut ait Hanna) mortificat et vivificat, deducit ad inferos et reducit.'

[5] *Instit.* 3.9.3. This is the great distinction between the Christian and the Stoic. Cf. *Comm. on John* 12.25, C.R. 75, p. 289: 'In summa, vitam hanc amare non per se malum est, modo in ea tantum peregrinemur semper ad scopum nostrum intenti. Nam hic legitimus est amandae vitae modus, si in ea manemus quamdiu Domino visum fuerit . . . si eam quasi manibus gestantes offerimus Deo in sacrificium.' [6] *Ibid.* Cf. C.R. 59, p. 19.

[7] *Instit.* 3.9.5; 3.25.1. [8] *Comm. on Rom.* 8.30, C.R. 77, p. 161.

of His resurrection',¹ for 'the order which God has begun with Christ His first-born He continues with all His children'.² Here and now 'Christ begins the glory of His Body in the world, and gradually increases it, and will complete it in heaven'.³ What is delayed is the *crown* of glory; the *final* result is suspended till Christ the Redeemer appear,⁴ but the glorification of the Church as the Body of the risen Christ is discerned by faith here and now in the *tolerantia crucis* itself. What is suspended, therefore, is not the περιποίησις, which means not only *possession* but *enjoyment*,⁵ so much as the full unveiling of our full inheritance in Christ. 'The sum is this—that Christ died with this in view, that He might bestow upon us His life, which is perpetual and has no end. It is not to be wondered, however, that Paul affirms that *we now live with Christ*, inasmuch as by entering through faith into the Kingdom of Christ, *we have passed from death to life* (John 5.24). Christ Himself into whose Body we are ingrafted, quickens us by His power, and the Spirit that dwells in us *is life, because of justification* (Rom. 8.10).'⁶

(2) It was characteristic of Luther that the whole relation between eternity and time should be understood in terms of the critical *Stündlein*, and that carried with it a paradoxical, abrupt apocalyptic. In Calvin's thought, however, it belongs to the covenant mercy of God to use the course of time in which, according to His purpose, the Church on earth has her life.⁷ This means that eschatology is concerned not so much with a dialectical relation⁸ but with a time-lag in the course of fulfilment between Christ the Head and the Church as His Body.⁹ Another way of putting the

---

¹ *Instit.* 3.25.3. Cf. *Comm. on Phil.* 3.12: 'What is it that Paul says he has not yet attained? For unquestionably as soon as we are by faith ingrafted into the Body of Christ, we have already entered into the Kingdom of God, and as it is stated in Ephesians 2.6, we already in hope *sit in heavenly places*' (C.R. 80, p. 51). ² *Instit.* 3.8.1. ³ *Instit.* 3.25.10. ⁴ *Instit.* 3.25.6.
⁵ *Comm. on 1 Thess.* 5.9, C.R. 80, p. 170. Cf. *Comm. on Eph.* 1.14, C.R. 79, p. 154. ⁶ *Comm. on 1 Thess.* 5.10, C.R. 80, p. 171.
⁷ This is in contrast to Luther's sharp division between Law and Gospel, Old Testament and New Testament. Cf. *Calvin's Comm. on Luke* 3.1-31f, C.R. 73, pp. 688f; on *Ezek.* 16.61, C.R. 68, p. 396; *Comm. on Exod.* 12.14, C.R. 52, p. 290; *Instit.* 2.10.2; *Comm. on Heb.* 8.6, C.R. 83, p. 10.
⁸ Calvin does speak of a *dialectica angelica*! C.R. 37, p. 221 and *Comm. on Ps.* 109.3, C.R. 60-147.
⁹ Cf., for example, *Comm. on Psalm* 75.3: 'Christ reigns, as we know, that He may destroy the old man, and He commences His spiritual Kingdom (*spirituale eius regnum incipere*) with the destruction of the flesh, in such a way, however, that there follows the restoration of the new man (*sic tamen ut deinde*

THE ESCHATOLOGY OF HOPE: JOHN CALVIN 143

same thing is to say that it is the ascension of Christ and His *sessio ad dextram* that are determinative.¹ Eschatology is concerned with the relation between the Heavenly Session of Christ wearing our humanity in glory and the course of the Church's pilgrimage and mission in history.² Because these two are related in terms of union with Christ, the course of the Church in history is to be understood in terms of *growth, advance, increase, edification*, that is to say, in terms of the Epistle to the Ephesians and the Epistle to the Hebrews.

It is above all in the doctrine of the Eucharist that this difference between Calvin and Luther comes out. In spite of all that Westphal and Heshusen had to say,³ the difference does not lie in the doctrine of the real presence or the actual eating of the Body and drinking of the blood of Christ,⁴ but in the *mode* of the presence and the participation.⁵ There is a mystery here which far transcends our understanding,⁶ but it is a mystery that is grounded upon and must be interpreted in terms of the mystery of Christ Himself—and that means in terms of *the hypostatic union* on the one hand, and the relation between *the ascension of Christ and His second advent* on the other. This involves three points of difference.

(*a*) The union between Christ and the Church through the

---

sequatur novi hominis instauratio). (C.R. 59, p. 702.) Cf. *on Heb.* 10.25, C.R. 83, pp. 133f. It is in terms of this *eschatological lag in time of fulfilment* that Calvin interprets Col. 1.24, C.R. 80, pp. 94f; cf. *Sermon on Gal.* 6.12f, C.R. 79, p. 117; also *Eph.* 1.23, C.R. 79, p. 160; cf. also *Serm. on Eph.* 1.23, C.R. 79, pp. 346f; *Comm. on 1 Cor.* 12.12, C.R. 77, p. 50.

¹ Cf. *Comm. on John* 20.18, C.R. 75, p. 435 and particularly the *Commentary on the Epistle to the Hebrews*, e.g. 1.13, 14, C.R. 87, pp. 19f.

² See *Serm. on Isaiah* 53.7f, C.R. 63, pp. 641f, where Calvin speaks of 'the *generation of Christ*' as *the continued and permanent life of the Church* for *the ascended Christ will not be separated from His Body, the Church on earth.*

³ See Calvin's *Defence of the Sacraments in answer to the Calumnies of Westphal*, *Last Admonition to Joachim Westphal* and *The True Partaking of the Flesh and Blood of Christ in the Holy Supper* (C.R. 37).

⁴ See especially *Instit.* 4.17.7ff; *Serm. on Luke* 2.1-14, C.R. 74, p. 966; O.S. I, p. 435.

⁵ 'The controversy with us is not as to reception but only to the mode of reception' (*Second Defence in answer to Westphal*, C.R. 37, p. 74).

⁶ The conceptions of mode and mystery belong together, for we can no more say just *how* Christ is present in Communion than *how* the divine and human natures are joined in His one person. That Chalcedon preserved the mystery by speaking negatively warns us not to destroy the mystery of the Supper by logical propositions. See *Instit.* 4.17.1; 4.17.7; 4.17.24; 4.17.32: 'Should anyone ask me as to the *mode*, I will not be ashamed to confess that it is too high a *mystery* either for my mind to comprehend or my words to express; and to speak more plainly, *experior magis quam intelligam.*' It is as great a miracle as the empty tomb (*Comm. on Matt.* 28.2, C.R. 73, p. 795).

Spirit reposes upon the union between God and Man in Christ through the *Spirit*.[1] Communion with Christ involves on the part of the Church participation in Christ, and therefore the nature of the Church as His Body is to be interpreted on the analogy of Christ.[2] That *Christological mystery (reconditum et incomprehensibile mysterium)*[3] must be respected in the communion of the Lord's Supper.[4] That means that the relation between the sign and the signified is to be understood in terms of *inconfuse* and *inseparabiliter*,[5] so that both Eutychian and Nestorian heresies are to be repudiated in a true doctrine of Holy Communion.[6] In terms of the Reformation movements this meant for Calvin a double battle, championing the *inconfuse* against Roman transubstantiation and Lutheran consubstantiation, championing the *inseparabiliter* against humanists and others.[7] In terms of the liturgy this meant a battle against the fusion of form and content so marked in the Roman Mass,[8] and on behalf of a proper doctrine of the Holy Spirit, felt to be lacking in Lutheran theology, particularly in the Eucharist.[9]

[1] This is why Calvin constantly insists on the 'spiritual' act, for it is only by the wondrous work of the Spirit that we can feed on the flesh and blood of Christ. See *Instit.* 4.17.31, 33.

[2] 'Non recusandam esse conditionem, quam Ecclesiae suae ordinavit Deus, ut membra Christi congruentem cum suo capite symmetriam habeant' (*Comm. on Col.* 1.24, C.R. 80, p. 94). Cf. O.S. II, p. 270.

[3] *Comm. on Exod.* 26.31, C.R. 52, p. 417. Cf. *Comm. on Isaiah* 7.14, C.R. 64, p. 158; *Comm. on 1 John* 1.1, C.R. 83, pp. 300f; *Serm. on Luke* 1.39f, C.R. 74, pp. 190f.

[4] See *Last Admonition to J. Westphal*, C.R. 37, pp. 208f, 219f, 239f; Cf. C.R. 16, p. 677: 'Christum secundum corpus suum in coelo manens, admirabili Spiritus sui virtute ad nos descendit et simul nos ad se sursum tollit'; and *Comm. on 1 Cor.* 11.27, C.R. 77, 49.1. *The True Partaking of the Flesh and Blood of Christ*, C.R. 37, pp. 507f; *Instit.* 4.17.5f; 13; 20; 30; 36, etc.

[5] Cf. *Mutual Consent of the Churches of Zürich*, C.R. 35, p. 738; C.R. 37, pp. 18f, 473f, O.S. II, p. 271; *LastAdmonition to J. Westphal*, C.R. 37, pp. 209f; cf. pp. 103f, 195f, 239f. *The True Partaking of the Flesh and Blood of Christ*, C.R. 37, p. 473, C.R. 35, pp. 738, 918; *Instit.* 4.17.20, etc.; *Comm. on Isaiah* 6.7, C.R. 64, p. 133. Calvin refuses to treat the proposition 'This is my Body' simply logically, as neither a proposition of identity nor of difference but of analogy; for the analogy reposes on the union wrought in Christ. Analogy without Christology is nothing. With Christology it is an *active analogy* or *ladder* which raises us up to Christ (*Instit.* 4.17.1-3).

[6] See the *Confession of Faith in Name of the Reformed Churches of France*, C.R. 37, pp. 767ff.

[7] Cf. *Comm. on 1 Cor.* 10.3, C.R. 77, p. 454: '*Confundunt papistae rem et signum; divellunt signa a rebus profani homines: nos mediocritatem servemus.*'

[8] Cf. Calvin's main argument against transubstantiation, that it destroys the analogy between sign and thing signified, and so destroys the Sacrament (*Instit.* 4.17.13ff, 16).

[9] *Instit.* 4.17.10f. *Comm. on Titus* 3.5, C.R. 80, p. 431. 'The efficacy and use

THE ESCHATOLOGY OF HOPE: JOHN CALVIN 145

(*b*) This understanding of union and communion, however, is given acute eschatological content by the doctrine of the Ascension and Final Advent. Granted that we have in the Holy Communion the real presence, the ascension tells us that we must distinguish between that real presence there and the real presence at the *Parousia*,[1] otherwise whenever we celebrate the Lord's Supper the final judgment would actually take place[2] and the hope of the resurrection would be destroyed.[3] '*Utilitas sacramentorum non restringenda ad tempus perceptionis.*'[4] It is highly significant that Calvin's insistence, as against the Lutherans, upon taking the ascension of Christ seriously has the same interest as his attack upon the teaching of Osiander on union with Christ, a *crassa mixtura* by which Christ transfuses Himself into us—'as if we now were what the Gospel promises we shall be at the "final advent of Christ" '[5]; and his attack upon the Chiliasts on the ground that no coming again of Christ to dwell and reign on an unredeemed earth even for a limited period is consistent with the transcendent majesty of His ascended Humanity, for His coming again in glory and power could only mean the complete transformation of the world and the unveiling of the new heaven and the new earth.[6] The Eucharistic presence of Christ is therefore to be understood eschatologically, in which the moment of real union and the moment of celestial glory are held somewhat apart until the final resurrection, although that eschatological distance is in-

---

of the sacraments will be properly understood by him who will connect the sign and the thing signified, in such a manner as not to make the sign unmeaning and inefficacious, and who nevertheless shall not, for the sake of adoring the sign, take away from the Holy Spirit what belongs to Him.' Cf. C.R. 37, pp. 22f; *Instit.* 4.15.14.

[1] *Instit.* 4.17.26f, 29f; 4.18.19f. Cf. *Second Defence of the Sacraments in answer to Westphal*: 'The question is, whether credit is to be given to the heavenly oracles which declare that we are to hope for a resurrection which will make our mean and contemptible body like unto the glorious body of Christ—that the Son of Man shall come on the clouds of heaven to judge the world—that Jesus of Nazareth after ascending to heaven, will in like manner come as He was seen to ascend' (C.R. 37, p. 79).

[2] For this reason Calvin understood the *manducatio impiorum* in terms of the 'savour of death unto death' (C.R. 37, pp. 25f; *Defensio Doctrinae de Sacramentis*, O.S. II, p. 277).

[3] O.S. II, p. 285: '... *quod spem resurrectionis evertit.*'

[4] O.S. II, p. 281. Cf. O.S. II, p. 251: '*Adeo non alligatur actioni sacramentorum gratia, ut fructus eorum percipiatur aliquando post actionem.*'

[5] *Instit.* 3.11.10.

[6] *Instit.* 3.25.5. *Comm. on* 1 *Thess.* 4.17, C.R. 80, p. 167; *on* 2 *Thess.* 2.1, C.R. 80, p. 195; cf. C.R. 76, p. 11.

comprehensibly transcended in the power of the Holy Spirit,[1] so that through a real and substantial union[2] we are given to feed even now upon the vivifying flesh of Christ.[3]

(c) The doctrine of the heavenly session of Christ in whom is lodged the perpetuity and continuity of the Church which is His Body,[4] means that in the course of its life on earth the Church united to Christ and nourished by communion with Him grows and increases in union with Him until His glorious advent.[5] In the doctrine of the Eucharist itself, the difference between Calvin and Luther comes out in regard to the continuity of union with Christ. Like Zwingli, Calvin held that the sixth chapter of John's Gospel refers to a continuous feeding upon the body and blood of Christ which we have through faith, for faith (through the wondrous action of the Spirit) incorporates us into Christ.[6] That faith-union grounded upon Baptism is presupposed by the Eucharist which nourishes and increases it, so that through sacramental communion in the Lord's Supper we are brought into closer and more intimate union with Christ.[7] In terms of the Church as the Body of Christ, that means that the Church grows up into the full stature of the manhood of Christ and is given progress and advance in its earthly life.

The difference here between Calvin and Luther becomes apparent when applied to the Apocalypse, which Luther so grievously misunderstood and mishandled because of a strange understanding of time and history in relation to Christology. Had Calvin written on the Apocalypse, he would (I feel sure) have interpreted it along two lines: (a) the application of Eucharistic eschatology to the

---

[1] *Instit.* 4.17.4f, 18f; *Comm. on Matt.* 28.30, C.R. 73, p. 826; C.R. 37, p. 193.

[2] *Instit.* 4.17.19 and 4.17.3; 4.17.7f; 4.17.11; 4.17.19f. Christ's Body thus becomes *una nobiscum substantia*, 4.17.3, 7ff.; *Comm. on 1 Cor.* 11.24, C.R. 77, p. 487.

[3] 4.17.8ff; C.R. 37, pp. 33, 76; 37, p. 48; O.S. II, pp. 265 and 282f. See also the long letter to Peter Vermiglio, 2266, C.R. 43, p. 723. It is on this ground that we are assured of the resurrection of the Body: 'Our flesh is vivified by His immortal flesh and stands in some manner in its immortality' (O.S. I, p. 413). Cf. C.R. 34, p. 129 and *Comm. on 1 Cor.* 6.15, C.R. 77, p. 398; *Instit.* 4.17.12.

[4] *Instit.* 4.17.1f, 5f: *Comm. on John* 6.53f, C.R. 75, pp. 154f; *Serm. on Isaiah* 53.11, C.R. 63, p. 671; O.S. II, p. 267; *Last Admonition*, C.R. 37, pp. 162f, 232f; *Mutual Consent*, C.R. 35, p. 698.

[5] *Mutual Consent*, C.R. 37, p. 17; *Instit.* 4.17.1f; 5; 33. One way Calvin has of expressing this is to say that 'Christ grows up in us in proportion to the increase of faith' (*The True Partaking of the Flesh and Blood of Christ*, C.R. 37, pp. 489f). Cf. *Instit.* 3.2.24; 3.3.9.

[6] *Instit.* 4.17.5, 30, etc.   [7] O.S. II, pp. 265, 269, 282f.

warfare of the Church in worship,[1] intercession, and proclamation through which the Kingdom of the Ascended Christ gains the victory over the kingdoms of this world; and (*b*) the application of the whole course of Christ's life and obedience from His birth to His death and resurrection to the course of the Church's life from birth at Pentecost, and growth through history to the fulness of Christ at His advent.[2] Certainly the ideas of Luther in his *Supputatio annorum mundi* were as far removed as anything could have been from the Christological eschatology of Calvin. To him that could only be a 'curious and unprofitable inquiry as to times'.[3] 'Believers do not desire to know more than they are permitted to learn in God's school. Now Christ designed that the day of His coming should be hid from us, that, being in suspense, we might be as it were upon the watch.'[4]

(3) Where Luther appeared to be content in his doctrine of the Church with a dialectical relation between the Word and historical forms, Calvin taught a doctrine of the Church as the Body of Christ continuously actualised within history. As we have seen, that dialectic is not wanting in Calvin. Indeed it is strengthened by his greater emphasis upon the doctrine of election, for as the society of the elect the Church is known only to God.[5] That is the eternal foundation of the Church which cannot be seen by the eye of man,[6] but because it is a 'sealed letter' which is to be read in the Gospel by which God calls us to Himself through the voice of man or the ministry of the Church,[7] the doctrine of election does not, in Calvin's view, detract from the visible actualisation of the Church on earth. It is as the voice of the Great Shepherd is heard

---

[1] Calvin notes in a comment upon Exod. 38.1f that liturgy and prayer can be spoken of as 'warring the warfare' of the sanctuary (C.R. 53, pp. 68f). Cf. C.R. 34, p. 179.

[2] Cf. *Instit.* 2.16.19; and *Instit.* 2.17.1: '*Ea gratia quisque ab initio fidei suae fit Christianus, qua homo ille ab initio suo factus est Christus.*' Cf. also '*puritas in eius conceptione, indulgentia in eius nativitate qua factus est nobis per omnia similis*' (2.16.19); and 4.16.18: '*a prima infantia sanctificatus fuit Christus, ut ex aetate qualibet sine discrimine electos suos seipso sanctificaret.*' Does this not mean that infant Baptism is to be grounded on the Virgin Birth of Christ?

[3] *Comm. on 1 Thess.* 5.1, C.R. 80, p. 168.

[4] Ibid. Cf. *on 2 Thess.* 1.10, C.R. 80, p. 192.

[5] *Instit.* 4.1.2, 7.

[6] *Serm. on 2 Tim.* 2.19, C.R. 82, p. 165. In the *Serm. on 2 Tim.* 2.19 Calvin says: 'He has given us the outward mark of Baptism that we may have the seal of the Holy Spirit: This is the *earnest of our election*: it is the pledge which we have of our being called to the heavenly inheritance' (C.R. 82, p. 174).

[7] *Serm. on 2 Tim.* 1.9f, C.R. 82, p. 57.

through the ministry of the Church that election is actualised on earth, so that the Church on earth occupies a place of prime importance in faith and salvation. 'Faith comes by hearing' (Rom. 10.9). God has deposited the treasure of forgiveness in the Church,[1] so that 'outwith the bosom of the Church no forgiveness of sins, no salvation, can be hoped for'.[2] The doctrine of election, therefore, does not only secure the hidden and eternal foundation of the Church, but involves belief in the *externa ecclesia* among the articles of saving faith.[3] The Church is the fruit of the death of Christ and proceeds from His atonement,[4] so that salvation through Christ and membership in the Church are inseparable. The *ecclesia visibilis* is to be spoken of as *mother*.[5] 'There is no other way of entering into life unless she conceive us in the womb and give us birth, unless she nourish us at her breasts, and in short keep us under her charge and government until, divested of mortal flesh, we become like the angels.'[6]

In contrast to Luther Calvin laid greater emphasis upon the *ecclesia externa sive visibilis*. The Kingdom of Christ consists not only in the Gospel, not only in a hidden community of believers, but in the historical communication of the Gospel, and the building up of the Church on earth by human agency (*humanitus*).[7] This carries with it several other differences between the teaching of Calvin and that of Luther.

(a) For Calvin, this means that 'in some measure', the heavenly Kingdom is already begun in us, even now on earth, and that in this mortal and evanescent life immortal and incorruptible blessed-

---

[1] *Instit.* 4.1.1, 5, 27; 4.15.4; C.R. 34, p. 40; *Serm. on 1 Tim.* 3.16, etc., C.R. 81, pp. 318f.
[2] *Instit.* 4.1.4.
[3] *Instit.* 4.1.3. Cf. O.S. I, pp. 88f. Cf. C.R. 29, p. 74: '*Sic credenda nobis est ecclesia, ut divinae bonitatis fiducia freti, pro certo habeamus, nos quoque ex ea esse ac cum caeteris Dei electis, cum quibus vocati, et iam ex parte iustificati sumus perfecte iustificatum ac glorificatum iri confidamus.*'
[4] *Catechism of Geneva*, C.R. 34, p. 39.
[5] See *Serm. on Gal.* 4.26-31 for an excellent exposition of the doctrine of the Church (C.R. 88, pp. 643ff).
[6] *Instit.* 4.1.4. 'Hence departure from the Church is always fatal' (ibid.).
[7] *Instit.* 4.1.4, 5. 'God reserves to Himself the power of maintaining faith, but it is *in evangelii praedicatione* that He brings it forth and unfolds it. With this in view, it pleased Him in ancient times that sacred meetings should be held in the sanctuary, *ut fidei consensus aleret doctrina per os sacerdotis prolata.* For among the many noble endowments with which God has adorned the human race, one of the most remarkable is, *quod dignatur ora et linguas hominum sibi consecrare, ut in illis sua vox personet*' (ibid.).

ness already commences.¹ Jesus Christ has already acquired permanent life for the Church in His flesh, has already accomplished our righteousness in His human nature, and because He transmits that to the Church even in the midst of its frailty on earth, the Church already begins to actualise its new life and being.² 'The Gospel brings with it the grace of regeneration, whose *doctrina* penetrates into the heart and reforms all the inward faculties, so that obedience is rendered to the righteousness of God.'³ 'True knowledge of God is of such a nature that it shows itself and yields fruit throughout our whole life. Therefore to know God, as St Paul said to the Corinthians, we must be transformed into His image.'⁴ And so, in a comment on Eph. 5.25-27, Calvin says: 'The Lord is daily smoothing the wrinkles of the Church and wiping away its spots. Its holiness is not yet perfect. Such then is the holiness of the Church: it makes daily progress but is not yet perfect; it daily advances, but has not yet reached the goal.'⁵

(*b*) For Luther the community of believers, the real Church, was wholly concealed under the *larva dei*, even though it could not have existence in this world apart from the *larva dei*. In the last resort the Church will be revealed when the *larva* is cast aside. The only face of the Church that shows here and now in history is sinful: '*ergo facies ecclesiae est facies peccatricis . . . et quidquid diaboli est.*'⁶ In contrast, Calvin would have nothing to do with the *larva dei* as applied to the Church or Sacraments,⁷ but spoke instead of the '*vera facies*' of the Kingdom of Christ and of the 'Church that is visible in history'.⁸

The operative factor here, in Calvin's thought, is the Word. 'God has imprinted His image in His Word, and it is there that He presents Himself to us and will have us behold Him, as it were face to face.'⁹ The preaching of this Word is 'a treasure common to the whole Church. Therefore we are keepers of the Truth of God; that is to say, of His precious image, of that which concerns

---

[1] *Instit.* 4.20.2; O.S. I, pp. 259f.
[2] See *Serm. on Isaiah* 53.7f, C.R. 63, pp. 636f; and 53.11, C.R. 63, pp. 661f; *Instit.* 4.17.8-9.   [3] *Comm. on Jer.* 31.33, C.R. 66, pp. 690f.
[4] *Serm. on Titus* 1.15-16, C.R. 82, p. 494.
[5] *Instit.* 4.1.17, C.R. 30. p. 760.   [6] W.A. 40/2, p. 560.
[7] *Vide supra*, pp. 34, 127. For Calvin's early use of *larvae* as contrary to the true order of the Church, see O.S. I, pp. 240f, 253, etc. *Institutio* 1536.
[8] Cf. *Comm. on Acts* 2.42: where along with '*vera et genuina Ecclesiae facies*' Calvin uses the expressions '*imago*' and '*publicus Ecclesiae status*' (C.R. 76, p. 57).
[9] *Serm. on* 1 *Tim.* 3.14-15, C.R. 81, p. 311.

the majesty of the doctrine of our salvation and the life of the world to come'.[1] Strictly speaking, it is Jesus Christ Himself, the Word made flesh, who is the Image of God, and through the Word and Sacraments He is delivered to us, and we behold Him and are transformed into His likeness through union with Him. We men have lost the image of God but He the Word has come into our defaced humanity in order to repair and reform us. Thus 'the Son of God did not refuse to be, as it were, disfigured—He who is the Image of God His Father—and all in order that His image might be repaired in us'.[2] That takes place by the power of the Spirit through the preaching of the Word and the dispensing and communication of the Sacraments, which are exercises through which we are more and more transformed into the likeness of Christ and are conformed to Him in mind and life. 'Jesus Christ is the true *Patron* of all believers. He has shown us the way we must go and we must therefore be *configurez à luy*.'[3] It is important to see that this configuration or conformity to Christ is not, for Calvin, a mere *externa larva* but is grounded in the real and substantial union of the Church with Christ. The new creation has ontological reality here and now in the Church, for, as we have seen, the Church participates in the vivifying flesh of Christ, in His new humanity, and is as such the society of glory. Its full glory is not yet publicly exhibited, but while the ultimate manifestation of the new creation is held in suspense, it is the function of *disciplina* under the power of the Word and Spirit to make the *vera facies* of the Church visible on earth.

(c) It *is* in this context that we see the difference between Calvin's view of the order of the Church and Luther's. In many ways the governing thought in Calvin's teaching is *rectitudo*, which describes the order and government of creation within which man is placed and within which he is made to reflect the image and glory of God in such a way that the divine order is manifest.[4] 'The image of God is imprinted in us,' he says, 'because men are born to have some common order and society among themselves.'[5]

---

[1] *Serm. on 1 Tim.* 3.14-15, C.R. 81, p. 311.
[2] *Serm. on Isaiah* 52.13-53.1, C.R. 63, p. 600.
[3] *Serm. on Matt.* 27.27-44, C.R. 74, p. 906.
[4] *Comm. on Col.* 3.10, C.R. 80, p. 121.
[5] *Serm. on Job* 10.7f, C.R. 61, pp. 489f. See also *Serm. on Eph.* 4.17-19, C.R. 79, pp. 591ff; and *Comm. on Gen.* 1.26, C.R. 51, pp. 25f.

THE ESCHATOLOGY OF HOPE: JOHN CALVIN

Being made in the image of God means being brought into a holy and sacred bond of order with God, to whom we are to submit ourselves obediently and thankfully, and in which the whole of our human nature receives its inner and outer *rectitudo* or *temperatura*, and *integritas*.[1] When that image of God is defaced 'the order of nature is inverted',[2] 'the legitimate order which God originally established',[3] and decay and ruin set in.[4] The whole life and integrity of man depends on keeping the divinely appointed order: complete dependence on the heavenly Father. The restoration of fallen man to this relation to God is a restoration to order or rectitude which is effected in Christ and through His Cross.[5] 'Out of Christ all things were disordered, and through Him they have been restored to order. And truly, out of Christ, what can we perceive in the world but ruins? We are alienated from God by sin and how can we but present a broken and shattered aspect? The proper condition of creatures is to keep close to God. Such a gathering together as might bring us back to regular order, the Apostle tells us, has been made in Christ. Formed into one body, we are united to God, and closely connected with each other. Without Christ, on the other hand, the whole world is a shapeless and frightful confusion. We are brought into actual unity by Christ alone.'[6]

Those are some of the basic ideas which govern Calvin's understanding of the order of the Church. Whether it be in regard to 'external order' or the Church or a civil and earthly government the basic factor is 'that *rectitudo* by which it comes that men are reformed according to God's image which is in righteousness and truth'.[7] But such *rectitudo* will not be fully established until Christ comes again, 'when He will appear openly to establish perfect order in heaven and earth'.[8] In one sense all that has been accom-

---

[1] See, for example, *Comm. on Dan.* 4.37, C.R. 68, pp. 690f; or *on Ezek.* 18.20, C.R. 68, pp. 440f.
[2] *Comm. on Gen.* 2.18, C.R. 51, p. 47.
[3] *Comm. on Psalm* 8.3f, C.R. 59, p. 89.
[4] *Comm. on John* 11.25, C.R. 75, p. 262.
[5] *Comm. on John* 12.31, C.R. 75, pp. 293f; *on John* 13.31, C.R. 75, pp. 316f; *on John* 17.21, C.R. 75, p. 387; *Serm. on Eph.* 4.6-8, C.R. 79, pp. 529f.
[6] *Comm. on Eph.* 1.10, C.R. 79, p. 151; *Serm. on Eph.* 1.7-10, C.R. 79, pp. 283f; *Comm. on Isaiah* 65.25, C.R. 65, pp. 433f.
[7] *Comm. on Jer.* 33.15, C.R. 67, p. 67. In the same passage he speaks of this as 'spiritual jurisdiction'. Cf. also *Comm. on Matt.* 6.10, C.R. 73, p. 197.
[8] *Comm. on Matt.* 25.31, C.R. 73, p. 686; cf. *Comm. on Matt.* 9.10: '*Regnum Dei secum affert plenam rectitudinem*', C.R. 73, p. 198.

plished in the Person of Christ has been accomplished on behalf of men,[1] as we have seen, and this has to be transferred to the whole body of the Church.[2] To be sure 'the final result is suspended until Christ the Redeemer appear',[3] but until then the Church that is ingrafted into Christ as His body through its configuration with Him already begins to wear the image which will be manifest fully in the *Parousia*. Of that ultimate rectitude the order and government of the Church are a real reflection and anticipation. In so far as the *vera facies ecclesiae* already appears in the Church, its order reflects or images its future state.[4] It is because the Church lives even now within the restoration of order wrought by Christ that the Church lives in the last times (the times that reach out to the new creation),[5] and that the whole question of order belongs to the obedience of the Church to the Will and Word of God as revealed in the Scriptures.[6] God has established in the Church a *rectus ordo*,[7] a perpetual order and government for His Church,[8] and in that order God's living image is to be seen,[9] so that refusal to submit to that order is tantamount to destroying the very *Dei facies*.[10] 'There is no other bond by which the saints can be kept together than by uniting with one consent to observe the order which God has appointed in His Church for learning and making progress.'[11] The order of the Church has to be seen, then, within the duality of the eschatological tension. A quotation from the Commentary on Phillipians may help to make that clear. 'The Kingdom of Christ is on such a footing, that it is every day growing and making improvement,

---

[1] *Comm. on John* 13.31, C.R. 75, pp. 316f; *on Heb.* 2.11, C.R. 83, pp. 28f, *on* 1 *Heb.* 7.25, C.R. 83, p. 94; *Instit.* 3.25.2.

[2] *Comm. on Acts* 8.33, C.R. 76, p. 194.

[3] *Instit.* 3.25.6. Cf. *Comm. on Eph.* 1.14, C.R. 79, p. 154; *on Rom.* 8.10f. C.R. 77, p. 151f

[4] *Instit.* 4.1.9: 'Hinc nascitur nobis et emergit conspicua oculis nostris ecclesiae facies.' See also 4.1.12. [5] *Vide supra*.

[6] O.S. I, pp. 234f, 240f. Cf. the expressions '*intra verbi Dei praescripta*', '*intra fines verbi Dei*', pp. 241, 243.

[7] *Instit.* 4.1.1; 4.2.10f; 4.3.1, etc.

[8] *Serm. on Psalm* 27.4, C.R. 36, pp. 409ff.

[9] *Serm. on Psalm* 27.4, C.R. 36, pp. 409ff; and *Serm. on Psalm* 27.8, C.R. 36, p. 426; *Instit.* 4.1.5.

[10] *Instit.* 4.1.5: 'Quod perinde est ac Dei faciem, quae nobis in doctrina affulget, delere.'

[11] Ibid. Commenting a little earlier on Eph. 4.11, Calvin says: '*Videmus ut Deus, qui posset momento suos perficere, nolit tamen eos adolescere in virilem aetatem nisi educatione ecclesiae.*' Cf. *Instit.* 4.8.1.

while at the same time perfection is not attained, nor will be until the final day of reckoning. *Thus both things hold true—that all things are now subject to Christ, and that thus subjection will, nevertheless, not be complete until the day of resurrection, because that which is now only begun will then be completed.*[1] The order of the Church is therefore the *rectitude* or *spiritual jurisdiction* of the *Regnum Christi* in actual operation. It is obedience to the resurrection of Christ and to the commencement of the new creation. 'Christ is the beginning because He is the first-born of the dead; for in the resurrection there is a restoration of all things and in this manner the commencement of the second or new creation, for the former had fallen to pieces in the ruin of the first man. As then Christ in rising again had made a commencement of the Kingdom of God, He is on good grounds called the beginning, for then do we truly begin to have a being in the sight of God when we are renewed so as to be new creatures.'[2] That is why the establishment of *order* in the Church was for Calvin a promotion of the Kingdom of Christ.[3] That is possible because the ascended Christ has sent through His Spirit such help to the Church that through it He promotes His own Kingdom,[4] and will always reign on the earth through the Church, which as His Body already bears the new order of the Kingdom of God.[5] Therefore the Church can be spoken of as the Kingdom, or the Kingdom as the renovation of the Church.[6]

This order of the Kingdom operates in the Church through the combination of *Regnum Christi* and *Sacerdotium Christi*. 'Let us learn to begin with the Kingdom and Priesthood when we speak of the state and government of the Church.'[7] The Kingdom of God is utterly opposed to all confusion,[8] and brings into confusion the *imperium* or *dominium* of God.[9] But that operates through the *Sacerdotium* of Christ, for it is through His mediation and death that all things are restored, as we have seen.[10] Thus apart from

[1] *Comm. on Phil.* 2.10, C.R. 80, p. 29.
[2] *Comm. on Col.* 1.18, C.R. 80, p. 87.
[3] O.S. I, pp. 363ff.   [4] C.R. 30, pp. 381f.
[5] C.R. 30, p. 23. Cf. 29, p. 21.
[6] C.R. 37, pp. 143, 430; 45, p. 172, 303, 520; *Serm. on 2 Tim.* 2.20-21.
[7] *Comm. on Jer.* 33.17f, C.R. 67, p. 68   [8] C.R. 45, pp. 197, 331.
[9] C.R. 1, p. 928; 2, p. 667; 45, pp. 197, 331, etc.
[10] Cf. *Serm. on Isaiah* 53.11: 'He was the Master of all creatures, and yet He brought a new dominion in the Person of the Mediator and in our nature' (C.R. 63, p. 666).

L

Regnum and *Sacerdotium* 'there can only be a maimed body and nothing but ruin'.¹ 'This then is the only true happiness of the Church, even to be in subjection to Christ, so that He may exercise toward us the two offices here described. Hence also we gather that these are the two marks of a true Church, by which she is to be distinguished from all conventicles, who falsely profess the name of God, and boast themselves to be Churches. For where the Kingdom and Priesthood of Christ are found, there, no doubt, is the Church. But where Christ is not owned as a King and a Priest, there is nothing but chaos as under the Papacy.'²

The working out of this in the order of the Church involves at once *doctrina* and *disciplina*. It involves *doctrina* because it is a true doctrine of the unique Priesthood of Christ that must govern the order of the Church,³ and so we see that 'the spiritual government of the Church can no more be separated from doctrine than any one of us can be separated from his own soul.'⁴ It involves *disciplina*, because the Church must learn that all its *potestas* is 'subject to and included in the Word of God'⁵ so that it exercises not *dominium* or *imperium* but *ministerium*, bearing the Cross of Christ, and each member of the Church, according to his measure of grace, may study the public edification assigned to him.⁶

In other words, Calvin does not forget that the *facies Ecclesiae* which we see belongs to the Church in its condition of humiliation under the Cross, and it is for that reason that when he discusses the form and ministry of the Church he insists that they must correspond to the humble form of a servant which Christ assumed before His exaltation. The Church manifests its face in history and orders its ministry as the suffering servant. Its visage is often marred more than any man's, although even in that humble condition there is such a transfiguration of the Church through suffering that rays of the divine glory of the Body of Christ break through. That is the way divinely intended. By the Word and

---

¹ C.R. 67, p. 68.   ² Ibid.
³ See especially *De sacerdotio papali abiiciendo*, 1537, O.S. I, pp. 329f.
⁴ *Comm. on 1 Tim.* 3.2, C.R. 80, p. 283; cf. *Comm. on Acts* 16.5, C.R. 76, pp. 372f.
⁵ *Instit.* 4.8.4, C.R. 30, p. 848. Discipline is the schooling of the Church to government by the Word in life as well as doctrine, for 'since the Church is the Kingdom of Christ He will not rule except by His own Word' (C.R. 29, p. 212. O.S. I, pp. 238f).   ⁶ *Instit.* 4.1.12.

Sacrament the Church is being continually nourished with the new humanity, the vivifying flesh of Christ, but by the bearing of the Cross, by discipline, the whole life of the Church in all its members is being refashioned in the image of that humanity and made to look beyond the present humiliation to contemplate the condition of glory at the advent of the Lord. It is because God continually gives His Church on earth anticipation of that future glory by way of *delibatio* that the Church is spurred on toward the perfection which is now concealed under hope. '*Quia regnum Dei per continuos progressus augetur usque ad mundi finem, necesse est quotidie optare eius adventum.*'[1]

(4) In the 1536 *Institutio* Calvin used language about the two Kingdoms or Regiments that was very like Luther's in his distinction between *geistliches und weltliches Regiment*. Calvin spoke of a '*duplex regimen in homine*',[2] but the words '*in homine*' show the difference between Calvin's view and Luther's. Like Luther he speaks of the difference between the *Regnum spirituale*, or the *spirituale et internum Christi Regnum*, on the one hand, and *regnum politicum*, or the *civilis ordinatio*, on the other hand. The one operates with a *jurisdictio spiritualis* and concerns eternal life, the other operates with a *jurisdictio temporalis* and concerns *externi mores* and *leges* of the present life.[3] The one is the realm of the *libertas Christiana*, and the other the realm of *politica administratio*.[4] These two realms are distinct,[5] and the political realm must not be allowed to invade the *Regnum Christi*. '*Sic autem Regnum Christi invaditur, sic libertas ab ipso fidelium conscientiis data, opprimitur penitus ac disiicitur.*'[6] This same language is carried over throughout the editions of the *Institutes* until 1559. The *duplex regimen* is emphasised and the distinction between the two kingdoms is brought out.[7] But the differences between Calvin's view and Luther's that appear in the early edition are clearer and more definite in the final edition of the *Institutes*. We may note the two main differences.

(*a*) Calvin thinks of the distinction between the two kingdoms

[1] C.R. 73, pp. 197f.   [2] O.S. I, pp. 232 and 258.
[3] Ibid. Cf. *Comm. on John* 18.36, C.R. 75, pp. 403f.   [4] O.S. I, pp. 223ff.
[5] O.S. I, pp. 258f: '*Qui inter corpus et animam, inter praesentem hanc fluxamque vitam et futuram illam aeternamque discernere noverit, neque difficile intelliget, spirituale Christi regnum et civilem ordinationem, res esse plurimum sepositas.*'
[6] O.S. I, p. 233.
[7] *Instit.* 3.19.15; 4.20.1. Cf. 1.15.8; 2.2.2, 6, 18, 24.

in terms of the overarching Kingship of God and in terms of His *providentia* and *singularis actio* by which He disposes all the kingdoms of the world.[1] That is to say, in modern terminology, Calvin thinks of them in terms of *Heilsgeschichte*, in a context that is at once historical and sacramental. This is where the whole thought of the *Regnum Dei* is linked up in Calvin's exposition with the *covenant*. There can be no doubt that here Calvin was somewhat influenced by Zwingli as well as by Butzer.[2] Calvin held that there was strictly but one covenant and one universal Kingdom of Christ from the beginning of creation which lasts to the end of the world.[3] The *form* that the covenant takes varies but its *substance* is essentially the same.[4] When the Scriptures speak therefore of a *new covenant*, we are to understand that in terms of fulfilment in Christ and in the Work of the Spirit.[5] 'The covenant of all the fathers is so far from differing substantially from ours, that it is the very same; it varies only in the administration.,[6] Throughout the history of this covenant reaching out to its change and fulfilment in Christ, who is its complete foundation,[7] Calvin thinks of the Kingdom of God or the Kingdom of Christ as operating in history and on earth. He speaks therefore of an '*oeconomia in dispensando foedere*',[8] of a '*successio gratiae*',[9] of a '*cursus salutis*'[10] or '*cursus regni*',[11] and of the whole movement as '*progressus usque ad mundi finem*',[12] to the '*ultimum punctum regni Dei: ut sit Deus omnia in omnibus*'.[13] The general pattern which Calvin seems to have in mind for this sacred progress of the covenant-Kingdom of God is that in the old covenant it operated by imaging itself in the out-

---

[1] *Instit.* 4.20.26.
[2] For Zwingli's views see mainly: '*In catabaptisarum strophas elenchus*', C.R. 93, pp. 1ff; *De peccato originali declaratio*, C.R. 92, pp. 359ff; and *Fidei Ratio*, *Zwingli Hauptschriften*, III, pp. 225ff.
[3] C.R. 36, p. 442.
[4] *Comm. on Jer.* 31.31, C.R. 66, p. 688; *Comm. on Ezek.* 16.61, C.R. 68, p. 396.
[5] *Comm. on Jer.* 31.33, C.R. 66, p. 691.
[6] *Instit.* 2.10.2. Cf. *Comm. on Exod.* 12.14, C.R. 52, p. 290; *Comm. on Heb.* 8.6, C.R. 83, p. 100.
[7] C.R. 2, p. 314, C.R. 50, p. 391; 64, p. 22.
[8] C.R. 30, p. 326; *Comm. on Gen.* 49.1f, C.R. 57, p. 592.
[9] *Comm. on Gen.* 48.1, C.R. 51, p. 579; cf. *Comm. on Isaiah* 60.17, C.R. 65, p. 366.
[10] *Comm. on Psalm* 89.25, C.R. 59, pp. 820; cf. *Comm. on Gen.* 49.1, C.R. 51, p. 592.
[11] *Comm. on Isaiah* 45.23, C.R. 65, p. 149.
[12] *Comm. on Gen.* 48.4, C.R. 51, p. 581; *Comm. on Psalm* 18.44, C.R. 59, p. 190; on *Psalm* 48.1, C.R. 59, p. 472; on *Psalm* 110.1, C.R. 60, pp. 161f; *Comm. on Phil.* 1.6, C.R. 80, p. 9.
[13] C.R. 33, p. 211.

ward forms of Israel's life and pilgrimage as a nation, as a kingdom especially under the Davidic dynasty, and as a priestly people with laws and ceremonies. All that pointed to the inward reality of the Kingdom of Christ, so that in these institutions and events in the old covenant, such as the Exodus out of Egypt, for example, God gave Israel a *prelude* of the Kingdom of Christ. The pattern of the old covenant is then this: 'What happened formerly in the Church, ought at length to be fulfilled in the Head.... It was then the full nativity of the Church when Christ came forth out of Egypt to redeem His Church. God, when He formerly redeemed His people from Egypt, only showed by a certain prelude the redemption which He deferred until the coming of Christ.'[1] The pattern of the new covenant is this: 'All that was accomplished in Christ, as in our Head, belongs to us, and the effect of it will show itself in each believer.'[2] In the new covenant the Kingdom is done into the Church by the power of the Spirit, and so it is spiritual and interior but it works from within out, insisting on manifestation in the daily life of man in the world, and pressing toward the full manifestation when Christ comes again, when we shall see Him and be like Him.[3] The important point in the progress of the Kingdom is thus actual incorporation into the Body of Christ, for it is the Body of Christ which is the substance and the form of the new covenant, the Kingdom of Christ which Calvin prefers to call it. All that had a *'praeludium ac umbratile specimen maioris gratiae'* in the old covenant, but it was suspended until Christ came.[4] But now in actual fulfilment the old shadowy forms and sacramental signs are abrogated and the covenant assumes the new form, which is the form of Christ.[5] This takes us to the other main difference.

(*b*) Under the overarching Kingdom of God, the two kingdoms, the spiritual and the political, overlap, not only in their common aim, the glory of God, but in their effect, which might be best described as *humanitas, humanité*, which is a constant theme in

---

[1] *Comm. on Hosea* 11.1, C.R. 70, p. 433; *Comm. on Matt.* 2.15, C.R. 73, p. 99.
[2] *Serm. on Isaiah* 53.7, C.R. 63, p. 641.
[3] *Serm. on 2 Tim.* 2.16-18, C.R. 82, pp. 153ff; *Comm. on 1 John* 3.2, C.R. 83, pp. 330f; *Comm. on 2 Cor.* 3.18, C.R. 88, p. 46f.
[4] *Comm. on Gen.* 49.10, C.R. 51, p. 958. Cf. *Comm. on Isaiah* 6.13, C.R. 64 pp. 140f.
[5] C.R. 30, pp. 322f. This is one of the main theses in Calvin's *Commentary on the Epistle to the Hebrews*, as one would expect.

Calvin's sermons.¹ While Calvin will not allow the political kingdom to invade the spiritual, he will not allow the spiritual to abrogate the political kingdom as the fanatics wanted to do. 'As that kind of government (the political or civil) is distinct from the spiritual and internal Kingdom of Christ, so we ought to know that they are not adverse to one another. The *former*, in some measure, begins the heavenly Kingdom in us, even now upon earth, and in this mortal and evanescent life commences immortal and incorruptible blessedness, while to the latter it is assigned, so long as we live among men, to foster and maintain the external worship of God, to defend sound doctrine and the condition of the Church,² to adapt our conduct to human society, to form our manners to civil justice, to reconcile us to each other, to cherish common peace and tranquility. All these I confess to be superfluous, if the Kingdom of God, as it now exists within us, extinguishes the present life.³ But it is the will of God that while we aspire to true piety we are pilgrims on the earth, and if such pilgrimage stands in need of such aids, those who take them away from man rob him of his humanity.'⁴ The aim of the political kingdom may be described then as follows: 'that a public form of religion may exist among Christians and humanity among men'.⁵ The task of the civil authority is a divinely appointed task and in obedience to it its magistrates wear the image of God and are bearers of His *gloria*.⁶ They are given authority to make room for the Church

[1] Cf., for example, *Serm. on Matt.* 25.51f, C.R. 74, pp. 859f. This common aim and effect is apparent in the exposition of the *adveniat regnum tuum* of the Lord's prayer. Cf. O.S. I, p. 109. How different this is from Luther is apparent in the very language Calvin uses when he speaks of using *humana politia* to establish *Christiana politia*. Cf. *Instit.* 4.20.3 and O.S. I, p. 260.

[2] But this defence of the *Regnum Christi* is done in a different manner from that in which worldly kingdoms are wont to be defended—in a way appropriate to its nature as spiritual. Therefore it is only *per accidens* that arms can defend the *Regnum Christi (Comm. on John* 18.36, C.R. 75, pp. 403f).

[3] 'This is how Jesus leads us into the heavenly Kingdom, after we have entered into the Kingdom of God in this world.' *Serm. on Acts* 1.1-4, C.R. 76, p. 590.

[4] *Instit.* 4.20.2. It is remarkable that in 1559, after all his experiences in Geneva, these words should still remain the same as they were in the 1536 *Institutio* (O.S. I, p. 259).

[5] Ibid. Cf. 1536 *Instit.*, O.S. I, p. 260: '*ut inter Christianos publica religionis facies existat, inter homines constet humanitas.*'

[6] *Instit.* 4.20.6, 24; *Comm. on* 1 *Pet.* 2.14, C.R. 83, pp. 245f; *on Jer.* 33.15, C.R. 67, pp. 66 and 257. Calvin even says of the magistrates: 'They have a commission from God; they are invested with divine authority, and in fact *represent the person* of God, as whose *substitutes* they in a manner act' (*Instit.* 4.20.4). Calvin uses the same words to describe the function of ministers (*Instit.* 4.3.1: *'personam suam repraesentent'* and *'quasi vicariam operam'*).

and to bring about *the conditions of humanity* on earth. The task of the Church is to hold forth Jesus Christ in the preaching of the Gospel and to dispense the Sacraments, for it is through communion with Him that the Church participates in His *new humanity*.[1] Under the Kingdom of God these two regiments overlap, and the area in which they overlap is *humanity*, the '*iustitia novi hominis*'.

This overlapping is so deep that for Calvin the operative eschatological distinction is not so much that between the two kingdoms in Luther's sense, as between the two conditions of the Church, which we have already discussed. In its way, the civil and political kingdom already wears something of the *gloria dei*, but it is endowed with *imperium*; the Church, however, operates in another way and is endowed with *ministerium*, following the example of Christ. In citing Matt. 20.25f and par., Calvin added: '*Quibus sane longissimo intervallo eorum ministerium ab omni mundi huius gloria et sublimitate divisit.*'[2] The Church exercises its ministry in the *Regnum Christi* between His two advents in humiliation and glory.[3] At His first advent Christ came in the form of a servant to suffer and endure reproach for the sake of the Gospel, but at His second advent He will come in the exaltation of His divine majesty and in the full manifestation of His glory.[4] Though the glory of Christ was revealed in His resurrection after He had taken the road of suffering in the mean and despicable condition of the flesh, the full revelation of that glory is suspended till the last day. In the same way, Calvin taught, the Church, which is the Body of Christ and which already shares in His ascension,[5] will be fully revealed in the glory only when it has gone through its period of humiliation and tribulation for the sake of the Gospel. Although the Church is already the new creation, and already participates in the world of the resurrection on the other side of the final judgment, the Church continues to live within the conditions of this world and so is sent out

---

[1] *Serm. on Luke* 2.1-14, C.R. 74, pp. 955-968, especially pp. 967f; *Comm. on Eph.* 4.25, C.R. 79, p. 209; cf. *Comm. on Jer.* 22.16: '*Ubi cognoscitur Deus, etiam colitur humanitas* (C.R. 66, p. 388).   [2] O.S. I, p. 251.

[3] *Serm. on Luke* 2.1-4, C.R. 74, pp. 955f; *Serm. on Acts* 2.13-17, C.R. 76, pp. 645f.

[4] On the other hand, there is a manifestation of God's glory now among all nations which is an anticipation of the final judgment and the full revelation of God's majesty (*Comm. on Dan.* 14.11, C.R. 77, p. 263).

[5] *Serm. on Acts* 1.9-11, C.R. 76, pp. 617f.

into the world bearing the Cross of Christ. Because it is united to the exalted Christ who is yet to come again in glory, the Church by the inner compulsion of its faith prays, 'Thy Kingdom come, Thy will be done on earth, as it is in heaven', and longs for the day of His advent,[1] but it must never confuse the two conditions, the mean and despicable condition under the Cross, and the condition of glory still to be manifested, for that would be to confound heaven and earth, and to drag the Kingdom of God down to earth rather than lift up our hearts and minds to heaven.[2]

It was the error of Romanism to confound these two conditions,[3] but it was also the error of the Disciples, as Calvin shows in his remarkable exposition of the *Little Apocalypse* and the early chapters of Acts. The Kingdom of Christ was perfectly realised in the resurrection and ascension of Christ, but the Disciples confused that with the end of the world (i.e. the outward revelation of the Church's glory). The problem, as Calvin expounded it, was not that of a delayed advent or the mistaken time of the end, but the confounding of the two conditions of the Kingdom of Christ. That the Kingdom had already come, Calvin held to be clear; the time problem refers only to the outward condition, to the fact that the road to the establishment of the Kingdom was that of suffering witness.

(5) Like Luther Calvin thought of the *Regnum Christi* as set in opposition to the *regnum satanae*,[4] but though he spoke of daily battles and struggles with Satan,[5] Calvin's conception of the *Regnum Christi* had a more persisting sense of complete victory, for 'it is to triumph that we are summoned'.[6] This optimistic

---

[1] C.R. 73, pp. 197f: '*Quia regnum Dei per continuos progressus augetur usque ad mundi finem, necesse est quotidie optare eius adventum.*'

[2] *Vide supra*, pp. 122f. 'Heaven', 'heavenly' refer as a rule in Calvin's thought not to some empyrean realm but to the new or celestial condition of God's creation. Thus the *regnum coelorum* is said to be the *status* or *conditio ecclesiae* (C.R. 73, pp. 172, 520). Cf. also C.R. 80, p. 55: '*Docet enim, nihili aestimanda omnia praeter spirituale Dei regnum: quia coelestem vitam in hoc mundo vivere debeant fideles.*'

[3] O.S. I, p. 250.

[4] O.S. I, p. 237; C.R. 38, p. 256; *Comm. on Luke* 10.18, C.R. 73, p. 315; *Comm. on Mark* 5.6, C.R. 73, p. 269; *Comm. on John* 12.31, C.R. 75, p. 293f; *Comm. on Acts*, Arg., C.R. 76, pp. viif.

[5] C.R. 43, p. 444; C.R. 59, pp. 28f; C.R. 76, pp. viif, etc.

[6] *Instit.* 2.15.4. *Comm. on Ps.* 18.38f, C.R. 59, pp. 187f; C.R. 46, p. 928; cf. C.R. 33, p. 426: '*Nos modica, imbellis, nuda exarmataque turba, horribiles veluti grex ovium ante lupos. An non mirifica est regis victoria Christi?*' And also *Comm. on 1 Tim.* 6.12, C.R. 80, p. 328.

THE ESCHATOLOGY OF HOPE: JOHN CALVIN 161

outlook based on the complete victory of Christ over all the powers of evil is irrepressible in Calvin.[1] He will never let *tentationes* obscure the fact that the victory over Satan has already been won, and that the Church is more than conqueror because it is the Kingdom of Christ.[2] The Kingdom of Christ is essentially militant and aggressive and all-conquering.[3] Typical is the prayer with which Calvin concluded one of his lectures on Micah: 'May we daily solicit Thee in our prayers, and never doubt, but that under the government of Thy Christ, Thou canst again gather together the whole world, though it be miserably dispersed, so that we may persevere in this warfare to the end, until we shall at length know that we have not hoped in vain in Thee, and that our prayers have not been in vain, when Christ shall manifestly exercise the power given to Him for our salvation and for that of the whole world.'[4]

That is a very important element in Calvin's view: the fact that the whole world belongs to the Kingdom of Christ and has come under His redemption, and that the triumph of Christ will soon be manifest everywhere among all nations. The *Regnum Christi* presses through the Church, in its obedience to the command of the risen Christ, to bring all mankind under its sway in the Gospel.[5] The missionary expansion belongs to the very nature of the Gospel and to the very nature of the Church in which the treasure of the Gospel is deposited. 'The Lord Jesus Christ did not come to reconcile a few individuals only to God the Father but to extend His grace over all the world.'[6] That means that 'the Church of

[1] C.R. 30, p. 12: '*Sed doctrinam nostram supra omnem mundi gloriam, sublimem, supra omnem potestatem, invictam stare oportet: quia non nostra est, sed Dei viventis, ac Christi eius, quem Pater regem constituit, ut a mari usque ad mare dominetur, et a fluminibus usque ad terminos orbis terrarum.*'

[2] Cf. especially *Comm. on Ps.* 18.42, C.R. 59, pp. 188f, or Calvin's letter to Melanchthon in 1555, C.R. 43, pp. 737f.

[3] This is strongly reflected in Calvin's prayers, and was written into the *Forme de Prières*, C.R. 34, p. 173. Cf. *Serm. on Matt.* 26.36f: 'He suffered in the weakness of His flesh but by virtue of the Spirit He was raised from the dead in order that we might be made partakers of His fight which He sustained and that we may realise the effect and the excellence of His power in us' (C.R. 74, p. 843). And cf. the following sermon on prayer, *on Matt.* 26.40f, C.R. 74, pp. 846ff.

[4] *Comm. on Micah* 7.10-14, *Opera Calvini*, 1667 edition, Amsterdam, V, p. 341.

[5] *Comm. on Rom.* 1.5, C.R. 77, pp. 11f, 16.21f; C.R. 77, pp. 289f.

[6] *Serm. on 1 Tim.* 2.5f. Cf. *Comm. on Isaiah* 12.4: 'The work of this deliverance will be so excellent, that it ought to be proclaimed not only in one corner only, but throughout the whole world' (C.R. 64, pp. 253f). Cf. also *Comm. on Micah* 4.3, C.R. 71, pp. 346f.

God will be expanded throughout the entire world',[1] and that is the supreme purpose of the ascension, to fill all creation with the *Regnum Christi*.[2]

It is that missionary urge armed with the irresistible triumph of Christ that accounts for the work which Calvin undertook from Geneva, arduously seeking everywhere 'to establish the heavenly reign of God upon the earth'.[3] 'May we attend to what God has enjoined upon us, that He would be pleased to show His grace, not only to one city or a little handful of people, but that He would reign over all the world; that everyone may serve and worship Him in truth.'[4] Several quotations may suffice to indicate that the heart of this urge to extend the Kingdom of Christ lies in the atonement, and begets the conception of a *universal Church*.[5] 'The office of our Lord Jesus Christ was to make an atonement for the sins of the world, and to be a Mediator between God and men. Having taken upon Him our flesh, and so far abased Himself as to become man, we should submit ourselves to Him in all His requirements. Our Lord Jesus Christ was made like unto us, and suffered death that He might become an Advocate and Mediator between God and us, and open up a way whereby we may come to God. Those who do not endeavour to bring their neighbours and unbelievers to the way of salvation plainly show that they make no account of God's honour, and that they try to diminish the mighty power of His empire, and set Him bounds that He may not rule and govern all the world; they likewise darken the virtue and death of our Lord Jesus Christ and lessen the dignity given Him by the Father.'[6] 'God sets up His Kingdom by humbling the whole

---

[1] *Serm. on Isaiah* 52.13f, C.R. 63, pp. 603f.

[2] See C.R. 30, pp. 381f: '*Et sane videmus quanto maiorem Spiritus sui abundantiam tum effuderit, quanto magnificentius regnum suum promoverit, quanto maiorem potentiam tum in adiuvandis suis tum in hostibus deiiciendis extulerit. In coelum ergo sublatus corporis sui praesentiam e conspectu nostro sustulit; non ut adesse fidelibus desineret, qui adhuc in terris peregrinarentur, sed ut praesentiore virtute et coelum et terram regeret. Quin potius quod pollicitus est se futurum nobiscum usque ad consummationem saeculi, id sua hac ascensione praestitit; qua ut corpus supra omnes coelos elevatum est, ita virtus et efficacia ultra omnes coeli ac terrae fines diffusa propagataque est. . . . Ibi enim sedet ad dexteram patris, et hic est : non enim recessit praesentia maiestatis.*' Cf. C.R. 29, p. 21; 30, p. 23.

[3] Letter to Nicholas Radziwill, 1555, C.R. 43, p. 429.

[4] *Serm. on* 1 *Tim.* 3.14f, C.R. 81, p. 161; cf. *Serm on Acts* 2.1-4, C.R. 76, p. 624: 'When the Holy Spirit descended, it was not only for a little handful of people, but in order that this might reach all the ends and extremities of the world.' [5] C.R. 30, p. 747. [6] *Serm. on* 1 *Tim.* 2.5f, C.R. 81, p. 161.

world, though in different ways, taming the wantonness of some and breaking the ungovernable pride of others. We should desire this to be done every day, in order that God may gather Churches to Himself from all quarters of the world, may extend and increase their numbers, enrich them with His gifts and establish due order among them.'[1]

As in Christ Himself, so in the Church the glory of God is amazingly joined to the grace of our salvation. *Regnum* is so joined to *Sacerdotium* that the Church is the movement of the Kingdom of God 'whose limits are wider than the whole world'.[2] Nothing could express Calvin's thought better than this concluding prayer to a Sermon: 'Or nous nous prosternerons devant la maiesté de nostre bon Dieu, en cognoissance de nos fautes: le prians qu'il luy plaise nous les faire sentir de plus en plus: et que nous despouillant de toutes nos mechantes cupiditez il nous retire pleinement à soy, et que nous profitions de iour en iour, et soyons augmentez en ses graces, iusques à ce qu'estans sortis de ce monde nous paruenions à sa gloire celeste. Et que d'autant que sommes maintenant un royaume sacerdotal, qu'il luy plaise nous reuestir de la iustice et integrité de nostre Seigneur Iesus Christ, et non point en figure, comme les sacrificateurs de la Loy: mais que par son S. Esprit nous soyons tellement renouuellez, que si nous ne sommes parfaits du premier iour, pour le moins nous aspirions à ceste perfection à laquelle il nous conuie. Que non seulement il nous face ceste grace, mais à tous peuples et nations de la terre,'[3] etc.

To sum up: The Church as the covenant community, the one Body of Christ which has already participated in His death, in His glorious resurrection and ascension, is compelled by an inner necessity to reach forth even in its present condition of humility and servitude towards that ultimate plenitude and harmony in all its members which is to be revealed. Calvin thinks of the activity of the Church under this eschatological impulse in three ways: (1) All members of the Church are engaged in the work of gathering the Church together on every side; everyone should strive to lead others to the truth, to restore the wandering to the right way, to extend a helping hand to the fallen, and to win over those that

---

[1] *Instit.* 3.20.41f. [2] *Comm. on Jer.* 33.16, C.R. 67, p. 68.
[3] *Serm. on Deut.* 33.7-8, 1567 edition (Geneva), p. 1135; cf. *Serm. on Deut.* 33.18-19, where Calvin says that even on the ground of *humanité* we must seek to bring all men on the earth to the knowledge of God (C.R. 57, p. 175).

are without. It is that impulse under what Calvin called the incredible force of the Gospel that accounts for the amazing extension of the Gospel to all parts of Europe from Geneva. (2) It is the business of the Church to be continuously restoring its true face, and in making that face public both in a godly life and in a form and order of the Church on earth through which by Word and Sacrament God may be known familiarly and face to face. (3) The Church should ever be engaged in ecumenical activity, which the whole idea of the *Regnum Christi* and the *facies Ecclesiae* carries with it.[1] From Calvin's letter to Sadoleto it is clear that this had long been in his mind, though there is little doubt that he learned much about this from Butzer, than whom Calvin was no less energetic in the work of bringing the Churches together into unity. It is not only brotherly love which behoves us to cultivate unity, for the last coming of Christ ought particularly to rouse us to the work of gathering the Church together. So he wrote in his *Commentary on Hebrews*, and then added: 'For to what end did Christ come except to collect us all into one body from that dispersion in which we are now wandering? Therefore the nearer His coming is, the more we ought to labour that the scattered may be assembled and united together, that there may be one fold and one shepherd.'[2]

[1] Cf. C.R. 77, p. 497; 38, pp. 68f; 42, pp. 313f; 59, pp. 572, 583; 30, pp. 178, 755ff, 760f.
[2] *Comm. on Heb.* 10.25, C.R. 83, p. 133.

GENERAL INDEX

Accidental result, reprobation as, 106f
Accommodation, 107f, 127f, 135
Advent of Christ, Second, Final, 12ff, 19f, 32, 54, 76f, 85, 103f, 119, 128ff, 140, 143ff, 147, 164
  between the Advents, 113f, 126f, 129, 135ff, 142ff, 152f, 157ff
Ambrose, 91, 99
Amsdorf, 36, 71
Analogy, 32, 46f, 60ff, 77, 101f, 114, 139ff, 144
Anfechtung, tentatio, 68, 72, 91, 160f
Ascension of Christ, Heavenly Session, 46, 57, 90, 101f, 108f, 129f, 143ff, 147, 159
Atonement, reconciliation, etc., 12, 75, 80, 148, 162
Augustine, 91, 93, 97, 99, 129

Baier, J. G., 27, 51
Baillie, J., 1
Basil, 98
Bernard of Clairvaux, 14, 91
Baptism, 27ff, 32, 35, 50ff, 54ff, 58f, 61, 64ff, 77, 91, 97, 101, 128f, 147
Body of sin, prison of the soul, etc., 13, 92f, 113

Charles V, the Emperor, 20
Chiliasm, 145
Church, *passim*
  Body of Christ, *corpus Christi*, etc., 4, 50, 52, 56f, 69f, 78, 98, 101, 114, 138, 143ff, 153, 163
  communio sanctorum, fidelium, renatorum, electorum, etc., 58ff, 61, 65, 74f, 78f, 79, 85f, 87, 89

Church,
  ecclesia, 24, 33, 58f, 66
  ecclesiola, 33, 66f
  duplex communio, 60
  duplex ecclesia, 18, 61
  facies ecclesiae, 66f, 73, 100, 138, 149, 152, 154, 164
  forma ecclesiae, etc., 57ff, 62f, 66f, 68, 71, 124f, 134f

Christology, 4f, 12f, 23, 26ff, 33, 38ff, 46ff, 50f, 80, 84, 88f, 90f, 93f, 101f, 108ff, 114f, 120f, 125, 129f, 133, 136ff, 139ff, 143f, 148f, 153f, 161f
Christenheit, 20, 23, 32f, 57, 70
Chrysostom, 91, 97f
Communicatio idiomatum, 47
Contemptus mundi, 141
Covenant, 26, 88f, 156f, 163
Copernicus, 1f
Cosmology, 1f, 7
Cross, under the, *tolerantia crucis*, etc., 64f, 67f, 122f, 136, 141, 154, 160
Cyprian, 5, 91, 99
Cyril of Alexandria, 91

Demetrianus, 5
De Wette, W. M. L., 33, 36, 44, 70f
Doctrina and *disciplina*, 80, 87, 154
Dialectical relation, 10, 15, 17, 23, 53, 71, 115, 126, 142f
Dufresne et du Cange, *Glossarium*, 35

Election, predestination, etc., 4f, 73, 78f, 82, 89, 95, 100, 104ff, 116, 147f
Erasmus, Desiderius, 11, 44

GENERAL INDEX

Eschatology, *passim*
  eschatological perspective, 1f, 29, 70ff, 91, 109f, 120, 126
  eschatological tension, 23, 103, 109ff, 133
  eschatological expectation, anticipation, 14, 44, 91, 100, 109f, 116, 119, 123, 135, 152, 155, 159
  eschatological suspension, 25, 71, 96, 108f, 138, 142f, 147, 150, 159f
Eusebius of Caesarea, 91

Fortunatus, 93
Fraticelli, 19

George, Duke, 44
Gregory the Great, 91

Hausmann, 19
Heilsgeschichte, 17, 156
Hierarchies, the three, 24, 58, 70
Heshusen, 130, 143
Hilary, 91
Hirsch, E., 39
Humanity, *humanitas*, *humanité*, etc., 87, 153f, 157ff

Imago Dei, *Christi*, 46, 74, 83, 112, 125ff, 128, 130, 138, 149ff, 158
Imitatio, 1
Imputation, *imputatio*, *reputatio*, etc., 11ff, 21, 49, 52
Incorporation, 39f, 47f, 50f, 56f, 69, 73f, 77, 80f, 82, 101f, 104, 129, 139f, 146, 157
Irenaeus, 91

Jerome, 91
Joachim of Fiore, 2f, 19
Judgment, the Last, Final, etc., 2f, 5, 8, 11, 15f, 24f, 44, 69f, 114, 119, 139, 159
Justification, *justitia*, etc., 11ff, 30, 39, 47, 74, 88, 94ff, 100f, 142, 149

Justification, *justus et peccator*, 10f, 15f, 53f, 65f, 72
justificandus, 14, 53

Kingdom of God, *passim*
  Regnum Christi, Kingdom of Christ, 18ff, 23f, 25ff, 29, 43, 51, 58ff, 69f, 75f, 78ff, 83ff, 91f, 98f, 110f, 114f, 121, 124f, 130, 136f, 147f, 152f, 160f
  initium regni et complementum, 33f, 70f, 111ff, 118f, 122
  two conditions of the Kingdom, 122ff, 136ff, 157ff
  regnum fidei, Reich der Glaube, 7, 9f, 22f, 26f, 29, 44f, 55
  regnum gratiae, Reich der Gnade, 23f, 26, 30f, 71
  regnum gloriae, 26, 71
  regnum caelorum, 18, 21, 67, 75f, 88, 134, 160
  regnum novum, 17f, 25f
Kingdoms, The Two, Regiments, Ages, etc., 11, 16ff, 23, 30f, 45, 56f, 87f, 155ff
  overlap of the two kingdoms, ages, etc., 17, 24, 78, 118f, 121, 134, 159
  the Spiritual Kingdom, *Geistliches Regiment*, etc., 16f, 23, 32f, 38, 43, 47, 155, 158
  the worldly kingdom, *weltliches Regiment*, etc., 16f, 18, 23f, 28f, 34, 38, 43f, 60, 77, 85f, 118, 155
Kerr, H. T., 16, 20, 30
Knox, John, 73
Kreutzer, M., 24

Lambert, F., 19
Larva, mask, veil, etc., 30, 34ff, 37ff, 40ff, 61, 64, 70, 127, 149
Last Day, 9, 11, 16, 21, 25, 29, 44, 69, 103f, 109, 113, 136
Last times, 3, 16, 19, 118f, 121, 126
Latomus, 69
Lombard, Peter, 34

GENERAL INDEX

Löwith, K., 3
Lord's Supper, the, Eucharist, Mass, Sacrament of the Altar, etc., 3, 7, 28f, 63f, 71, 81, 97, 101, 128, 130f, 143f

Macchabaeus, J., 33
Manducatio impiorum, 145
Martyr, Peter Vermiglio, 73, 146
Melanchthon, P., 18f
Melito of Sardis, 91
Meditatio vitae futurae, sursum corda, etc., 83, 91f, 102f, 107f, 130, 138f, 141
Müntzer, T., 37
Mystery, *mysterium, arcanum consilium*, etc., 5, 79, 84, 90, 100, 106f, 142

Nature and grace, 2f, 10, 46, 52f
New creation, age, 4f, 6, 13, 52, 72, 88f, 93, 133, 150, 153, 159
  grammar, 6, 47
  man, humanity, 6, 48ff, 66, 82f, 94, 101, 140

Oeconomia, Hausregiment, 24, 58f
Order, *ordo*, 32ff, 57ff, 110, 131f, 134ff, 150ff, 163
Ordinatio, 33, 41f, 62
Ordnung, 75
Origen, 91
Osiander, 4, 19, 145

Pauck, W., 85f
Persona, person, 34ff, 37ff, 158
Pilgrimage, 54, 142, 157
Politia, polity, 24, 30, 36, 58f, 62, 68, 133f, 158
Priesthood of Christ, *Sacerdotium*, 78, 83, 123, 153, 163
Priesthood of believers, 13, 81
Progress, increase, growth, etc., 51f, 54ff, 66, 72, 77, 82, 94ff, 98f, 103, 105, 115, 143, 146, 152, 156

Punctus mathematicus, 19, 46

Reason, 8, 10, 28, 38, 47, 50, 103, 123
Respublica, 70, 81f, 85f, 88
Resurrection, 5, 21, 29, 38, 48ff, 52f, 72, 93, 102f, 107, 111f
Rückert, H., 39
Rupp, G., V, 11, 14

Sacraments, 3, 23, 27, 41, 47, 51, 55f, 60ff, 66f, 70, 80f, 100f, 128f, 143ff, 164
Sadoleto, Cardinal, 64, 97ff, 164
Sanctification, 49, 52, 65f, 100f
Schlink, E., 16
Schwärmer, 30f, 36, 44, 57
Spalatin, 11, 22, 33
Spirit, 5
Stephanus, H., 35
Strohl, H., 74
Spirit, the Holy, 13f, 25, 29, 36, 49f, 56, 74, 78, 82f, 86, 97f, 100f, 104, 111, 141, 125, 130f, 133, 142, 143f, 157
Stündlein, 9ff, 27, 55

Tauler, 74
Taubes, J., 1
Theologia crucis, 28, 71
Tertium comparationis, tertium datur, third dimension, etc., 32ff, 45ff, 47f, 71
Tertullian, 91, 93
Thomas Aquinas, 3f
Törnvall, G., 16
Totum simul, 8f, 19
Transubstantiation, 3, 61, 97
Tuveson, E. L., 2, 4

Union with Christ, 39f, 46, 56, 59, 69, 94f, 100f, 116, 130, 139ff, 144ff, 150

Von Hutten, Ulrich, 44
Von Schubert, Hans, 56, 71

Walch, J. G., 19
Walther, C. F. G., 51
Watson, P. S., V
Wendel, F., 74f
Westphal, J., 129f, 143f
Word of God, *passim*

Worst, H., 64
Word and Spirit, 25, 56, 62, 74, 78, 80, 89, 97ff, 133

Zwingli, Ulrich, 146, 156

www.ingramcontent.com/pod-product-compliance
Lightning Source LLC
Chambersburg PA
CBHW051933160426
43198CB00012B/2136